The Five-Minute Linguist

The Five-Minute Linguist

Bite-sized essays on language and languages

Edited by
E.M. Rickerson and Barry Hilton

LONDON   OAKVILLE

Published by

Equinox Publishing Ltd.
UK: Unit 6, The Village, 101 Amies Street, London, SW11 2JW
USA: DBBC, 28 Main Street, Oakville, CT 06779
www.equinoxpub.com

First published 2006
Reprinted 2007

British Library Cataloguing-in-Publication Data
A catalogue record for this book is available from the British Library.

ISBN-10   1 84553 199 X   (paperback)
ISBN-13   978 1 84553 199 7   (paperback)

Library of Congress Cataloging-in-Publication Data
The five-minute linguist : bite-sized essays on language and languages /
edited by E.M. Rickerson and Barry Hilton.
    p. cm.
Includes bibliographical references and index.
ISBN 1-84553-199-X (pbk.)
1. Language and languages--Miscellanea. I. Rickerson, E. M. II.
Hilton, Barry. III. Title: 5 minute linguist.
P107.A15 2006
400--dc22
                              2006022397

Typeset by Catchline, Milton Keynes (www.catchline.com)
Printed and bound in Great Britain and USA

'Wherever you are
and whatever you do,
language makes a difference!'

— The Five-Minute Linguist

The radio series that served as the foundation for
this book was jointly sponsored by the School
of Languages, Cultures, and World Affairs at the
College of Charleston (Charleston, SC) and the
National Museum of Language.

Contents

Foreword

This book is for anyone who has a question about languages or the nature of language—which means just about all of us. But it's not just a musty academic text for specialists. While written by leading experts on the subject of language, *The Five-Minute Linguist* is a user-friendly exploration of the basics, a linguistic start-up kit for general readers. It assumes nothing on your part except interest in the subject. Its bite-sized chapters (no more than a few pages each) give authoritative answers to the most frequently asked questions people have about language, and tell the story in a lively and colloquial style. It is a delightful read.

Although the main purpose of the book is to inform, it also aims to encourage the study of language and raise awareness of the nature and diversity of languages on the planet—which is why it is of special interest to us at the American Council on the Teaching of Foreign Languages (ACTFL). You may be aware that the U.S. Senate and House of Representatives designated 2005 as the 'Year of Languages' in the United States, to call attention to the importance—and the benefits—of language study. Throughout that year, ACTFL promoted activities aimed at jump-starting a sense of urgency about language. There were lectures and films at universities, poster contests in schools, billboards on highways, statewide language competitions, essay contests, folk festivals, cultural programs, national roundtables, and many other events. There was even established (at the college of Charleston in South Carolina) a new School of Languages, Cultures, and World Affairs. One of the more ambitious projects—a radio series called *Talkin' About Talk*—was broadcast on public, commercial, and college radio stations around the country. Members of the ACTFL Board of Directors and staff took part in that project, and ACTFL supported it by posting audio files of the entire series on our national Web site (www.actfl.org). The book you have in your hand is an adaptation of that series: enriched versions of the original fifty-two broadcasts, augmented by several new essays.

In addition to more lofty goals, there are some very practical reasons to encourage language study. The U.S. is the only industrialized nation whose children routinely leave secondary school knowing only one language (the stereotype of the monolingual American is not entirely untrue). The latest enrollment survey tells us that only one American in three studies a foreign language in school at all. Meanwhile, the government has great backlogs in materials waiting for translation, a shortage of language specialists everywhere, and a readiness level of only 30 per cent in the most critical languages. Beyond considerations of global commerce, in a post-9/11 world the lack of attention to languages other than English has very serious consequences. Americans can't afford *not* to study foreign languages and cultures at a time when economic necessity and national security depend more than ever on clear communication with trading partners, allies and potential adversaries.

To increase its language capacity, the U.S. has to build a pipeline of students who start language study early in life and continue it through college. There need to be language-learning opportunities for all students, especially in the elementary schools. State and local officials need to look at priorities and put to rest the notion that language is an 'extra' in the school curriculum, a frill that can easily be cut when funding is tight. The paradigm has changed. Every day 70 per cent of Americans interact with someone whose native tongue is a language other than English. In a global economy, no matter what job a student seeks, he or she will be just as likely to do business with South Korea as with South Carolina.

Understanding what other people think, and why, helps us— Americans and others—be better friends and better negotiators worldwide. And language is the key.

But to change perceptions about the importance of language is not easy, and it will take more than a single year's effort to bring it about. The 'Year of Languages', therefore, was just a first step. To raise public awareness about the critical role that languages play in a shrinking world, what was initiated in 2005 will continue for many years as a national—and, we hope, international—campaign with the theme *Discover Languages ... Discover the World!*

The Five-Minute Linguist is a welcome contribution to that campaign.

Bret Lovejoy, Executive Director
American Council on the Teaching of Foreign Languages

Introduction

Language. All of us are immersed in it, like fish in water, and yet almost all of us have questions about it, such as 'how many languages are there in the world?' Or 'why do languages die?' Or 'do animals use language?' Every year there are thick books published about such topics, some of which can be technical or tedious, or perhaps aimed at a narrow audience of scholars. *The Five-Minute Linguist* is not that kind of book. Although it's the work of language experts, authoritative and full of facts, it was designed for non-specialists who want to read for enjoyment as well as for knowledge. It is divided into short chapters, suitable for browsing or reading on the run, and its style is intentionally light—more like a series of fireside chats than a college textbook. In fact, that's how it started—as a series of radio chats called *Talkin' About Talk*, which ran through the year 2005 as part of a celebration of the 'year of languages' in the United States. The essays have a chatty quality because of the broadcast persona of the narrator, a knowledgeable and amiable guide whose task was to demystify the sometimes complex subject of language for a wide range of listeners. Each week the narrator talked in a relaxed, conversational style about a language-related topic for exactly five minutes—thus the title of the book.

The editors had never intended to create yet another book about language; but neither did we know that the radio series would be so warmly received. It turned out that the essays appealed not just to radio listeners, but to a variety of people with a personal or professional interest in language. The material was used in basic language and linguistics courses, introductory anthropology classes, pre-service training for language teachers, adult education centers, English as a Second Language programs, and classes for younger students in Language Arts. Secondary schools broadcast the programs through speaker systems to their student bodies, and a U.S. foreign affairs agency put them online for its employees worldwide. The American Council on the Teaching of Foreign Languages (ACTFL) posted the audio files on its Web site as a resource for language teachers. There was even an enterprising book club that started its meetings—well before this book existed—by playing the audio essays to stimulate discussion. The creators of *Talkin' About Talk* were especially honored when the series was nominated for the Linguistic Society of America's prestigious 'Linguistics, Language, and the Public' award.

A major difference between *Talkin' About Talk* and other discussions of language—and one of the reasons for its popularity—was that the series spoke to a general audience. Along with up-to-date content, its greatest strengths were brevity and clarity. Thus, when it was suggested that the essay collection be made into a book, we felt it important to preserve the directness and down-to-earth tone of the radio talks. Although the resulting words in print are not always quite as colloquial as the original chats, we believe the book shares the virtues of the radio broadcasts—that it is authoritative, succinct, clear, and fun to read.

Let us be clear that there is no such person as the 'Five-Minute Linguist'. The radio voice and architect of the project was Dr. Rick Rickerson, Professor Emeritus at the College of Charleston; but the 'Linguist' is actually a consortium of fifty-five experts from twenty-five U.S. states and the United Kingdom. They're an impressive array of talent by any measure, and we encourage you to read their brief biographies at the end of each chapter. Many have written highly-acclaimed books of their own that discuss, at greater length and with narrower focus, the topics discussed in this book. Most are on university faculties or otherwise professionally engaged with language. They include Scientific Linguists (linguistics professors, field linguists, philologists, phoneticians, psycholinguists and others primarily interested in linguistic theory and linguistic data); Language Educators (specialists in second language acquisition, foreign-language education, and teachers of various languages); and Applied Language Professionals (translators/interpreters, language officers in government agencies, lexicographers, anthropologists, directors of resource centers and language programs, and members of advocacy groups or professional organizations). Despite their common interest in language, these groups tend to occupy separate orbits. We believe it to be a unique feature of this book that its contributors represent the entire breadth of the language profession.

Keeping such a large group speaking with a relatively consistent stylistic voice, on the air and later in print, was the responsibility of a Review Board that examined, edited, and commented on drafts of each essay. The Board consisted of the then-president of the Linguistic Society of America, Joan Bybee, Distinguished Professor of Linguistics at the University of New Mexico; Frank Borchardt, Duke University Professor of German and specialist in language-teaching technology; Sheri Spaine Long, Professor of Spanish at the University of Alabama at Birmingham, and Editor-in-Chief of *Foreign Language Annals*; and the multilingual freelance writer and independent scholar Barry Hilton (co-editor of this book, along with Rick Rickerson).

The Board's job was *not* to purge the collection of all contradictions or repetitions. (It's not unusual, in areas of lively academic research, for different inquiries to overlap, or for the same evidence to be interpreted differently by different experts.) Nor was the goal to make *The Five-Minute Linguist* an encyclopedic work. The five-minute broadcast format ruled out in-depth coverage of any one topic, and even sixty topics are far too few to cover the field in any detail. Instead, the creators of the radio series and book decided early on to limit their focus to a few guiding principles: What do people who are *not* in the language field want to know about language? What are some of their major misconceptions? What specific languages or language groups are of most interest to this audience? What do our readers want to know about *learning* or *using* languages? The resulting sixty chapters, each with a question as its title, are what we like to think of as a savory platter of *hors d'oeuvres,* something to whet your appetite and invite you to go on to a more substantial dish.

How to read this book

The Five-Minute Linguist does not have to be read from the beginning. Since the chapters are essentially free-standing, they may be read in any order. That does not mean, however, that each is unconnected to the rest. Chapters may be related to adjacent chapters and to other parts of the book as well. To help readers pursue the connections, we have provided both an index at the back of the book and, after each chapter, a few suggestions for further browsing. For those whose appetite has been stimulated by the book's bite-sized essays and who want to try something more substantial, each is followed by a short list of relevant books, articles, and Web sites that are accessible to a non-specialist reader.

While the book is not formally divided into sections, you will see that adjacent chapters tend to fall into groups with similar subject matter. Approximately the first half of the book discusses language in general, from the perspective of scientific linguists. Topical groups include the nature of language (chapters 1–12), language's relationships with brain function and thought (chapters 13–16), the social context of language (chapters 17–25), and the sounds of language (chapters 26–28). In the second half, chapters 29–34 address language learning and teaching; chapters 35–41 are a miscellany of articles on language in the U.S.; and chapters 42–47 discuss language 'applications' such as lexicography, translation, and forensic investigation. The last thirteen chapters of the book are devoted to commentary on a selection of specific languages and language families.

Acknowledgements

It has taken many people and organizations to make *The Five-Minute Linguist* a reality. It should first be noted that the project was jointly— and enthusiastically—sponsored by the College of Charleston and the National Museum of Language. We are particularly grateful to Dr. Samuel M. Hines, Founding Dean of the College's new School of Languages, Cultures, and World Affairs, who provided resources and facilities at the School for much of the basic work on the radio series; to Dr. Amelia Murdoch, President of the National Museum of Language, and to members of the Museum's Board, who embraced the *Talkin' About Talk* project from the start and provided funding to support it. It is our hope that the School and the Museum, both recently arrived on the U.S. national language scene, full of potential, will find ways to continue their fruitful partnership.

We would like to express appreciation to the language and linguistic organizations in the U.S. that actively supported the project. Our thanks especially to Maggie Reynolds, Executive Director of the Linguistic Society of America, and to the dozens of LSA members who made contributions to either the radio series or the book, or both; to Bret Lovejoy, Executive Director of the American Council on the Teaching of Foreign Languages (ACTFL), for graciously contributing a Foreword to the book; and to Marty Abbott, Director of Education at ACTFL, who wrote an essay for the radio series and was one of the project's most consistent supporters. Other national language organizations that endorsed the radio project and encouraged us to carry it through to completion included the Modern Language Association (MLA), the Center for Applied Linguistics, the National Foreign Language Center, the American Translators Association, the Joint National Committee for Languages, the Indigenous Language Institute, and the National Council of State Supervisors of Foreign Language. The project also enjoyed the support of regional organizations: the South Carolina Council on Languages; a long list of foreign-language teacher associations, including many of MLA's regional affiliates; and especially the Southern Conference on Language Teaching, which recognized *Talkin' About Talk* through a special Year of Languages Award.

We would also like to acknowledge some of the many individuals who gave their time or in other ways contributed to the project's success: Steve Ackley at ACTFL; Sarah Haynes in Charleston and consultant Wilson Rickerson in Boston; Professors Moore Quinn at the College of Charleston, Eric Bakovic at the University of San Francisco, Jill

Morford at the University of New Mexico, Margaret Winters at Wayne State University; independent scholars and writers Michael Erard and Amalia Gnanadesikan; radio host Joan Mack in Charleston; College of Charleston Language Resource Center Director, Georgia Schlau; our Web site manager, Sam Tyson; and our talented professional indexer, Joyce Henderson. The editors owe particular thanks to Eve and Barbara, who commented on parts of the manuscript, kept things in perspective, and helped us preserve our sanity.

We are especially indebted to Professors Deborah Tannen at Georgetown University and G. Richard Tucker of Carnegie Mellon, internationally-known linguists and authors who generously read and commented on the final draft; and to Professors Walt Wolfram and Robert Rodman of North Carolina State University, two of America's most respected linguists, whom we think of as the book's godfathers. They were actively engaged in the radio project from its earliest days and gave it much-valued impetus and encouragement. Both contributed multiple essays to the anthology and freely shared their wisdom and experience to keep the project on track during the inevitable tribulations.

Finally, we would like to give special applause to the book's fifty-plus distinguished contributors. The authority and clarity of the essays in *The Five-Minute Linguist* will be obvious to readers. Not observable, except to the editors, is the collegiality and selflessness that characterized the writing and shaping of them. Contributors joined the project voluntarily for the benefit of the profession, and did so without reserve. They embraced the project so wholeheartedly that the modest goal of raising the profile of language in the public consciousness became, ultimately, a celebration of language itself.

E. M. Rickerson and Barry Hilton

1

Why learn about language?

Robert Rodman

Have you ever wondered which language is the oldest?
Or how babies learn to talk?

Language is universal, and each of us is a kind of expert in using the language we were raised speaking, but there's a lot more to language than what we use in everyday life, and it raises a lot of fascinating questions. Whatever happened to Esperanto? Can machines translate languages? Are some ways of speaking or writing better than others? The chapters of this book will address all these questions and many more.

Let's start with a big question: What is it that makes us human? Is it walking on two legs? Or living in society? Is it our ability to love and hate? To some degree, all of those. But none is unique to the human species. Birds walk on two legs. Ants live in society. And my dog loves me, and hates the cat next door.

It's language that distinguishes us from all other creatures. Whatever else people do when they're together—whether they play, or fight, or make love, or serve hamburgers, or build houses—

they talk. We're the only creatures on the planet with the power of speech.

Every human being, rich or poor, is capable of language. Every child learns his or her native tongue, be it English or Zulu, just by being exposed to the talk around them. Most children are fluent before they're ten years old, sometimes in more than one language. Equally impressive is that as they grow up they master different styles of speech: everything from formal, job-interview talk to street slang.

Among the questions to be taken up in this book is how something as complex as language can be so easy for children to learn, yet so difficult for adults. We do know that certain areas of the brain specialize in language, and that children are born with a capacity to learn any human language to which they are exposed. Moreover, as will be discussed later, a child who is isolated from language while growing up may never learn to speak well as an adult. Based on that evidence, many scientists believe that the capacity for language is genetic, but that much of that capacity is lost by adulthood.

Our discussion pertains to spoken language. Learning to read and write—literacy—is another matter entirely. Writing—though it's closely related to spoken language and will be addressed in several chapters of this book—is a human invention, like the bicycle, and has to be studied. Talking is a biological trait, like walking, and comes naturally.

Something you'll see clearly in the course of the book is how much variety there is in the world's tongues, and how constantly they change over time. There are thousands of languages on the planet, all descended from earlier languages that spread and changed and split up into dialects as people moved. Given enough time, the separation of groups and the dialects they speak inevitably leads to the birth of new languages, the way French, Romanian, and Spanish grew out of the Latin spoken by the Romans.

You'll also read what linguists have discovered about how and when language began. What do you think? Was there once a single 'Ur-language' spoken by some brilliant ancestor? Or did aliens come to earth long ago and teach our forebears to speak? There's no shortage of theories, ranging from the supernatural to the imitation of animal sounds.

Do animals talk? Clearly, apes and other animals communicate with each other, and can be taught to do some language-related tasks, but they lack the linguistic flexibility of humans—our amazing ability to express new thoughts, without limits on subject matter.

And what about computers? In some ways they seem very clever. But can we teach a machine to speak and understand like a human? Not quite. Although they're capable of some flashy simulations of human-like skills, computers are limited in their ability to understand and produce meaningful speech. And they certainly lack the spontaneity and creativity of human language.

Think about it: almost every time you speak—except for a few set phrases such as exclamations of pain or anger, or things you recite from memory like poems or prayers—you're creating a sentence different from any other sentence you've ever heard or spoken. Each one is unique. And every day you create hundreds, or even thousands, of them! One reason language is special is that it's a universal form of human creativity. Happily, even without being great poets, authors, or orators, we can be creative every day of our life when we speak.

There is no human trait more pervasive, or in many ways more valuable, than language. It's capable of expressing all of human thought, even thoughts about itself—which is what this book is all about. So start reading!

About the author

Robert Rodman is a UCLA-trained linguist who is currently a Professor in the Department of Computer Science at North Carolina State University. He is co-author of a popular linguistics textbook, *An Introduction to Language* (Thomson/Wadsworth, eighth edition 2007). Dr. Rodman is also a forensic linguist and consults with the judiciary in matters of speaker identification based on recordings and wiretaps of criminal activity.

Suggestions for further reading

Fromkin, Victoria, Robert Rodman, and Nina Hyams. *An Introduction to Language* (Thomson/Wadsworth, eighth edition 2007). This is a comprehensive book about language and linguistics written for persons with no previous background in languages. It is written in a light, readable style and makes copious use of cartoons, pithy quotations, poems, and song lyrics to make its linguistic points. Nearly one million copies of this book have been bought.

Pinker, Steven. *The Language Instinct: How the Mind Creates Language* (HarperCollins/Perrenial Classics, 1994). This is a fascinating, witty treatment of the nature of the human mind as it pertains to language. It is well written enough to be a page-turner despite its technical subject. It's a must-read for anybody in the language field, and a joyful read for the linguistically curious.

2

How many languages are there in the world?

M. Paul Lewis

How many languages are there in the world? Who counts them? Where are they spoken? Which have the most speakers?

How many languages are there? That's one of those 'it all depends' questions: how you answer it depends on what we call a language, and deciding what is and what isn't a language is not as easy as you'd think.

Suppose you like to eat, for breakfast, thin round cakes of grilled batter with butter and syrup. You call them 'pancakes'. Your neighbor, who likes the same meal, might call them 'griddlecakes'. If you or he travelled to a restaurant in a nearby town you might find that you have to ask for 'flapjacks'. Now imagine that chain of contacts stretching out further. Even tiny differences wouldn't have to accumulate for more than a few hundred miles before it could become hard to understand people. They might even say something

11

like 'Wassup?' to mean 'Hello!' Where do you draw the line between a dialect and a language? Where does one language leave off and another begin?

Sometimes it's not so hard. People in Iraq speak Arabic; their neighbors in Iran speak Farsi, a completely unrelated language. At other times, though, the linguistic differences are small, and the answer becomes a matter of politics and sociology. Swedes and Norwegians can understand each other easily. But they have different histories, customs, and governments, and they see themselves as two nations, speaking two languages, not one. The same thing, more or less, goes for Malaysians and Indonesians; or Macedonians and Bulgarians. Some groups go to great lengths to distinguish themselves from their linguistic cousins across a border: Serbs and Croatians understand each other's speech perfectly well, but they use two different writing systems. Other groups do just the opposite: A billion people live in China, with at least seven mutually unintelligible forms of regional speech. But they're reluctant to see themselves as separate nations, so they've clung to a unique ancient writing system that can be used anywhere in the country and lets them think of themselves as united by a single language.

So it's not easy to define what is or isn't a language, and counting is a matter of definitions. How many languages there are also depends on when you count them. Languages, like people, are born, they change and grow and sometimes have offspring, and they eventually dwindle and die. We'll never have an exact answer to the slippery question of how many languages there are, but among the most dedicated counters are the researchers at *Ethnologue*, a comprehensive directory of the world's languages that released its fifteenth edition in 2005. Their estimate, based largely on how well speakers can understand each other, is that a total of close to seven thousand languages are spoken or signed in the world today.

Some of those thousands are just about extinct, with only a handful of speakers left. In fact, about *a quarter* of the world's languages have fewer than a thousand speakers. A small population, however, doesn't necessarily mean that a language is on its way to extinction. Many of those small groups are using their languages quite vigorously. It is more difficult to maintain a language, however, when there are fewer people to speak it with and when another language is being picked up and used for communication with outsiders.

At the other end of the scale is a group of very dominant languages. Over the next century they'll probably drive hundreds, or even thousands, of the smaller languages to extinction, just as superstores drive small shopkeepers out of business. The largest by far is Mandarin—nearly 900 million people in China speak it as a native tongue. Hindi, English, and Spanish each have over 300 million native speakers. The other leading languages—all of which have between 100 and 200 million native speakers—are Bengali, Portuguese, Russian, Indonesian, Arabic, Japanese, German, and French.

In addition to simply counting how many languages there are, it is interesting to observe how those languages are distributed around the world. We often think of Europe as a very multilingual place. And it does have 238 different languages. But it doesn't compare with Asia, which has 2,269—nearly a third of the world's languages—or with Africa, which has almost as many. Some linguists are very interested in exploring why different regions of the world are so different in their levels of linguistic diversity. Clearly, groups that differ socially and culturally, as we've described above, may be motivated to emphasize their linguistic differences as well, gradually becoming speakers of different languages. In recent years, some linguists have also been looking at the apparent correlation between environmental (ecological and biological) diversity and the number of languages in a particular region. They hypothesize that where there are more plant and animal species to talk about, there are likely to be more linguistic forms as well, and that people who live in different ecological settings will develop different languages.

The number and *diversity* of the world's languages are amazing and are constantly changing. You might yearn for the days before the Tower of Babel, when it's said that everyone spoke the same tongue, but *every* language is a window on the culture (and environmental setting) in which it's spoken and a window on the human mind as well. So there are good reasons for us to study them—and to preserve what we can of *all* of them.

About the author

M. Paul Lewis is a sociolinguist with SIL International (a non-profit, faith-based language development organization). Born in the U.S., he is the child of a multilingual, multicultural family with parents and grandparents born in England, Wales, and Argentina. He lived for nearly twenty years in Guatemala, where he studied and did research on the Maya-K'ichee' language. He holds a Ph.D. in linguistics from Georgetown University. He resides near Dallas, Texas, with his wife and four (Guatemala-born) children and has recently taken on the role of Editor of *Ethnologue: Languages of the World*. The fifteenth edition of *Ethnologue* was published in 2005.

Suggestions for further reading

In this book: Various languages of the world are described in chapters 50 (Latin), 51 (Italian), 52 (Spanish, Portuguese, and others), 53 (Russian), 54 (Icelandic), 55 (Arabic), 56 (languages of Africa), 57 (Chinese), and 58 (Japanese); Also relevant are chapters 24 (language death), 25 (language rescue), 35 (languages of the U.S.), and 47 (the National Museum of Language).

Elsewhere:

Crystal, David. *Language Death* (Cambridge University Press, 2000). A good overview of the dynamics of language maintenance and death and related issues.

Grenoble, L. A. and L. J. Whaley. *Endangered Languages: Language Loss and Community Response* (Cambridge University Press, 1998). Looks at the ways in which various communities have responsed to the endangerment of their languages.

Nettle, Daniel and Suzanne Romaine. *Vanishing Voices: the Extinction of the World's Languages* (Oxford University Press, 2000). Another look at language maintenance, endangerment and death which makes an explicit connection between linguistic diversity and biological eco-diversity.

Web site:

http://www.ethnologue.com
Gordon, Raymond G., ed. *Ethnologue: Languages of the World* (SIL International, 2005). Also online at the Web site above. Possibly the most comprehensive inventory of the languages of the world.

3

What's the difference between dialects and languages?

G. Tucker Childs

Is it better to speak a language than a dialect?
Which one do you speak?

Strange as it may seem, there is no generally agreed-upon way to distinguish between a 'language' and a 'dialect'. The two words are not objective, scientific terms, even among linguists. The lay community is no different, and people often use the terms to mean different things. As used by many people, 'language' is what 'we' speak and 'dialect' is the linguistic variety spoken by someone else, usually someone thought of as inferior. There is no linguistically objective difference between the two. In other contexts, 'language' can mean the generally accepted 'standard' or government and radio-broadcast language of a country, while 'dialects' are homelier versions that vary from region to region and may not be pronounced in the same way as by radio announcers. Language varieties tend to be labeled 'dialects' rather than 'languages' for non-linguistic reasons, usually political or ideological. Oftentimes they are not written, or they are spoken by people who don't run the country. They are generally regarded as being not so 'good' as the standard language and consequently have little prestige. In short, the distinction is subjective. It depends on who you are and the perspective from which you judge the varieties.

From a linguistic perspective, no dialect is inherently better than another and thus no dialect is more deserving of the title 'language' than any other dialect. A language can be seen as a group of related dialects. For example, the dominant position of the Parisian dialect in France is largely an accident of history. When the Count of Paris was elected king of France in the tenth century, the language of his court became the 'standard'. If things had gone differently, the dialect of Marseille or Dijon might have become the national language of France today.

Dialects can be *socially* determined, as Eliza Doolittle learned in *My Fair Lady*. In this play and film, as will be remembered, a snobbish phonetics professor (based on the real-life phonetician Daniel Jones; Rex Harrison in the movie version was coached by the real-life phonetician Peter Ladefoged) agrees to a wager that he can take a flower girl and make her presentable in high society. He succeeds, primarily by changing her speech.

Similarly, dialects can be *politically* determined. The linguist Max Weinreich is often quoted as saying, 'A language is a dialect with an army and a navy.' His point was that politics often decide what will be called a 'dialect' and what will be called a 'language'. Powerful or historically significant groups have 'languages'; their smaller or weaker counterparts have 'dialects'.

The status of a language can be *arbitrarily* determined by a person or a government, typically a person or entity endowed with the power to do so. In southern Africa an early twentieth-century missionary created a language now known as 'Tsonga' by declaring three separate languages to be dialects of a single tongue. Conversely, the government of South Africa created two languages by arbitrary declaration—Zulu and Xhosa—even though there is no clear linguistic boundary between them. In many parts of the world dialects form what is called a 'dialect continuum', where no two adjacent dialects are wildly different, but at the ends of the continuum the dialects are mutually unintelligible.

Dialect differences are often relatively minor—sometimes just a matter of pronunciation ('You say tomayto, I say tomahto') or slight differences in vocabulary (Americans say 'elevator', Britons say 'lift'). Such differences are crucial to understanding George Bernard Shaw's famous quip that America and Britain are 'two countries separated by a common language.' But dialects can also differ so greatly from one another that they are incomprehensible. German speakers from Cologne and German speakers from rural Bavaria can barely understand one another, if at all. Although the Swiss speak German as one of their national languages, few Germans can understand them when they speak their local dialects.

One of the tests people use to differentiate 'language' from 'dialect' is mutual intelligibility. Many would say that people speak the same language, meaning dialects of the same language, if they understand each other without too much difficulty. If they don't understand one another, they are considered to be speaking different languages. That seems like a good rule. So why are Cologne German and Bavarian German, which are *not* mutually intelligible, not considered separate languages? Or why are Swedish and Norwegian considered separate languages, when Swedes and Norwegians have no trouble understanding one another?

Such questions become even more unanswerable when speakers of Dialect A just don't *want* to understand speakers of Dialect B, and sometimes vice versa. One or both groups insist that they speak separate tongues, even though they—judging by objective linguistic criteria—are speaking mutually intelligible dialects of the same language.

It is thus easy to conclude from all this that the terms 'dialect' and 'language' are politically and socially *loaded*. You might want to ask yourself whether you speak a language or a dialect. It's a trick question, of course, because ultimately, *all* languages are dialects. You speak both at the same time.

About the author

G. Tucker Childs is a professor in the Applied Linguistics Department at Portland State University in Portland, Oregon, where he teaches courses in phonetics, phonology, language variation, pidgins and creoles, African American English, and sociolinguistics. He and several of his students have begun researching the dialects of Portland in their 'Portland Dialect Study' (http://www.pds.pdx.edu). Dr. Childs also has interests in African languages, including the pidgins and new urban varieties spoken on the continent. His most recent book in that area is *An Introduction to African Languages* (Benjamins, 2003), and in 2004 he began a project documenting the moribund Mani language of Guinea and Sierra Leone (see: http://www.hrelp.org). He has taught at universities in the United States, Canada, Europe and Africa, and has been a visiting researcher at the interdisciplinary *Langage, langues et cultures d'Afrique noire* (LLACAN) unit of France's National Council for Scientific Research (CNRS) in Paris.

Suggestions for further reading

In this book: dialects are discussed in chapters 18 (English in Britain, America, and elsewhere), 26 (U.S. Southern English), and 41 (Are dialects dying?).

Elsewhere:

Crystal, David. *The Cambridge Encyclopedia of Language* (Cambridge University Press, second edition 1997). A fascinating and accessible introduction to language and linguistics with numerous illustrations and quotable facts.

Joseph, John E., and Talbot J. Taylor, eds. *Ideologies of Language* (Routledge, 1990). A collection of articles illustrating how power and ideology control the status of such languages as Afrikaans and French.

Trudgill, Peter. *Sociolinguistics: An Introduction to Language and Society* (Penguin Books, Ltd., 2000). A sociolinguistically informed introduction to languages and dialects written for those with little knowledge of linguistics.

Web site:

http://www.ethnologue.com/
Online version of Gordon, Raymond G., Jr., ed. *Ethnologue: Languages of the World. Fifteenth edition* (SIL International, 2005). A useful reference cataloguing and classifying all known languages of the world, with some information on dialects.

4

What was the original language?

Barry Hilton

*When did language begin, and how? What language
did the earliest humans speak?*

Questions like these were easier to answer back when supernatural
explanations were in fashion. You could just say that language was
a gift granted to humans when they first appeared in the world, like
their senses and their limbs. The answer to 'when?' was 'when Adam
and Eve lived in the Garden of Eden'; and as for identifying that
first language, chapter 6 of this book describes some of the theories
advocated during the era when older ways of thought prevailed.

Beginning in the eighteenth and nineteenth centuries, though,
a different way of thinking about the history of languages began to
develop: the science of Historical Linguistics. As described in more
detail in chapter 5, its practitioners have identified relationships
among existing languages and shown how they fit into 'family trees'
reflecting thousands of years of changing and splitting from previously existing languages.

In many cases, these language genealogies point back to ancestral
languages that no longer exist. Historical linguists have developed

a method of reconstructing those long-dead languages from clues surviving in their descendants, and almost all of them believe it allows valid deductions about languages whose descendants have been separated for up to about five to seven thousand years. Some think that it's possible to look, cautiously, even further into the past. Most, though, believe that languages separated for ten thousand or more years have changed too much for the method to be reliable; and modern humans have been around five or ten times that long.

This leaves a large gap to bridge: what happened to change wordless early humans, or near-humans, into the talkers that we've since become? And what was their speech like? There's been no shortage of speculation on these subjects, beginning in the late nineteenth century. Maybe, it was suggested, early people invented speech by imitating animal calls or other natural sounds and, over time, attaching meaning to them; or by attaching meaning to their own inarticulate grunts of emotion or exertion. Guesses like these are a legitimate step in scientific inquiry if they generate hypotheses that can be verified, but there didn't seem to be any way of finding relevant concrete evidence. Critics, even friendly ones, applied mocking names like 'the "bow-wow" theory', 'the "ding-dong" theory', 'the "pooh-pooh" theory' and 'the "yo-he-ho" theory'. For several decades, the Origin of Language was an unfashionable field of study.

Beginning around the last quarter of the twentieth century, though, increasing amounts of brainpower—and more and more *kinds* of brainpower—have been devoted to the question, and interest is picking up.

Paleontologists studying fossils and ancient artifacts have improved our chronology of humanity's early past, sharpening debate over *when* language is most likely to have emerged: with the first tool-using members of genus *Homo* some two million years ago? or with the artistic flourishing that accompanied the appearance of anatomically modern humans some 50,000 years ago?

Other researchers have looked for modern analogues to the earliest human language origins: Psychologists have intensively studied how infants make the transition from wordless creatures into talking children; primatologists have devised ingenious experiments to determine how much or how little human-like linguistic behavior apes can learn; and neurologists and anatomists are making clearer to us just how extensively human language is enabled and limited by the human body and brain.

The anatomists, in particular, have suggested that language was impossible until humans had both the right kind of vocal tract to produce speech sounds and the right kind of nervous system to control them. One physical distinction between modern humans and all other animals, even chimpanzees and earlier humans, appears to be critical: a lowered larynx. Your dog can eat his food in a few quick gulps, but he can't talk. You can talk, but you can also choke from food lodged in your larynx. The human ability to make speech sounds is not a bonus provided by the body systems designed for breathing, chewing, and swallowing—it's just the opposite: the lowered larynx (with associated changes in the pharynx and mouth) is a handicap to the usual animal uses of mouth and throat, but on balance this handicap is far outweighed by the great survival value in speech. You can talk—and participate in civilization—because you *can't* wolf your food.

It's unlikely that these multidisciplinary efforts will allow us to reconstruct what words our ancestors said, or what their speech sounded like. But some interesting late twentieth-century research suggests that we may be able to know something about the *gram mar* of the earliest languages—how words came together to form sentences. Within the past few centuries several new languages of a special kind have been born. European colonists arriving in the third world communicated with their local laborers using pidgin languages, a kind of adult babytalk using a hodgepodge of words from different languages, strung together with a rudimentary grammar. When children are raised speaking a pidgin as their native language, they turn it into a full-fledged language called a creole, with a broader vocabulary and a more elaborate grammar. Now here's the fascinating part: Unrelated creole languages in places as far apart as Surinam, Haiti, Hawaii, and Papua New Guinea have radically different vocabularies, but some researchers find their grammars very similar, suggesting that the human brain may be hardwired to create particular patterns of speech. Could this be a clue to how the earliest languages worked?

About the author

Barry Hilton is the Associate Editor of this book and was a member of the review board of the radio series from which it was adapted. He is a freelance writer/editor and independent scholar living in Maine and working as a marketing specialist for a small publishing company. He is an honors graduate of Harvard College who after graduate studies at Cornell, Yale, and George Washington Universities and the Foreign Service Institute has travelled extensively and lived in both Europe and Asia. In a variety of U.S. government assignments he has made professional use of Vietnamese, Chinese, Japanese, French, and German. He describes himself as an 'armchair philologist and recovering polyglot.'

Suggestions for further reading

In this book: The origins and history of languages are also discussed in chapters 5 (language relationships), 6 (the language of Adam and Eve), 7 (language change), 8 (pidgins and creoles), 48 (origins of English), and 54 (Icelandic).

Elsewhere:

Crystal, David. 'The origins of language', in *The Cambridge Encyclopedia of Language* (Cambridge University Press, second edition 1997), pp. 290–3. A compact account of the history of scientific inquiry into how language began.

Bickerton, Derek. *Roots of Language* (Karoma, 1981). A readable, serious presentation of the by-no-means-mainstream theory that evidence for the prehistoric origins of language can be found in language learning processes observable today.

5

Do all languages come from the same source?

Allan R. Bomhard

What does it mean to say that two languages are related? Are all languages related?

Have you ever studied German, or Spanish, or French? If you have, you were probably grateful for cognates, foreign words that sound and look like English words with related meanings. In German, your parents are your *Mutter* and your *Vater*. In Spanish, they are your *madre* and *padre*. In French, they are your *mère* and *père*.

These resemblances not only make language learning easier, they tell us something about the history of languages. English and German share some similar vocabulary because they are both descendants of a language called Proto-West-Germanic, spoken by tribes in northern Europe well over two thousand years ago. Over time, migrations split that language into dialects, and some of the tribes moved across the North Sea into the British Isles. Fifteen centuries of separate development turned the speech of the British

Isles into varieties of English, while the language of the Mainlanders turned into varieties of German. So we have two languages, obviously different, but also so alike that they are clearly part of the same language family.

Language families, like families of people, can be connected into larger and larger groupings, spreading outward in territory and backward in time, as our relatives do on a genealogy chart. The Germanic family that English, German, and several other languages belong to has a cousin, the Romance family, which includes not only French and Spanish but also several other languages that have Latin as their common ancestor; and there are other cousins as well.

Now let us go back a step further in time. The Germanic and Romance language families share a common ancestor called Proto-Indo-European. It was spoken by tribes living some six to seven thousand years ago, probably in the steppes north and east of the Black Sea. From there, the tribes spread westward across Europe and eastward and southward into Iran and northern India. As they spread and lost contact with each other, their language changed into languages like Greek, Armenian, and Albanian, and into families like Germanic, Romance, Celtic, Slavic, Indian languages, and Iranian languages. Taken together, they make up the Indo-European language family, the most widely-spoken group of languages in the world today.

As different as the Indo-European languages were from one another, they all preserved bits of ancient vocabulary and grammar. Linguists have used these bits to figure out relationships and actually reconstruct the older languages. Sir William Jones opened the way at the end of the eighteenth century through a remarkable analysis of the classical Indian language Sanskrit, showing that Sanskrit was related to languages in Europe such as Latin and Greek. And now, even though no one has seen or spoken the original Indo-European parent language for thousands of years, we have a fairly good idea of what it may have sounded like. Moreover, by cracking the code of Indo-European, we have taken a big step toward answering the question, Can all language families be linked in a super family tree that begins with a single ancestral language?

To find out, linguists have increasingly studied and compared *non*-Indo-European languages, asking, What families do they belong to? How far back can those families be traced? Clearly, many non-Indo-European languages can be grouped together. For example, Finnish, Estonian, and Hungarian, which are surrounded by Indo-Europeans in the heartland of Europe, are not in the Indo-European language family. But they do group together with several other languages to form a non-Indo-European language family called Uralic. Similarly, there is a family called Turkic, which takes in Turkish, Azerbaijani, Uzbek, Uighur, Kazakh, and some other languages in Central Asia. In East Asia, the Sino-Tibetan family includes over two hundred and fifty languages, the largest of which is Mandarin Chinese. Linguists think that at least two hundred language families exist; the obvious next question is, Are any of those families related to each other?

There are theorists who believe that we can lump all of the languages of the world—including even language isolates like Basque, which seems to fit nowhere—into a handful of giant families.

But maybe we cannot go that far. The fact that the word for 'dog' in an Australian native language called Mbabaram is 'dog' does not mean that Mbabaram is related to English; it is just a random resemblance. The fact that Chinese calls coffee *kāfēi* does not mean that Chinese is related to English, either; the origin is a Turkish word that happens to have been borrowed by both Chinese and English. Furthermore, we know that languages change continuously; new words join the vocabulary, while older words, including cognates, disappear, and the same thing has happened to grammar. After tens of thousands of years of change, can we reliably find a common ancestor? Do all languages come from the same source? The answer is: Maybe … and maybe not. It is too soon to know.

About the author

Allan R. Bomhard is a linguist living in Charleston, South Carolina. His main areas of interest are distant linguistic relationship and Indo-European comparative linguistics. He has published over forty articles and five books and is currently preparing a new book on Nostratic comparative phonology, morphology, and vocabulary.

Suggestions for further reading

In this book: Chapters on the history and origins of language include 4 (earliest language), 6 (the language of Adam and Eve), 7 (language change), 8 (pidgins and creoles), 48 (origins of English), and 54 (Icelandic); chapters focusing on language families include 49 (Native American languages) and 56 (African languages).

Elsewhere:

Baldi, Philip. *An Introduction to the Indo-European Languages* (Southern Illinois University Press, 1983). This book presents an excellent overview of the Indo-European language family. Both beginners and knowledgeable readers will find much of interest here.

Comrie, Bernard, ed. *The World's Major Languages* (Oxford University Press, 1987). This book is a comprehensive survey of the major languages spoken in the world today.

Lehmann, Winfred P. *Theoretical Bases of Indo-European Linguistics* (Routledge, 1993). This book is a more advanced treatment of the issues involved in the reconstruction of the Indo-European parent language. Beginners should start by reading Baldi's book listed above before tackling this work.

Pedersen, Holger, translated by John Webster Spargo. *The Discovery of Language: Linguistic Science in the Nineteenth Century* (Indiana University Press, 1931). Though dated and lacking information about more recent scholarship, this book remains the most comprehensive introduction to the history of the study of languages.

Ruhlen, Merritt. *A Guide to the World's Languages, Vol. 1: Classification* (Stanford University Press, 1991). Though this work is a comprehensive and reliable guide to the classification of nearly all known languages, some of the proposals regarding larger groupings remain controversial.

6

What language did Adam and Eve speak?

E. M. Rickerson

Does the language of Adam still exist? What language did God speak in the Garden of Eden? Did Adam and Eve speak Indo-European?

In the Old Testament story of the Garden of Eden, Adam was created as a fully-formed modern being, with all the faculties of *homo sapiens*, including the ability to speak. We can only guess what Adam might have said to Eve in their early chats, but we do know that both of them could talk. Eve had a fateful conversation with a persuasive snake, and one of Adam's first tasks on earth was linguistic: '... *and Adam gave names to all cattle, and to the fowl of the air, and to every beast of the field*' (Genesis 2:19). But what language did Adam use? Presumably it was the same one in which the serpent's words were couched and which the first couple heard when they were sternly evicted from Paradise.

It certainly wasn't English, which is a relatively young language, nor was it any of the world's languages that you might think of as 'old', such as Chinese or Greek. Leaving aside the question of how the first language-using people came into being, it is now fairly well accepted that humans were physiologically *able* to speak—that the vocal apparatus was ready to produce more than the calls or growls of our fellow mammals—at least as early as fifty thousand years ago, or more. Because we can trace languages only as far as their early written records, and because writing itself emerged only around five thousand years ago, we are left with a gap of thousands of years. And throughout those millennia, the language of the first human beings was undergoing constant and profound change. Therefore, whatever else we may say about the original language, it is clear that *none* of the languages currently spoken on the planet bears any resemblance to what may have been spoken in the legendary Garden of Eden.

That is the modern view, based on what we have learned about language since religious explanations gave way to the patient collection of linguistic data. But before the eighteenth century—from the earliest days of Christianity and through the Middle Ages and Reformation—it was taken for granted that Adam spoke the first language, and that the *lingua adamica*, the language he used, still existed. For most of that time, the leading candidate for the honor was Hebrew, if only because it was the language in which the Old Testament was handed down. In the fourth century St. Jerome asserted that only the family of Eber had not been so foolish as to help build the Tower of Babel. As a result, when God destroyed the Tower and scattered its builders, Eber's people—the Eberites, or Hebrews—were not punished, and continued to speak the original tongue. St. Augustine and other Christian church fathers accepted without question that Hebrew was the *lingua adamica* and, for the next thousand years or so, almost everyone agreed. I find it ironic that the scholarly discussion of this topic took place in Latin, which was as close to a universal language as there was in Europe during that time—yet no one suggested that Latin could have been the original tongue. The idea of Hebrew as the Adamic language had a firm hold on the imagination throughout the Renaissance, and even beyond.

The nature of Adam's language was an especially hot topic in the sixteenth and seventeenth centuries, when it was thought to be a divine or 'perfect' language, in which words coincided so harmoniously with the things they identified that people understood them without having to be taught their meanings. But not everyone accepted that this perfect language was, or had been, Hebrew. With the Renaissance came a sense of nationhood in Europe, and the *lingua adamica* idea served as a way to build national pride. In Germany, people rallied to the language of Luther's Bible and asserted that German was closest to the language of Adam; some even claimed that Hebrew was derived from German. Linguistic nationalism also prompted a claim for Dutch or Flemish. The theory ran that citizens of Antwerp were descendants of Noah's son Japeth, who had settled in northern Europe after the Flood and *before* the Tower of Babel, so that Dutch preserved the purity of the Adamic tongue. Improbable arguments were also made for the divine status of Celtic, Basque, Hungarian, Polish and many other languages. This was the time when Sweden was making itself felt as a world power, so it is not surprising that Swedish too was proposed as the original language, again based on the story of Japeth. And that leads us to my favorite theory: the suggestion that God spoke Swedish in Paradise, Adam Danish, and the snake … French.

After the Age of Reason loosened the grip of religion on philosophical thinking, the divine origins of language became a lesser concern. In the eighteenth and nineteenth centuries it was gradually understood that words and the things they stand for are not magically connected, and that languages are not divinely given. They are created by human communities, not a heavenly force. It became clear that language was a matter of agreement that certain combinations of sounds would be used to mean whatever a community decided they should mean. Instead of theological debates, scholars in Europe used scientific criteria to compare known languages, figure out how they are related, and how they developed over time. It is telling that when they discovered Indo-European, they made no claim that it was the original language. That discovery made it clear that it would be difficult if not impossible to penetrate the linguistic past to its absolute beginnings—and that the quest for the Adamic language was over.

About the author

E. M. ('Rick') Rickerson is the General Editor of this book. He is Professor Emeritus of German, Director Emeritus of the award-winning language program at the College of Charleston (South Carolina), a former Deputy Director of the U.S. government's Center for the Advancement of Language Learning, and an Associate of the National Museum of Language. In 2005 he created the radio series on languages (*Talkin' About Talk*) from which *The Five-Minute Linguist* has been adapted. He is currently a consultant on the development of language programs at the university level.

Suggestions for further reading

In this book: The origins and history of languages are also discussed in chapters 4 (earliest languages), 5 (language relationships), 7 (language change), 8 (pidgins and creoles), 48 (origins of English), and 54 (Icelandic).

Elsewhere:

Rickerson, Earl. *The Lingua Adamica and its Role in German Baroque Literature* (unpublished Ph.D. dissertation, 1969; available at UMI Dissertation Services: http://www.umi.com/products_umi/dissertations). Chapters 1–3 provide an overview of how the Adamic language was viewed before the Age of Reason.

Eco, Umberto. *The Search for the Perfect Language* (Blackwell, 1995). A comprehensive and very readable history of the ways in which the idea of an original or perfect language occupied European thinkers for close to two thousand years.

Olender, Maurice, *The Languages of Paradise: Race, Religion and Philology in the Nineteenth Century* (Harvard University Press, 1992). A scholarly discussion of ideas that underlay the comparative study of languages in the nineteenth century. Chapter 1 touches briefly on the *lingua adamica*.

7

Why do languages change?

John McWhorter

Why is our English different from Shakespeare's? What can English spelling tell us about language change? What kinds of changes do languages undergo? Can we stop English from changing?

Have you ever left a Shakespeare performance feeling worn out from trying to understand what the characters were saying? It wasn't just because Shakespeare's English is poetic, but because the English that Shakespeare knew was, in many ways, a different language from ours. When Juliet asked 'Wherefore art thou Romeo?' she wasn't asking where Romeo was—after all, he's right there under the balcony! *Wherefore* meant *why*. But we no longer have that word because languages shed words all the time. And they also take on new ones, like *blog*.

Languages are always changing. It's as inevitable for them to change as it is for cloud patterns in the sky to take on new forms. If we see a camel in the clouds today and walk outside and see the same camel tomorrow, then something's very wrong. It's the same way with languages—every language is in the process of changing into a new one.

In English, you can see this easily because our spelling often preserves the way the language was pronounced seven hundred years ago. The word *name*, for instance, used to be pronounced 'NAH-muh.' But we stopped saying the final /e/ and the AH sound (NAHme) drifted into an AY sound (NAYm).

Pronunciation is not the only area of impermanence: grammar changes, too. English used to be a language where verbs at the end of the sentence came. That is, a thousand or so years ago that's how you would have said that last sentence, with 'came' at the end. We also used to have more pronouns. *You* was only used to mean 'y'all'; for talking to an individual person, the word used was *thou*. And for the 'generic' *you*—as in a sentence like 'You only live once'—the pronoun was *man*. Now we just use *you* for all those meanings.

This kind of change is why we face the task of learning foreign languages. If language didn't change, we'd still all speak the first language that popped up in Africa when humans first started to talk. But once the original band of people split off into separate groups, the language took on new forms in each new place—different sounds, different word order, different endings. The result was that Chinese has tones; some Australian languages have only three verbs; some African languages have click sounds; many Native American languages pack a huge amount of information into single words; and English uses the same word *you* whether one or two or many people are involved.

The only thing that makes it look as if a language stays the same forever is print, because print *does* stay the same way forever. We think of Latin as a dead language, because we see it written on the page and we know that the particular language captured on that page is not spoken by anybody any more. But technically, the Latin we struggle with in classrooms was just one stage in a language that never died. It just drifted into several new versions of itself like French, Spanish, and Italian. We don't think of the language of the opera *Don Giovanni* as 'street Latin'—it's a new language altogether. There was never a day when people in Italy woke up and proclaimed 'We were speaking Latin last night but today we're speaking Italian!' Latin just morphed along like cloud formations, which might look like a camel one day and like a weasel the next.

But within our lifespans, it's hard not to think of changes in our language as mistakes. There was a time, fifteen or twenty centuries ago, when Latin was the official language of the territory we now call France. The bureaucrats and scholars who lived there and spoke it heard the beginnings of French around them but to them it sounded like just Grade-F Latin, not like a new language in its own right. Gray zones are always tricky. So, when young people say things like 'She's all "don't talk to me like that" and I was like "you shoulda known anyway"', they're pushing the language on its way to new frontiers. It was through the exact same kinds of changes that English got from *Beowulf* to Tom Wolfe.

About the author

John McWhorter, Senior Fellow at the Manhattan Institute, earned his Ph.D. in linguistics from Stanford University in 1993 and became Associate Professor of Linguistics at the University of California, Berkeley, after teaching at Cornell University. His academic specialty is language change and language contact. He is the author of *The Power of Babel: A Natural History of Language* (Perennial, 2003), an account of how the world's languages arise, change, and mix; and *Doing Our Own Thing: The Degradation of Language and Music in America and Why We Should, Like, Care* (Gotham, 2003). He has also written a book on dialects and Black English, *The Word on the Street* (Plenum, 1998), and two books on Creole languages: *The Missing Spanish Creoles* (California, 2000) and *Defining Creole* (Oxford, 2005). Dr. McWhorter has appeared often on radio and television programs such as *Dateline NBC, Good Morning, America, The Jim Lehrer Newshour,* and *Fresh Air,* and he does regular commentaries for National Public Radio's *All Things Considered.* E-mail: communications@manhattan-institute.org.

Suggestions for further reading

In this book: The origins and history of languages are also discussed in chapters 4 (earliest languages), 5 (language relationships), 6 (the language of Adam and Eve), 8 (pidgins and creoles), 48 (origins of English), and 54 (Icelandic); other chapters specifically focusing on language change include 11 (grammar), 41 (dialect change), 50 (Latin), and 51 (Italian).

Elsewhere:

McWhorter, John. *The Power of Babel* (Perennial, 2003). A book-length survey of how one original language became five thousand, with discussion of what dialects and creoles are and why writing slows down language change.

Bryson, Bill. *The Mother Tongue* (Morrow, 1990). A great way to get a handle on how English became what it is after starting as a close relative of German that is now a foreign tongue to English speakers; witty and goes down easy.

Ostler, Nicholas. *Empires of the Word* (HarperCollins, 2005). A chronicle of the birth, spread and sometimes decline of languages of empire like English, Arabic, and Sanskrit, lending a nice sense of how language change is natural and eternal.

8

Are pidgins and creoles real languages?

John M. Lipski

What's a pidgin language? Is creole more than just food? Are pidgin and creole the same thing?

How una dé? Uskain nius? These two greetings, the first from Nigeria and the second from Cameroon, both mean roughly 'Hi, what's happening?' Both use words from English, but combine them in new ways. They're the kind of language we're using when we greet someone by saying 'long time no see,' or when we invite a friend to come have a 'look-see,' or use 'no can do' when something's not possible. When we do that, what we're speaking is no longer English—it's a new language, based on English words but with simpler grammar and vocabulary. 'Look-see' and 'no can do' come from a language once called *China Coast Pidgin English*, which was used by sailors and merchants throughout the Pacific. But what kind of bird is this 'pidgin'?

Imagine for a moment that everyone reading this article spoke a different native language, and that the only English any of us knew was the result of a year or two of limited exposure somewhere earlier in our lives. If we all got stranded on the proverbial desert island, we might well find that the only way we could communicate would be to use our bits of English with one another. As the years went by, with no grammar books and no native speakers to correct us or teach us new words, we'd all develop survival skills in this way of talking, and we'd invent combinations that a true native speaker of English would barely recognize.

A language formed like this—among people who share no native language and are forced to communicate using elements of one that none of them speaks well—is what linguists call a pidgin. The word probably comes from South Sea traders' attempt to pronounce the word *business*. Most pidgins do not form on desert islands; they are formed when speakers of different languages have to speak to one another using bits and pieces of a language imposed on them—for example as slaves, contract laborers, or itinerant vendors. Pidgins have been used on slave plantations in the Americas, on South Pacific islands that imported laborers from widely scattered islands, and in Africa and the Pacific where urban marketplaces bring together people speaking a wide variety of languages.

Pidgins start out as simplified languages, but something happens when children are born to pidgin-speaking parents. Like children everywhere, as they grow they absorb the language they hear around them and make it their own. Unlike other children, though, as they learn their parents' language they expand and transform it from a makeshift jargon into a full-fledged new language. These new languages, spoken natively by the next generation in the family, are called *creole* languages by linguists (although sometimes the name 'pidgin' continues to be used in non-specialist contexts). There are dozens of creole languages scattered around the world, derived from European languages such as English, French, and Portuguese, but also from Arabic, Swahili, and other non-European tongues.

English-based creoles are used in the South Pacific from Papua New Guinea to the Solomon Islands and northern Australia. Gullah in South Carolina and Georgia and Hawaiian Pidgin are creole languages native to the U.S., while Cape Verde Portuguese Creole in Massachusetts and Haitian Creole in Miami and New York are among our country's immigrant languages.

Creole languages have millions of speakers. And they aren't 'broken' versions of what you might think of as 'real' languages. They have established grammars, they're taught in schools, and they're used in radio, television, and the press. They even have their own names and may serve as official languages, such as Tok Pisin in Papua New Guinea, Bislama in Vanuatu, and Papiamentu in Aruba, Curaçao, and Bonaire. The language used in the first sentence of this article is spoken in much of West Africa. While many people mistakenly refer to it as 'broken English,' it's the language of African popular music and literature, and of novels by the Nobel laureate Wole Soyinka.

Creoles and pidgins often include words and expressions that speakers of languages like English or French would recognize, but with very different meanings. For example, *beef* in West African Pidgin English refers to any animal whose meat can be eaten. So a pig could be a 'beef'. In Papua New Guinea the word *Meri* (from the English name 'Mary') is a word for woman, any woman.

Speakers of languages with long literary traditions sometimes laugh at creole languages, thinking of them—and their speakers—as inferior. But that kind of viewpoint has no basis in fact. Creoles are new languages, at most a few hundred years old, and deserve the same respect as the world's new nations, many of which also emerged through struggle.

Article 1 of the United Nations Universal Declaration of Human rights, translated into Nigerian Pidgin English, begins: *Everi human being, naim dem born free and dem de equal for dignity and di rights wey we get, as human being.* Speaking a creole language with pride and dignity is one of those basic human rights.

About the author

John M. Lipski is Professor of Spanish Linguistics in the Department of Spanish, Italian, and Portuguese at the Pennsylvania State University. He received his B.A. from Rice University, in Texas, and his M.A. and Ph.D. from the University of Alberta, Canada; he has taught Spanish, Romance, and general linguistics, translation, language acquisition and methodology, Latin American literature, and a variety of language courses at colleges and universities in New Jersey, Michigan, Texas, Florida, and New Mexico. His research interests include Spanish phonology, Spanish and Portuguese dialectology and language variation, the linguistic aspects of bilingualism, and the African contribution to Spanish and Portuguese. He is the author of eleven books and more than two hundred articles on all aspects of linguistics. He is also Editor of the journal *Hispanic Linguistics* and has served as Associate Editor of *Hispania* for Theoretical Linguistics. He has done fieldwork in Spain (including the Canary Islands), Africa, the Caribbean, Central and South America, the Philippines, Guam, and many Spanish-speaking communities within the United States.

Suggestions for further reading

In this book: The ways languages begin and develop are also discussed in chapters 4 (earliest languages), 5 (language relationships), 7 (language change), 11 (grammar), 41 (dialect change), 43 (dictionaries), 48 (origins of English), 50 (Latin), and 51 (Italian). Chapter 23 (sign languages) discusses the importance of children in transforming an invented language into a natural one.

Elsewhere:

Todd, Loreto. *Pidgins and Creoles* (Routledge and Kegan Paul, 1974). A very basic book, still not outdated in terms of the general concepts.

Holm, John. *An Introduction to Pidgins and Creoles* (Cambridge University Press, 2000).

Romaine, Suzanne. *Pidgin and Creole Languages* (Longman, 1988). Either of these books would be a good place for readers to pursue the topic of this chapter in greater detail. Holm is more accessible, Romaine more comprehensive.

9

How many kinds of writing systems are there?

Peter T. Daniels

How do writing systems differ? Which one is used the most? Could we use a system for English other than an alphabet?

Around the world, a little over thirty different writing systems are in official or widespread use today (counting all the different roman alphabets, like English and French and even Vietnamese as variants of a single one; likewise for all the varieties of Cyrillic and Arabic and so on). Unlike languages, which are all basically alike because every language has to fit into everyone's brain, writing systems are human inventions, and about half a dozen different kinds have been devised over the past five thousand years.

Most familiar, and most widespread, is the alphabet. In an alphabet, each letter represents one consonant or one vowel, and (theoretically) all the consonants and vowels in a word are written down, one by one, from left to right. But since you read and write English, you know that we are very far from that ideal! Why should *though*, *through*, *tough*, and *cough* all be spelled with *o-u-g-h*? Because we've been spelling pretty much the same way for more than five hundred years—since printing got started in England in the year 1475—while the pronunciation of English has been changing gradually over the centuries. Spanish and Finnish and Czech do a lot better in keeping the spelling the same as the sounds. The first language to be written with an alphabet was Greek—and to this day, Greek is written with the Greek alphabet. Every other alphabet in the world is descended from the Greek! Russian and many languages of the former Soviet Union are written with the Cyrillic alphabet, and the languages of western Europe, with the Roman alphabet.

So, too, are many languages that have only recently started being written. Hundreds and hundreds of them, such as Massachusett and Maori, Zulu and Zomi, have had alphabets created for them, usually the Roman alphabet with maybe a few extra letters or some accent marks, by missionaries translating the Bible. These alphabets usually don't have much use outside the Bible texts and related materials. But sometimes they also get used for personal correspondence, newspapers, and even books and the Internet—and a literate culture has been created.

Before there were alphabets, there were scripts of the kind I call 'abjads'. This seemingly simpler kind of writing can be seen in news photos from the Middle East. If you open a Hebrew Bible or a Qu'ran, you'll see the letters surrounded by dots and dashes and curls, but if you look at billboards and placards, you'll just see the letters—Hebrew ones all squared up separate in a row, Arabic ones gracefully joined together to make whole words without lifting the pen. The difference between the holy texts and the street signs, or ordinary books, is that ordinary writing in Hebrew and Arabic only writes letters for the consonants. If you know the languages, you can fill in the vowels on your own as you read. But getting the pronunciation exactly right is very important in holy books, and devout scholars in the early Middle Ages wanted to add helps to the reader. They wouldn't change the spellings they inherited, so they added in the vowels using dots and dashes around the letters.

The Greek alphabet developed out of the Phoenician abjad. The scripts of India developed out of the closely related Aramaic abjad—but with a difference. In India, linguists *without the benefit of writing* had already created a very sophisticated analysis of the Sanskrit language, and by the third century B.C.E. they had invented a very sophisticated way of writing the vowels (I call this type the 'abugida'). For languages of India and its neighbors in South and Southeast Asia, such as Sanskrit and Hindi and Bengali, Tamil and Thai, you write a plain letter and it reads as a consonant plus 'ah'. If you want it to read as the consonant plus a different vowel, you add a mark to it; and if you want it to read as two consonants in a row with no vowel in between, as in *chakra* or *Mahatma*, you attach a piece of the letter for the first consonant in front of the whole letter for the second consonant. It *can* get complicated!

If we go back before the Phoenician abjad, back to the very beginning of writing, we find that the first writing systems are always 'logographic'—instead of individual sounds (consonants or vowels), entire words (or word elements, called 'morphemes') are represented by a single syllable-sign. The one writing system based on the logographic principle that's still used today is the Chinese.

Look closely at the characters on a Chinese menu. If you compare them with the English names for foods, you might see which ones correspond to '*kung pao*' and which ones correspond to 'chicken' or 'shrimp'. With a logographic system you don't 'spell' words, because each character corresponds to a whole word or part of a word. It works very well, but it takes a *lot* of characters, since you need one or two for virtually every word in the language, and all languages have thousands of words. In the case of Chinese, you can read almost anything published in the language today if you learn about three thousand to four thousand characters.

Now look at a Japanese menu. Alongside the complicated characters that look like Chinese characters (in fact, they *are* Chinese characters, but each one stands for a whole Japanese word), you'll mostly see simpler characters. These represent the endings on the words, and each of these simpler characters stands for a whole syllable, a consonant plus a vowel. There are just fifty of these symbols, because Japanese syllables are just that simple: a consonant plus a vowel. *Su-shi, sa-shi-mi, ki-mo-no.*

Other languages are written with this kind of syllable-character, such as the American Indian language Cherokee and the Liberian language Vai. It would be hard to use syllable-writing for English, because English can make really complicated syllables, like 'strengths' and 'splint'. You'd need a lot of different characters to write them all.

Maybe the best writing system ever devised combines the syllable approach learned from China with the consonant-and vowel-letter approach learned from India: Korean writing, or *hangul*. On a Korean menu, you'll see squarish shapes that look like simple Chinese characters—but look at them closely and you'll see just forty simple designs (the letters) combined into blocks (the syllables). A great deal of information in a small space!

Different types of writing system work more or less well with different languages; but languages change over time, while spelling systems tend not to, so over time a writing system works less and less well. A glimpse of the history of writing is found in the next chapter.

About the author

Peter T. Daniels is one of the few linguists in the world specializing in the study of writing systems. He has published articles in a variety of journals and edited volumes, and contributed to several encyclopedias. He co-edited *The World's Writing Systems* (Oxford, 1996) with William Bright and was Section Editor for Writing Systems for the *Encyclopedia of Language and Linguistics* (Elsevier, 2006).

Suggestions for further reading

In this book: Other chapters about writing include 10 (origins of writing), 57 (Chinese) and 58 (Japanese).

Elsewhere:

Diringer, David. *The Alphabet* (Funk & Wagnalls, third edition 1968).

Jensen, Hans. *Sign, Symbol and Script* (George Allen & Unwin, 1969). These two books may take some effort to find, but each offers a very full history of writing. Diringer is more readable, Jensen more reliable and scholarly.

DeFrancis, John. *Visible Speech: The Diverse Oneness of Writing Systems* (University of Hawaii Press, 1989). Stresses that all writing is based on the *sounds* of languages.

Daniels, Peter T., and William Bright, eds. *The World's Writing Systems* (Oxford University Press, 1996). A standard reference for facts about writing systems, past and present.

Rogers, Henry. *Writing Systems: A Linguistic Approach* (Blackwell, 2005). Preferable among the small number of textbooks on writing.

10

Where did writing come from?

Peter T. Daniels

When did writing begin? How did it start? Was it invented more than once?

Dozens of writing systems have been used over the ages around the world, in a bewildering variety. They're written from left to right or right to left or top to bottom or even from bottom to top. Their symbols come in many shapes and sizes. Unlike spoken language, which started tens of thousands of years before writing and whose origins are cloudy, we have a very good idea of how and when writing began. Because fragments of some of the earliest writing still exist, carved on rocks, we can trace its evolution through time.

The discovery of writing was almost inevitable when a society grew complex enough to need it. As long as people are in small groups, everyone knows who did what for whom. But when people settle in towns, commerce becomes more complicated. A potter makes pots, a weaver makes cloth, an administration collects taxes. At some point, there's a need to keep track of everyone's contributions. Records might be kept with knots in string, or with notched sticks. And everywhere, people draw pictures to represent things. In Stone Age caverns, we drew pictures of prey animals. In modern times, we make pictures of things we want people to *buy*.

A second condition for discovering writing is a certain *kind* of language, one in which words are likely to consist of only one syllable. The reason seems to be that if you don't already know how to read with an alphabet, you aren't able to break down a syllable into its individual consonants and vowels. And if the words (or morphemes) of your language are mostly just one syllable, then when you write a picture standing for one of them, you're also writing its sound, and its sound can get reused for writing words it's not so easy to make pictures of.

These conditions gave rise to writing at least three times that we know of, and probably more that have left no trace. Writing appeared over five thousand years ago in ancient Mesopotamia (now southern Iraq), representing a now-dead language known as Sumerian. A completely different writing system was created in China close to four thousand years ago for a linguistic ancestor of modern Chinese. And in Middle America around the fourth century c.e. yet another system was developed to write down the Mayan languages. That system died a few centuries later with the Mayan empire. So all the writing systems in the world today can be traced back to just two places: China and Ancient Iraq.

Writing turns out to be a pretty useful thing to have. And once one group discovers it, nearby peoples tend to adopt it too. Japan adopted Chinese characters and started writing Japanese words with them. On the other side of the world, Sumerian writing was adopted for many languages between about 2500 and 1000 b.c.e., early in its history changing in form from pictures to easier-to-write abstractions. Sumerian inspired the Egyptian hieroglyphs we know from temples and tombs. And hieroglyphs became the raw material for the Phoenician abjad that gave the world its alphabets and abugidas.

There are hundreds of such scripts in use today (now counting each variety of Roman alphabet, say, separately). In addition to Europe and the western hemisphere, they're used across southern and southeastern Asia and on into Oceania. Most of them use twenty to thirty symbols. But they range in size from a language of the Solomon Islands, with eleven letters, to the Khmer abugida of Cambodia, with seventy-four. They look as different as English, Russian, or Hebrew, but it's fairly easy to show that *every* abjad, alphabet, and abugida—the ones I named and many more—has a common origin: ancient Phoenicia on the eastern shores of the Mediterranean.

The Phoenicians brought their abjad to the Greeks, who (accidentally!) turned it into an alphabet and passed it via the Etruscans to the Romans, who gave our letters the shapes they have to this day. Greek was also the model for alphabets in Eastern Europe, such as the Cyrillic alphabet of Russian and other tongues. Another descendant of Phoenician was the Aramaic abjad, from which came writing systems as different-looking as Hebrew and Arabic—and all the writings of India and beyond.

Writing originated from some pretty basic characteristics of human beings and human society. And yet it is not found everywhere. Despite writing's obvious uses, fewer than half of the world's languages even have a writing system! Most languages are only spoken. But that's changing. And as more languages become written, it's mostly the Roman alphabet, brought to the less-developed world by missionaries and linguists, that's spreading writing across the globe.

Where would we be without writing? It's a remarkable part of language—and of human history. Without writing, you could reasonably ask, would history even exist?

About the author

Peter T. Daniels is one of the few linguists in the world specializing in the study of writing systems. He has published articles in a variety of journals and edited volumes, and contributed to several encyclopedias. He co-edited *The World's Writing Systems* (Oxford, 1996) with William Bright and was Section Editor for Writing Systems for the *Encyclopedia of Language and Linguistics* (Elsevier, 2006).

Suggestions for further reading

In this book: Other chapters about writing include 9 (kinds of writing systems), 57 (Chinese) and 58 (Japanese).

Elsewhere:

Diringer, David. *The Alphabet* (Funk & Wagnalls, third edition 1968).

Jensen, Hans. *Sign, Symbol and Script* (George Allen & Unwin, 1969). These two books may take some effort to find, but each offers a very full history of writing. Diringer is more readable, Jensen more reliable and scholarly.

DeFrancis, John. *Visible Speech: The Diverse Oneness of Writing Systems* (University of Hawaii Press, 1989). Stresses that all writing is based on the *sounds* of languages.

Daniels, Peter T., and William Bright, eds. *The World's Writing Systems* (Oxford University Press, 1996). A standard reference for facts about writing systems, past and present.

Rogers, Henry. *Writing Systems: A Linguistic Approach* (Blackwell, 2005). Preferable among the small number of textbooks on writing.

11

Where does grammar come from?

Joan Bybee

Does grammar change? What is grammar anyway? Do all languages have it?

All languages have grammar, by which we mean those little function words (*the*, *a*, *will*, *some*) or prefixes and endings that signal meanings such as past, present and future. Grammar also includes the way we arrange words so effortlessly yet consistently in our native language; for instance, the fact that we say 'the dog is sleeping on the couch' rather than 'is dog ingsleep couch the on'. Although most of us are aware of words changing, we tend to think of grammar as more stable. But in fact, grammar is also constantly in flux.

The Language Police always deplore the loss of grammar—for instance, the fact that we don't know when to use *whom* anymore—but it's barely noticed that languages also develop *new* grammar. And yet they do! All the time.

For example, English has some old ways to indicate future tense by using *will* and *shall*. But these days American English speakers and younger Britons hardly use the word *shall* at all. A new way to mark future has evolved in the last few centuries from the expression *be going to* plus a verb. So when we say 'it's going to rain', we mean it purely as a prediction about a future event—it doesn't mean that something or someone is going anywhere at all. In Shakespeare's time, on the other hand, if you used *going to*, it always meant literally that someone was going from one place to another for some purpose.

How did this change happen? It is a process that linguists call 'grammaticalization', through which a word or sequence of words like *be going to* may acquire a change of meaning and take on a grammatical function. Such changes happen very gradually, over long periods of time, and several things usually happen at once.

The change of meaning often starts when inferences get associated with certain phrases. For instance, if I say 'I'm going to visit my sister' I am telling you both where I am going and what my intentions are. After a while, the intention meaning becomes even more important than the movement meaning. From the intention meaning in turn you can make an inference about what will happen in the future. So eventually, we can use *be going to* to indicate future.

Humans are very interested in other people's intentions, so expressions of intent are a more important piece of information than expressions about movement in space. So when *be going to* began to be used for intention it was used more often. When phrases are used a lot they begin to lose some of their impact, and the original meaning seems to get bleached away. They also tend to be said faster, and pronunciation erodes: so when *going to* came into constant use as a main way to express the future, it started to turn into *gonna*—a new bit of grammar. Not everybody has yet recognized *gonna* as a future tense marker, but that is clearly the function it is serving, especially in spoken language. In another hundred years it will no doubt be firmly entrenched in our grammar books—until another way to express future develops.

Grammaticalization happens over and over, and in all languages. In fact, many languages use a phrase with a verb such as *go* to signal the future. You can see it in Spanish, French, the African languages Margi, Krongo, Mano and Bari, the Native American languages Cocama and Zuni, the Pacific language Atchin, and many more. One thing that languages have in common is that they develop over time in very similar ways.

And it is not just markers of future time that develop this way, but all kinds of grammatical markers. For instance, it is common for the indefinite article *a/an* as in 'a dog' to develop from the word for 'one'. In English, you can still hear the 'n' of 'one' in the 'an' of 'an apple'. Similarly, in Spanish, French, German and other European languages, the relation between the word for 'one' and the indefinite article 'a' or 'an' is quite clear. Spanish *un/una*, French *un/une* and German *ein/eine* all mean both 'one' and 'a/an'.

Or think about prepositions, those little words like *at, over, with, above* or *through* that link up with a noun to talk about when, where or how something was accomplished ('at ten o'clock', 'over the bridge', 'with daring speed'). They too are what we think of as part of 'grammar' and have undergone changes in their meaning and use. Our words *before* and *behind*, for example, are composed of an old preposition *be-* and the noun *fore* meaning 'front' and *hind* meaning 'the back part of a body'. While these prepositions started out with meanings having to do with space ('before the castle', 'behind the ramparts'), they are now also used for time ('before noon', 'I'm running behind schedule').

There are many features of grammar whose origins we don't know, but because the process of grammaticalization is so common, it's safe to assume that all words and parts of words that have a grammatical function … came from other words.

And that helps us explain how the very first language got grammar. The earliest language was no doubt fairly 'telegraphic' in nature,

WHERE DOES GRAMMAR COME FROM? 53

a collection of individual words, supplemented with gestures to convey meaning. But soon after human beings could use words as symbols and join two words together, they surely used some combinations very frequently. With the making of inferences and inevitable changes in pronunciation, the development of grammar was put in motion. And that was a great thing, because—despite its bad reputation among those who struggled with it in school—it is the existence of grammar that makes fluent, connected speech possible.

About the author

Joan Bybee (Ph.D., UCLA) is a Distinguished Professor of Linguistics at the University of New Mexico. At the University of New Mexico she has served as Associate Dean and Department Chair. In 2004 she served as President of the Linguistic Society of America. Professor Bybee is considered a leader in the study of the way language use impacts language structure. She has authored books and articles on phonology, morphology, language typology and language change. Her book *The Evolution of Grammar* (University of Chicago Press, 1994) uses a database of seventy-six languages to study the way in which languages spontaneously develop new grammatical structures.

Suggestions for further reading

In this book: Other chapters discussing grammar include 12 (universal grammar), 14 (animals and language), and 22 (language deprivation); chapters 7 (language change) and 8 (pidgins and creoles) discuss how grammar changes over time.

Elsewhere:

Deutscher, Guy. *The Unfolding of Language* (Henry Holt and Company, 2005). A lively popular introduction to linguistics from the point of view of language change.

Hopper, Paul, and Elizabeth Traugott. *Grammaticalization* (Cambridge University Press, 2003). A textbook for linguistics students about grammaticalization.

12

Do all languages have the same grammar?

Mark C. Baker

Is there a universal grammar that underlies all languages? What do English, Mohawk, and Japanese have in common?

Probably no one would claim that all languages have the same grammar. But many linguists believe that all languages have certain basic design features in common, and that it is worth looking seriously into a concept often called 'Universal Grammar'.

If there were such a thing as a set of rules underlying all languages, might that help explain how children can so easily learn their mother tongue—without graduate courses or government funds—even though language is one of the most complex systems of knowledge that any human being acquires?

Perhaps, but it's not easy to see what all languages might have in common—especially if we look beyond the Western European languages, which have many similarities because they share a common history. Each language obviously uses different words, and it seems no less obvious that the rules and patterns for assembling words into phrases and sentences differ widely from one language to the next. Let's look at a couple of non-European examples.

In English, one says 'John gave a book to Mary'; the Japanese equivalent is *John-ga Mary-ni hon-o yatta*. The words for 'book' (*hon-o*) and 'gave' (*yatta*) are different, of course, but so are their positions in the sentence. In English, the verb 'gave' is the second word of the sentence; in Japanese it is the last word. In English, 'book' comes after the verb; in Japanese it comes before the verb. In English the gift recipient 'Mary' comes after the preposition 'to'; in Japanese the recipient comes before *ni* (the equivalent of 'to'). Not only do you need to learn a new set of words to speak Japanese, you also need to learn a new set of rules for how to combine the words—a new grammar.

The Mohawk language differs from English in a different way. In Mohawk, the sentence 'The man gave a blanket to the baby' could be expressed as *Owira'a wa-sh-ako-hsir-u ne rukwe*. Word order is not grammatically important in Mohawk: you can put *owira'a* ('baby'), *washakohsiru* ('he-her-blanket-gave'), and *rukwe* ('man') wherever you like and still get the same meaning. What's crucial in Mohawk is the form of the verb: if you replace *washakohsiru* with *wahuwahsiru*, the sentence then means 'The baby gave a blanket to the man,' whatever order the words are put in. Stranger still, the direct object 'blanket' is not even a separate word in these sentences. It is indicated by *hsir*, which combines with the verb root *u* to make a complex verb ('blanket-gave')—something that is not usually possible in English or Japanese. Indeed, a complex verb can be a sentence unto itself in Mohawk: *washakohsiru* can stand alone to mean 'He gave a blanket to her.'

Despite differences like these, linguistic research is discovering that the grammars of different languages are much more similar than they appear at first.

The subject in Japanese is at the beginning of the sentence, as it is in English. Did you notice that apart from that, the words in Japanese are in the exact mirror-image order of the English order? The recipient 'Mary' comes next to the word meaning 'to' in both languages. The direct object 'book' comes next to the word meaning 'gave' in both languages. Overall, the same kinds of words combine with each other to form the same kinds of phrases in English and Japanese. The only difference is a systematic difference in order—whether verbs and prepositions are put at the beginning of their phrases (as in English) or at the end of their phrases (as in Japanese). That's why it is right to say that the grammars are almost the same. After all, a picture and its mirror image are not completely different, even though the pixels don't match up. On the contrary, they are almost the same image—a truth we take advantage of when brushing our teeth or combing our hair.

What about Mohawk, where word order doesn't seem to matter? The fact that the subject can come before or after the verb does not seem so strange if you have studied Spanish or Italian. In all these languages, the verb changes its form to agree with the subject, so the subject can go anywhere in the sentence and you can still recognize it. How about the way the direct object gets incorporated into the verb in Mohawk? Even here Mohawk is not completely unlike familiar languages. Recall that the direct object appears next to the verb in both English and Japanese. This is also true in Mohawk, with a slight twist: the direct object combines so closely with the verb that the two of them become a single word. The three languages are the same in that the verb combines with the direct object more readily than it does with the subject or some other part of the sentence. The only difference is whether the result of that combination is a verbal *phrase* (English and Japanese) or a verbal *word* (Mohawk).

The fact that verbs always combine more closely with direct objects than they do with subjects is a good example of a general law of grammar, which seems to hold for all human languages.

It turns out that there are many such universal laws. In fact, over the past several decades, linguists have uncovered dozens of them. The laws provide the basic skeletal structure of language, which individual languages then flesh out in various ways. Once we dig beneath the surface, languages seem to have as many similarities in their structure as they have differences. So, while it is not quite true that all languages have the same grammar, it is much closer to being true than you might have thought.

About the author

Mark Baker was trained in linguistics at MIT under Noam Chomsky. He is now professor of linguistics and cognitive science at Rutgers University, where he specializes in the word structure and sentence structure of less-studied languages, especially those spoken in Africa and the Americas.

Suggestions for further reading

In this book: Other chapters discussing grammar include 11 (grammar in general), 14 (animals and language), and 22 (language deprivation).

Elsewhere:

Baker, Mark. *The Atoms of Language* (Basic Books, 2002). A non-technical book-length discussion of the similarities and differences among languages, showing in more detail than this chapter how different-looking languages can be derived from almost the same grammatical rules.

Pinker, Steven. *The Language Instinct* (Harper Collins, 1994). Chapter 8 addresses the question of how languages differ, putting this question in the context of the overall view that language is an instinct hard-wired into the human brain.

Whaley, Lindsey. *Introduction to Typology* (SAGE Publications, 1996). An introductory textbook that gives some of the history and main results that come from comparing a wide range of historically unrelated languages.

13

How do babies learn their mother tongue?

Roberta Michnick Golinkoff and
Kathryn Hirsh-Pasek

*When do babies start learning to talk? How do they do
it? Can babies learn any language they are exposed to?*

'Goo goo gaa gaa' might be what you think is the beginning of how
babies learn to talk, but if so, you're wrong! Language learning starts
well before babies utter their first words or babbles. Once babies can
hear, they respond to sounds. There's no question that babies in the
womb *jump* in response to noises, such as fireworks. Even before
they're born, they eavesdrop on every conversation their mother
has. When they emerge, we can trick them into showing us that they
recognize their mother's voice as well as stories and songs they've
heard in the womb. At first, language is only like a melody for them,
but they enter the world prepared to learn any of the world's nearly
seven thousand languages.

With the melody imprinted, the first problem babies face is finding the *units* in the speech they hear. Where does one word end and the next begin? By four and a half months of age, they're well on the way to finding words in the stream of speech that washes over them. They start by recognizing their own name. The first clue is its stress pattern ('Irving' is clearly different from 'Annette'); in very little time, they can distinguish their name (e.g., 'Irving') even from other names with the same stress pattern ('Wilson', for example). Researchers can demonstrate this by showing that, given a choice, little Irving consistently prefers listening to his own name. Having mastered their names, babies begin to recognize other frequently occurring words—like 'mama'—that can serve as anchors in the mass of sounds coming at them. (You may have had a similar experience as you began learning a foreign language.) Research tells us that at six months of age babies can recognize a word they hear when it comes *after* their own name.

Having learned to distinguish words, babies need to figure out what they mean. Naturally enough, some of the first words babies understand the meanings of are 'mama' and 'daddy'. Research tells us that by six months, they attach the word 'mama' to their own mother and not to just any woman. Likewise for 'daddy'. But as their internal vocabularies expand, learning what words mean can be complicated. Imagine yourself in a foreign country where you know very little of the language. A rabbit hops by, and a native says 'zoxil'. What might 'zoxil' mean? 'Rabbit' is a pretty obvious guess, but it might not be right. She could be saying 'look', or 'hopping' or 'ears'. Picking up the new language this way, it'll take time for you to sort out the possibilities and add 'zoxil' to your vocabulary. Babies are in the same situation. But by twelve months, they seem to interpret words as labels for objects—usually whole objects (like rabbits) as opposed to parts (like ears) or actions (like hopping).

After babies find words and know some meanings comes the step that marks true language acquisition: they begin to learn how words go together to make sentences. They know more about their language than what they can say—just as you could understand more in a foreign language than you could speak. So while their first spoken words appear at around twelve months of age, they may already understand hundreds of words. By eighteen months, they can understand five- and six-word sentences when they may be saying only one or two words at a time themselves.

Picture an oversize TV screen, split between two moving images: on the left side, Cookie Monster is hugging Big Bird; on the right, Big Bird is hugging Cookie Monster. Babies watch the screen with rapt attention. When they hear 'Where's Big Bird hugging Cookie Monster?' they look more at the right side of the screen than at the left. This means that babies, amazingly enough, are already using *grammar*, the order of the words in English, to figure out who's doing what to whom—even if they aren't *saying* much at all.

So here's a paradox: Babies can't tie their shoes or be left alone for more than thirty seconds, and yet they're like sponges when it comes to learning languages. The next time you're tempted to think of a newborn baby as a vegetable, think again! They're paying attention—and they learn languages better than their older and wiser parents!

About the authors

Roberta Michnick Golinkoff holds the H. Rodney Sharp Chair in the School of Education at the University of Delaware and is also a member of the Departments of Psychology and Linguistics. She directs the Infant Language Project, whose goal it is to understand how children tackle the amazing feat of learning language. Having obtained her Ph.D. at Cornell University, she has produced nine books and many research articles. The recipient of a prestigious John Simon Guggenheim Fellowship and a James McKeen Cattell Sabbatical award, she is frequently quoted in newspapers and magazines and has appeared on *Good Morning America* and many regional morning television programs.

Kathy Hirsh-Pasek is the Stanley and Debra Lefkowitz Professor in the

Department of Psychology at Temple University, Pennsylvania, where she serves as Director of the Infant Language Laboratory. Her research projects in the areas of early language development and infant cognition have been funded by the National Science Foundation and the National Institutes of Health and Human Development and have resulted in nine books and numerous journal publications. She has appeared on *Today*, *20/20*, and other national television programs and is often quoted in newspapers and magazines. She is a Fellow of the American Psychological Association and serves as Associate Editor of *Child Development*.

Suggestions for further reading

In this book: Other chapters discussing language acquisition by children include 8 (pidgins and creoles), 15 (language and the brain), 22 (language deprivation), 23 (sign languages), and 33 (children and second languages).

Elsewhere:

Golinkoff, R. M. and K. Hirsh-Pasek. *How Babies Talk: The Magic and Mystery of Language in the First Three Years of Life* (Dutton/Penguin, 1999). This is a fun read that reviews the latest research in language acquisition and offers tips to parents.

Hirsh-Pasek, K. and R. M. Golinkoff. *Einstein Never Used Flash Cards: How Our Children Really Learn and Why They Need to Play More and Memorize Less* (Rodale, 2003). This award-winning book shows how important language is for reading, expressing emotion, and succeeding at school.

14

Do animals use language?

Donna Jo Napoli

*Do animals talk among themselves? If so, what systems
do they use? And how do they differ from human
language?*

Parrots talk. So the answer is yes, animals use language, right?
Well, not so fast. There are two issues here, both interesting from
a linguistic point of view. One is whether animals use language
among themselves; the other is whether animals can learn human
language. Before addressing them, we have to decide what should
count as language.

Human languages have well-defined characteristics. First, they
are systematic; that is, they all have rules that we call grammar.
('Chased dog the nasty a cat' is made of English words, but it isn't an
English sentence—the words have been thrown together randomly,
rather than according to the rules of English syntax.)

Human language is also innate. Children are born hard-wired
to acquire language. No one needs to teach them. This ability
depends on the plasticity of the infant brain, though: a child not
exposed to language by the age of five may never fully acquire it.

A third striking characteristic is what linguists call 'displace-ment'—humans can talk about objects that aren't present, like the man in this sentence: 'The weird man you followed last week told me he's considering writing an exposé of existentialism.' Still another feature of human language is its ability to talk about abstract notions—like 'weirdness', 'exposé', and 'existentialism'. Finally, the 'weird man' sentence is one I never used before I wrote it just now. You probably never heard it before, either. All human languages have the ability to create new expressions.

If language necessarily involves all five of those criteria, we have to say that animals do not use language, even though they communicate with one another in ways that share some of its characteristics.

Bees have elaborate dances to tell other bees the location and quality of a food source. The dances have regulated paths and speeds. The orientation of the dancer's head and the vigor of its waggle are significant. Clearly these dances follow rules. They are about food that isn't present (so we have displacement) and about how good the food is (so we have abstraction). And researchers seem to assume that dancing is innate. But creativity is lacking; the amount of information bees can pass on is extremely limited. They cannot communicate, for example, that a new food source is near another well-known one, or that other bees are already approaching the source so that the hive had better hurry if they want any.

Birdsong has also rules. Robin song, for example, has motifs which have to occur in a certain order (a kind of grammar) or other birds will find them unintelligible. The ability to sing is innate, and birds not exposed to song within the first several months of life never develop typical courtship-territorial song. Birdsong does convey emotion, so to that extent it refers to abstractions. We have no evidence, however, that birdsong allows displacement (birds never seem to tell each other that something scary happened to them on the other side of the barn, for example); nor do they make up new songs.

Whales and dolphins sing and whistle. The form of their songs follows rules (the complex songs of some whales can go on all day long), and they can convey limited meaning (distress or warning calls), but there's no evidence of the novelty or creativity characteristic of human language. The songs are signatures, simply identifying the members of a pod.

Chimpanzees have grunts, barks, pants, wails, laughs, squeaks, hoots, and calls. They use them to alert others to the location of food sources, to announce a successful kill, to express alarm or danger, to identify themselves, or to express satisfaction. Their postures, facial expressions, and limb gestures play an even greater role in communication. But nothing so far has indicated that any of this follows a set of grammar-like rules.

Turning to the second question, there have been many attempts to teach human language to birds, sea mammals, and primates.

Alex, an African grey parrot that Dr. Irene Pepperberg of the University of Arizona has worked with, has an extensive vocabulary. He can identify objects with English words, by their material, color, shape, and number. He can ask for food that isn't present. He apologizes when he's misbehaved. He is quite facile at language and clearly understands what some words mean. Yet, his verbal behavior is erratic in ways unlike even a very young human's.

Dolphins have been taught to respond to hand gestures and are able to interpret new utterances correctly. For example, dolphins who learned that the sequence of gestures PERSON SURFBOARD FETCH means 'bring the surfboard to the person' were able to interpret SURFBOARD PERSON FETCH as 'bring the person to the surfboard'—and quite easily. They recognized a system and used it.

Chimpanzees, gorillas, and bonobos (closely related to chimps) have been taught to use and respond to sign language. The famous chimp Washoe, who learned a simple sign language from her trainers, adopted a baby named Loulis; and Loulis is said to have learned to sign from Washoe. A gorilla named Koko is reported to have amassed a vocabulary of over a thousand signs. A bonobo named Kanzi, featured in cover stories in *Time*, *Newsweek*, and *National Geographic* because of his language-like ability, learned to use a keyboard with symbols on it. We are told he could understand over five hundred spoken English words and use about two hundred keyboard symbols to represent set words or actions.

While experiments in teaching human language to animals are suggestive, they leave the basic question unresolved. How great is the ability of animals to use language? Kanzi demonstrates that primates can learn language to some extent; but even if animals have such a capacity, they do not use it among themselves. There seems to be no chimpanzee grammar in the jungle. Nor is there evidence that animal communication systems can express new ideas, a key feature of human language. Language remains the most profound distinction between animals and humans.

About the author

Donna Jo Napoli, trained at Harvard and MIT, is Professor of Linguistics at Swarthmore College. She publishes widely in theoretical linguistics, primarily on the structure of Italian and, more recently, of American Sign Language (ASL). Her books include *Language Matters* (Oxford, 2003) and *Linguistics: An Introduction* (Oxford, 1996). She also writes novels for children: http://www.donnajonapoli.com

Suggestions for further reading

In this book: Chapters discussing grammar include 11 (grammar in general), 12 (universal grammar), 13 (infant language acquisition), and 22 (language deprivation).

Elsewhere:

Anderson, Steve. *Dr. Doolittle's Delusion: Animals and the Uniqueness of*

Human Language (Yale University Press, 2004). Clarifies the distinction between communication and language and argues that while animals have the former, they do not have the latter.

Web sites:

http://www.cwu.edu/~cwuchci/
The site of Central Washington University's Chimpanzee and Human Communication Institute, where scientists use ASL with chimps.

http://www.bga.com/~pixel/fun/alex.htm
An article by Kenn Kaufman about Alex the parrot and his communication with humans.

http://polarization.com/bees/bees.html
About bee dances.

15

How does the brain cope with multiple languages?

Henk Haarmann

*Is there such a thing as **too much** language learning?*
How does the brain deal with multiple languages?

Have you ever been faced with uncomfortable amounts of new or complicated information, and said something like 'I feel my head's going to explode'? Well, I don't want to blow anybody's head up, but one of the major aims of many of the chapters of this book is to encourage readers and their children to learn new languages. So, in case you detect cerebral pressure building, let me offer some words of comfort about the magnificent flexibility of the human brain.

Researchers today compare the brain at birth to a kind of ready-to-assemble computer kit: it comes with working components, but they have to be connected before you have a fully functioning computer. In this view the brain comes with *readiness* for language in general, but acquiring the actual sounds, words, and grammar of a particular language means growing new connections between neurons, the individual brain cells. This connection-building is what happens as a toddler learns to associate the word 'dog' with a four-legged animal and 'milk' with what's in his drinking cup; or as another toddler learns the words 'perro' for the same animal and 'leche' for the same liquid.

But you may wonder, if a child is hearing *both* languages, will her brain mix them up and thereby hinder speech? Here's the comforting fact: the brain—especially in early childhood—has a huge, virtually inexhaustible capacity for making such connections. The more talk children are exposed to in the first three years of life, the better their language skills later. In fact, children exposed to more than one language grow not only the connections that build vocabulary in each language; they also grow connections that help them sort out which language to use in different situations.

They learn, for example, to ask their English-speaking mother for 'milk' and their Spanish-speaking grandmother for 'leche'.

In the past few years we've seen some tragic cases in which people adopted babies from orphanages in Eastern Europe and found that, as they grew into childhood, they were handicapped in talking to their American mothers. That wasn't a result of being confused by hearing a new language. It happened because the orphanages were thinly staffed. People watching the babies gave them minimal care and had little or no time to talk to them. The babies were linguistically starved, and didn't have the verbal stimulation that leads to normal use of language. Hearing talk, lots of talk, in infancy and later is healthy activity for the human brain, and that seems to be true no matter how many languages are involved.

But there's more to the story. It seems that there are cognitive advantages in training oneself to keep two or more languages separate. A recent study found that brain regions important for fluent speech were better developed in bilingual speakers than they were in monolinguals, especially when two languages were learned early in life.

Here's why: When a bilingual child wants to express a word in one language, the brain also activates the corresponding word in the other language. To prevent the word in the other language from being unintentionally spoken aloud, the brain has to suppress it. By having to perform this kind of control, the developing bilingual brain gets a kind of exercise that the monolingual brain does not.

To repeat, learning two languages at an early age is *good* for the brain—and, you'll be interested to know, not just for learning to *talk*. Studies at York University in Canada suggest that early bilinguals also have better cognitive control in certain types of *non*-verbal tasks. And that was true not just for children but also for middle-aged and older adults. Bilingualism seems to protect healthy older adults from some of the negative effects of aging on the brain. That in itself is an excellent reason to be born into a bilingual family—or to start learning a second language while you're still in diapers.

About the author

Henk Haarmann is an associate research scientist at the Center for Advanced Study of Language (CASL) of the University of Maryland. He is a cognitive psychologist who has studied language memory through computer modeling and measurement of brain activity. He was born in the Netherlands. He received doctoral training at the Max Planck Institute for Psycholinguistics and the University of Nijmegen in the Netherlands and post-doctoral training at Carnegie Mellon University. Email: hhaarmann@casl.umd.edu

Suggestions for further reading

In this book: Other chapters discussing adult language learning include 27 (foreign accents), 30 (how to study languages), 31 (history of language-teaching methods), 32 (study abroad), and 34 (language-teaching technology); chapters discussing children's language learning include 8 (pidgins and creoles), 13 (babies and language), 22 (language deprivation), 23 (sign languages), and 33 (second-language learning in elementary schools).

Elsewhere:

Bialystok, E., F. I. M. Craik, C. Grady, W. Chau, R. Ishii, A. Gunji, and C. Pantev. 'Effect of bilingualism on cognitive control in the Simon task: Evidence from MEG', in *NeuroImage* (2005) 24: 40–9.

16

Does our language influence the way we think?

Geoffrey K. Pullum

*How are language and thought related? Do you **think**
the way you do because of the language you speak?
What's the real story on Eskimo words for 'snow'?*

A surprising number of the things people say about thinking are
actually expressed as claims about language. People say 'We didn't
even speak the same language' when they really mean that our
thoughts were totally different; 'I was speechless' nearly always means
that I was astonished rather than that my voice stopped working;
and so on.

Of course, language and thought are doubtless quite closely
related. Language permits thoughts to be represented explicitly in
our minds, helping us reason, plan, remember, and communicate.
It's communication that gets all the press when we talk about language, but could it be that the language we use causes us to think
in certain ways?

Different languages do put things differently. But does that mean some thoughts can only be expressed in one language? Is it possible to have thoughts in one language that can't be translated into another? Most of the people who think the answer to these questions is yes turn out to have nothing in mind other than word meanings.

It is pretty easy to find words in one language that don't have exact equivalents in another. The German word *Schadenfreude* is a famous example (it refers to a kind of malicious pleasure some people find in other people's misfortunes). But does the lack of a one-word exact English equivalent mean that English speakers aren't able to experience that feeling themselves or recognize it in others? Surely not (and I believe I just explained in English what it means, too).

Another familiar example concerns color: some languages have far fewer words than English for naming primary colors. Quite a few use the same word for both 'green' and 'blue'. Some have only four, or three, or two color-name words. Does this mean their speakers can't physically distinguish multiple colors? It seems not. An experiment in the 1960s found that members of a New Guinea tribe (the Dani people) whose language named only two colors were just as good at matching a full spectrum of color chips as English speakers.

And lest we forget, I'd better mention the tired old claim that Eskimos see the world differently because they have some huge number of words for different varieties of snow. You may be disappointed to learn that there's hardly any truth to this. The eight languages of the Eskimo family have only a modest number of snow terms. Four were mentioned in a 1911 description of a Canadian Eskimo language by the great anthropologist Franz Boas: a general word for snow lying on the ground; a word for 'snowflake'; one for 'blizzard'; one for 'drift'; and that was it. His point had nothing to do with numbers of words or their influence on thinking, but just with the way different languages draw slightly different distinctions when naming things.

But after years of exaggeration and embellishment of Boas's remarks, a seductive myth has arisen. People with no knowledge of Eskimo languages repeat over and over in magazines, newspapers, and lectures that the Eskimos have X words for snow, the number X varying wildly from the dozens to the thousands between different tellings of the story. They offer no evidence, and they ignore the fact that English, too, has plenty of words for snow—words like 'slush', 'sleet', 'avalanche', 'blizzard', and 'flurry'.

Do the vocabularies of Eskimo languages really give their speakers—the Inuit and Yup'ik peoples of arctic Siberia, Alaska, Canada, and Greenland—a unique way of perceiving, unshared by English speakers? Perhaps it's true in some subtle way, but people overstate the possibility grossly. Some go as far as claiming that your language *creates* your world for you, and thus that speakers of different languages live in different worlds. This is relativism taken to an extreme.

The idea that our language inexorably shapes or determines how we think is pure speculation, and it's hard to imagine what could possibly support that speculation even in principle. For one thing, there is surely some thought (in the minds of animals, for instance) that is done without the aid of language. But notice also that in order for you to know there was a thought that was understandable for a speaker of (say) Hindi but not for you as an English speaker, you'd need to have that Hindi thought explained to you

Take as an example the Hindi word *kal*. It's a word that picks out a particular region of time: if today is the 8th of the month, surprisingly *kal* refers to either the 9th or the 7th, whichever is appropriate. Does that give Hindi speakers a unique and special sense of time that you can never share, where time is seen as spreading outward in both directions, and *kal* is one day away from now in either direction? Well, if so, then I have just explained it to you, and that means you can understand it after all.

Certainly, it is not impossible that your view of the world may be influenced in some subtle ways by the way your native language tempts you to classify concepts; but that doesn't mean that your language defines a shell within which your thought is confined, or that there are untranslatable thoughts that only a speaker of some other language can have. If you find yourself trying to think an unthinkable thought, don't give up and blame your language; just think a little harder.

About the author

Geoffrey K. Pullum is a linguist with broad scholarly interests in language, especially in topics relating to the grammar of English. He was born in the U.K., and worked there and in Europe as a rock musician for some years before going to college. He received his B.A. in Language at the University of York and earned the Ph.D. in General Linguistics at the University of London. He has taught at University College London, the University of Washington, and Stanford University, and since 1981 has been a tenured faculty member in the Department of Linguistics at the University of California, Santa Cruz (UCSC), where from 1987 to 1993 he also served as Dean of Graduate Studies and Research. He was elected a Fellow of the American Academy of Arts and Sciences in 2003. He has published over two hundred articles and books, ranging from technical works on syntactic theory to a handbook on phonetic transcription (*Phonetic Symbol Guide*, Chicago, second edition 1996) and a collection of satirical essays about the study of language (*The Great Eskimo Vocabulary Hoax*, Chicago, 1991). His most recent books (both co-authored with Rodney Huddleston) are *The Cambridge Grammar of the English Language* (Cambridge University Press, 2002) and a textbook based on it, *A Student's Introduction to English Grammar* (2005). *The Cambridge Grammar*, a 1862-page detailed description of the linguistic structure of international standard English, revises the traditional description of English in numerous ways. It was awarded the Linguistic Society of America's Leonard Bloomfield Book Award in January 2004.

Suggestions for further reading

Whorf, Benjamin Lee., ed. by John B. Carroll. *Language, Thought and Reality: Selected Writings* (MIT Press, 1964). Edited collection of the (fairly accessible) writings of Whorf, who was perhaps the most important popularizer of the idea that language shapes thought.

Preston, John, ed. *Thought and Language* (Royal Institute of Philosophy Supplement 42) (Cambridge University Press, 1997). A collection of serious papers on language/thought relations by some important modern philosophers.

Lucy, John Arthur. *Language Diversity and Thought: A Reformulation of the Linguistic Relativity Hypothesis* (Cambridge University Press, 1992). Major book-length study of the 'linguistic relativity' hypothesis that the grammar of our native language affects the way we think about reality; it contrasts English with the Yucatec Maya language of Mexico.

17

What's the right way to put words together?

Dennis R. Preston

Is there a 'right' way to use a language? What authority determines it?

The U.S. has no shortage of linguistic gatekeepers. Language pundits warn in the press, on the air, and even on the inside of matchbook covers that if we don't clean up our linguistic acts, the doors of opportunity will be closed. Fear of not saying things the 'right' way causes some of us to break out in a sweat when choosing whether to say 'between you and me' or 'between you and I'. (*Answer below.)

What makes us so linguistically insecure? It's the idea that a language has only one correct form, and that we're not in step with it. But let's remember that the choice of the 'best' or 'most correct' way of speaking is just a matter of history. Saying 'between you and me'—like not wearing sneakers with a coat and tie—is a convention, not a divine law. Power, money and prestige cause one variety of language to be preferred and therefore prescribed. In England, the focus of wealth, commerce, and government in London caused a variety of southern British English to be thought of as the best. In the U.S., where there was no such center, the language of the well-educated, higher classes became the preferred variety. Over time, that variety came to be seen as the only acceptable way for people to express themselves.

There will always be people who prescribe how we should talk, and who point out what they see as flaws in other people's speech. Because they think the preferred language is the only one that's acceptable, prescriptivists try to prove that other varieties of language are deficient.

If you say 'I don't have no money,' for example, one of them may tell you that 'two negatives make a positive,' but even in simple arithmetic, minus two plus minus two equals *minus* four. Besides, does anybody really believe that people who say 'I don't have no money' mean that they *do* have some money? Are people who say such things frequently misunderstood? Not likely. The test of a language's effectiveness is not whether its arbitrary noises or scribbles meet a standard but whether it communicates. A speaker of impeccable English may say silly and illogical things; a speaker of a down-home variety may be logical and precise.

One must feel sorry for the watchdog pundits who try to tell us when to use 'whom' instead of 'who'. It's a losing battle, because how language will be used can't be legislated. Such attempts fail because words and combinations of words don't have a 'real' meaning. They only mean what we agree they'll mean, and there may be differences from one group to another about that agreement. Besides, language isn't a fixed system. It evolves. Some of yesterday's poorly-thought-of language may become today's preferred English. You may deplore it if you're a speaker of the preferred variety of a language, but most often, as language evolves, it adjusts in the direction of how lower-status speakers use it. That doesn't make it wrong or deficient. It's just what language does.

That said, another aspect of language is that it happens in societies, and societies always make judgments. It's a reality in English-speaking countries that speakers who use double negatives will earn disapproval from certain people, some of whom have power over what we hope for in life. If you're not a native speaker of the preferred variety of language, there are social and economic advantages to learning it, even though it's only a historical convention, no more logical or beautiful than the one you already speak.

Prescriptivists even want us to give up our native varieties. But we shouldn't let ourselves be bullied. Prescriptivism comes out of a desire for uniformity in behavior, in language as in other areas. It can lead to elitism, racism, and even silliness. When told not to end sentences with prepositions, Winston Churchill is said to have remarked, 'This is arrant pedantry, up with which I shall not put.' So should we all.

* 'Between you and I' is said to be wrong by prescriptivists, who point out that the 'I' should be 'me', since it is the object of the preposition 'between'. They forget to tell us that such constructions have an ancient and glorious history. It was after all Shakespeare who wrote 'All debts are cleared between you and I.'

About the author

Dennis R. Preston is University Distinguished Professor of English at Michigan State University and has been a visiting professor at several U.S. universities and a Fulbright Senior Researcher in Poland and Brazil. He has served as President of the American Dialect Society and on the Executive Boards of that Society and the Linguistic Society of America, the editorial boards of *Language*, the *International Journal of Applied Linguistics*, and the *Journal of Sociolinguistics*. His work focuses on sociolinguistics, dialectology, ethnography, and minority language and variety education. He is perhaps best known for the revitalization of folk linguistics and attempts to provide variationist accounts of second-language acquisition. His most recent book-length publications are, with Nancy Niedzielski, *Folk Linguistics* (De Gruyter, 2000), with Daniel Long, *A Handbook of Perceptual Dialectology*, Volume II (Benjamins, 2002), *Needed Research in American Dialects* (Duke, 2003), and, with Brian Joseph and Carol Preston, *Linguistic Diversity in Michigan & Ohio* (Caravan, 2005). He is a fellow of the Japan Society for the Promotion of Science and was awarded the Officer's Cross of the Order of Merit of the Polish Republic in 2004.

Suggestions for further reading

In this book: Other chapters touching on the theme of this one include 18 (British and American English) and 43 (dictionaries).

Elsewhere:

For non-linguists, the belief that there is simply a right and a wrong way to use language is a very strongly held notion. There are a number of excellent books that document the history of this prescriptivism and its current status. The ones recommended here should require no specialized knowledge of linguistics.

Battistella, Edwin L. *Bad Language* (Oxford, 2005). A catalog of how 'bad language' extends even to 'bad citizens', highlighted in media reflections of popular attitudes to language.

Bauer, Laurie, and Peter Trudgill, eds. *Language Myths* (Penguin Books, 1998). Professional comment on twenty-one popular beliefs about language—all of which turn out to be false.

Bolinger, Dwight. *Language: The Loaded Weapon* (Longman, 1980). A book by one of America's most insightful linguists on matters of language and public usage. Bolinger tells you what bad language really is.

Cameron, Deborah. *Verbal Hygiene* (Routledge, 1995). A vigorous exposé of numbskull commentary on language use.

Finegan, Edward. *Attitudes toward English Usage* (Teachers College Press, 1980). A thorough investigation of the nastiness that ensued when professionals dared to tell the public what was really going on in language.

Lippi-Green, Rosina. *English with an Accent* (Routledge, 1997). Use bad language; go directly to jail (lose your job, go to the back of the line, etc...).

Milroy, James, and Lesley Milroy. *Authority in Language* (Routledge, 1985). Who gets to say what's right and wrong? Why?

Niedzielski, Nancy, and Dennis R. Preston. *Folk Linguistics* (Mouton de Gruyter, 2000). A survey and analysis of what real people (i.e., not linguists) had to say about language in America in the waning days of the twentieth century.

18

Is British English the best English?

Orin Hargraves

Is British English superior to other versions of the language? How should we judge between different versions of a language? Who owns English anyway?

Suppose you had the chance to record a sample of human language for aliens to listen to. What language would you choose? You don't have to make that choice, because someone has already done it: when the Voyager space probes were launched in 1977, they carried recordings of short greetings in fify-five human languages—including English—for the benefit of other-worldly beings. But what sort of English did they record?

You may be thinking, surely English today is one language: we all understand the written form of it and we do reasonably well with spoken varieties of it other than our own. English is written with a single alphabet and the core of its grammar and vocabulary are commonly understood. But like any language, English comes in a number of flavors, and a couple of flavors dominate the rest: American and British. These two titans of English vie, in a very refined and civilized way, for world domination, and the coming decades will be crucial in determining which of the dialects is going to come out on top.

In a sense, American English already has the upper hand. How has it happened that the American dialect of English—one of the many offspring of British English—should grow up to compete with, if not overwhelm, the island version of the mother tongue? The truth of the matter is that American English has gotten (yes: *gotten*) the upper hand by might, rather than by right. Great Britain gets the credit for successfully spreading English around the world during the glorious days of its empire. But the cultural and economic empire of the U.S. has pushed its dialect to the forefront. We read of people lining up on the docks in nineteenth-century New York to read the latest installments in the serialized novels of Charles Dickens. Today the situation is reversed: Americans who happen to be on the other side of the Atlantic will see a line (or rather, a queue) of people waiting for the premiere of the latest Hollywood blockbuster in London's Leicester Square.

American English has pretty much won the numbers game, but Britons are inclined to think that their strain of the language is the *purer* one: in other words, the New World may have won on quantity, but the Old Country still holds all the aces on quality. Is there anything to this argument? The British have been arguing for the superiority of their dialect since before the ink was dry on America's Declaration of Independence, but Americans have been just as vehement in insisting that their variety of the language is as worthy as any dialect to be the standard-bearer of world English.

Let's look at the canon: the British do have things that Americans can never take away from them: the King James Bible, Shakespeare, the romantic and metaphysical poets, the great tradition of nineteenth-century novelists. But despite British English's impressive credentials, Americans have never shown any sign of subservience to it. American English has gone its own way from the beginning. As one twentieth-century American writer observed, 'Why should we permit the survival of the curious notion that our language is a mere loan from England, like a copper kettle that we must keep scoured and return without a dent?'

The British, of course, take a different view of American linguistic independence and innovation. As one of their writers put it: 'The Americans are determined to hack their way through the language, as their ancestors did through the forests, regardless of the valuable growths that may be sacrificed in blazing the trail.'

Leaving aside the questions of quality and quantity, the question that remains is this: What is the future of these two dialects of English? It turns out that the wild card that will have the most weight in determining that future is held not by the Brits or the Yanks, but rather by those who will speak English as a second or foreign language. In a few years, that third group will outnumber the native speakers of English. And it turns out that those learners may not want *any* 'branded' variety of English; they just want a kind that they can use. Consider this: in 2000, a Chinese training program for steel engineers chose neither Americans nor Britons, but rather *Belgians*, to teach them English: the Chinese saw it as an advantage that the Belgians, like the Chinese themselves, were not native speakers. The Belgians, they thought, would have a feel both for the difficulties of learning the language in adulthood, and for using it with other non-native speakers.

Imagine, then, a conversation between a Belgian teacher of English and a Chinese engineer: if a pronoun fails to decline and there is no native speaker there to hear it, does it make a difference? The heyday of the big-brand dialects of English is probably over. In this century, the chief demand placed on English will be for an ability to adapt to the needs of the millions of speakers who use it as a second language.

And what about that clip recorded for the denizens of outer space? Well, the aliens lucky enough to decode it will hear the voice of a schoolgirl—who sounds to our ear as though she lives closer to Cape Canaveral, Florida, than to Sloane Square in London—saying, 'Greetings from the children of Earth.'

About the author

Orin Hargraves is a tenth-generation American of almost undiluted British Isles ancestry, and has lived for considerable periods in London. He is the author of *Mighty Fine Words and Smashing Expressions* (Oxford University Press, 2003), which explores the differences between British and American English. He has made substantial contributions to dictionaries and other language reference works from publishers including Berlitz, Cambridge University Press, Chambers-Harrap, HarperCollins, Langenscheidt, Longman, Merriam-Webster, and Oxford University Press. He now lives in Carroll County, Maryland.

Suggestions for further reading

In this book: The contrasts between different regional versions of languages are discussed in chapters 3 (dialects and languages), 26 (U.S. Southern English), and 41 (dialect change); linguistic standards are discussed in chapters 17 (prescriptivism) and 43 (dictionaries).

Elsewhere:

The author's book, noted above, is a good place to start exploring the subtle and pervasive differences between the two main dialects of English. Other suggestions:

Fiske, Robert Hartwell, ed. *Vocabula Bound* (Marion Street Press, 2004). A book of essays about English, one of which (a longer article by the author, entitled 'Who owns English?') inspired this chapter.

Bragg, Melvyn. *The Adventure of English* (Hodder & Stoughton, 2003). An enjoyable overview of the subject.

McArthur, Tom, ed. *The Oxford Companion to the English Language* (Oxford, 1992). This book is the place to go for one-stop shopping concerning all things English.

Graddol, David. *The Future of English?* (British Council, 1997). Forecasting the popularity of the English language in the twenty-first century.

19

Why do people fight over language?

Paul B. Garrett

Is language important enough to fight about? How do conflicts over language get started? What are the underlying causes?

The idea of fighting over language might seem strange, but it's all too common. Why do people sometimes feel so strongly about their language that they take up arms against speakers of another? What is it about language that can generate tensions that last for generations? The answers to these questions lie in the close relationship between language and identity, particularly ethnic identity.

Many of us who speak only English tend to think of monolingualism as the normal state of affairs. We may also tend to think that there is a one-to-one correspondence between language and nation: in France they speak French, in Japan they speak Japanese, and so on. But worldwide there are close to seven thousand languages—and only about two hundred nations. That means a lot of multilingual nations! And because languages tend to coincide with ethnic groups, that means a lot of multi-ethnic nations as well. Of course, some are more multilingual and multi-ethnic than others. At one extreme are countries like Japan, where the vast majority of people are ethnically Japanese and speak Japanese. At the other extreme are countries like India and Nigeria, each of which has about four hundred languages and ethnicities within its borders.

In many areas of the world, people of different language backgrounds interact every day. For the most part things go smoothly enough; but sometimes tensions arise, and sometimes these tensions erupt into outright conflicts. This is especially likely when speakers of one language feel threatened or oppressed by speakers of another. When that's the case, language differences become powerful markers of social, cultural, and political difference. And wherever you find language conflict, you're sure to find struggles over other issues as well, such as territory, religion, and political power.

The weapons used in these conflicts may be far more than harsh words. Language conflicts can escalate into riots, wars, even genocide. Conflicts over language played a major part in the separation of Bangladesh from Pakistan in 1971. What began as a Bengali language movement escalated into a nine-month war for independence in which more than three million people died.

In other parts of the world today, language is at the heart of ongoing conflicts characterized by constant tensions and sporadic outbreaks of violence. In Sri Lanka, the Tamil Tigers (speakers of the Tamil language) have been rebelling for decades against a government dominated by the Sinhala-speaking majority. And in Spain, the separatist group ETA has sometimes used acts of terrorism in pursuit of its goal of an independent Basque homeland, where Basque would be the national language.

Language conflicts don't always lead to violence. But they can create tensions that persist for years, affecting the lives of millions on a daily basis. Take the case of Canada—generally a peaceful place, but one that has had its share of language conflict. Canada as a whole is officially bilingual, but most French-speaking Canadians live in the province of Quebec. Surrounded by English-speaking provinces, they often feel that their language and culture are under siege. They feel particularly threatened by the presence of English speakers within Quebec itself, where historically, English speakers have been a disproportionately powerful minority.

In 1977, French speakers in Quebec tried to protect their language by passing a law that in many ways restricted the use of English. For example, it required that all signs in public places be in French, and French alone. This became a focal point of resentment among English speakers, including small business owners like Allan Singer. For years, Mr. Singer had run his modest shop beneath a simple handpainted sign that read, 'Allan Singer Limited—Printers and Stationers'. Under the new law, Mr. Singer's sign became illegal; he would have to replace it, at his own expense, with a sign in French.

Well, Mr. Singer refused to do that—and he took his case all the way to Canada's Supreme Court. The court's ruling was a compro mise of sorts, but it reflected the realities of Canadian society in a way that most Canadians found fair and just. The court decided that Mr. Singer did *not* have the right to keep his sign in English only. But the new law could *not* require him to replace it with a sign in French only, to the exclusion of English—or of Spanish, Chinese, or any other language that he might wish to use in addition to French. So business owners in Quebec *could* be required to use French on their signs, but the law *could not* interfere with their freedom to post bilingual or multilingual signs—signs reflecting the linguistic diversity of Quebec, and of Canada as a whole.

Ultimately, this brouhaha over signs provided an opportunity for Canada to clarify its commitment to protecting the language rights of *all* of its citizens. But the underlying tensions haven't gone away. On two occasions—in 1980 and 1995—Quebec's citizens even went to the polls to vote on whether their province should secede from Canada, and become an independent French-speaking nation. It didn't happen; but the 1995 vote was extremely close, with a margin of less than one percent.

In these and other conflicts, much more than language is at stake. The language that we speak is part of who we are. It gives us a powerful sense of belonging with those who speak like us, and an equally powerful sense of difference from those who don't. Little wonder, then, that when someone attacks our language—or even just our accent—we feel that *we* are being attacked. And we respond accordingly. Discriminate against a language, and you discriminate against its speakers; disrespect my language, and you disrespect me.

About the author

Paul B. Garrett, Assistant Professor of Anthropology at Temple University, Pennsylvania, is a linguistic anthropologist whose research focuses on the creole languages and cultures of the Caribbean—particularly the island of St. Lucia, where he has conducted long-term ethnographic fieldwork. His other research interests include language contact, ideologies of language, and the political economy of language. For more information see his Web page: http://www.temple.edu/anthro/faculty. htm#garrett

Suggestions for further reading

In this book: The topic of how social contexts influence the way languages function and interact is addressed in chapters 8 (pidgins and creoles), 21 (glossolalia), 38 (Cajun), 39 (German in the U.S.), and 40 (Gullah).

Elsewhere:

Harris, Roxy and Ben Rampton, eds. *The Language, Ethnicity and Race Reader* (Routledge, 2003). This collection of classic and contemporary readings examines the relationships between language and such issues as identity, ethnic diversity, nationalism, colonialism, and migration.

Joseph, Brian D. et al., eds. *When Languages Collide: Perspectives on Language Conflict, Language Competition, and Language Coexistence* (Ohio State University Press, 2003). Fifteen essays examine cases of language contact worldwide (due to trade, migration, war, etc.), considering the factors that give rise to both peaceful and conflictual outcomes.

Schmid, Carol L. *The Politics of Language: Conflict, Identity, and Cultural Pluralism in Comparative Perspective* (Oxford University Press, 2001). Focusing on the many languages spoken within the U.S., this book examines both historical and contemporary conflicts and controversies.

20

What does it mean to be bilingual?

Dora Johnson

Is everybody who knows two languages bilingual?
Can you be bilingual for life?

If you speak just one language, you probably think that you're
pretty normal, and that people who speak more than one are an
exception, or at least a minority. In fact, it's just the opposite. Three-
quarters of the people in the world, including many in the U.S. and
Britain, are bilingual or multilingual. It's *monolinguals* who are a
minority breed.

Bilingualism, of course, can mean different things. And not all
bilinguals speak two languages at the same level. For example, after
September 11, 2001, bilinguals responded to U.S. government calls
for people who could handle both English and Arabic. But some
had skills that weren't good enough to meet the need. Some spoke
both languages fluently but couldn't read and write one of them

well; others turned out to have full skills in one language but limited ability to translate to or from the other.

So how do you get to be bilingual? Often it happens early in life, in a home where two languages are spoken. Parents sometimes speak both languages to the child; sometimes one parent uses one language and another uses the other. There also exists what linguists call 'additive' bilingualism, where you add a new language to your repertoire later in life. You can obviously do that by learning a language in school. Or maybe your parents move to Armenia when you're little and you learn Armenian while continuing to develop English skills at home.

A bilingual capability may also wither away, for example if you move to a new country and the language of the majority largely *replaces* your original language. We call this 'subtractive' bilingualism, and we see it often in immigrant families. For example, you may overhear a parent speaking to a child in the 'old country' language, with the child responding in English. The child is *subtracting* her first language from her repertoire. This begins quite early. By about age two and a half a bilingual child starts to make choices in language use, and it's usually in favor of the majority language. Think of little Quang who moved to the U.S. from Vietnam. He runs errands for his grandmother when she speaks to him in Vietnamese, and may even answer her in Vietnamese, but not in the presence of his friends! He's decided that English is the language he's going to use most, and his skill in Vietnamese starts to fade. It can be revived, and he'll *re*-learn it more quickly than someone who starts learning Vietnamese from scratch, but it'll take some serious effort on his part.

Parents often worry that their child will become confused if exposed to different languages. They needn't be concerned. There are moments when a child's language development can cause some anxiety for parents and other adults in their lives, but the advantages of using two languages in the home rather than only one far outweigh any disadvantages. Children are amazing in their ability to code-switch, that is, transfer back and forth between two systems. They will sometimes mix them up, but they quickly learn to use each language appropriately.

Immigrant families who want their children to retain their community's *heritage* language, as well as English, have to consciously work at it. Children rarely have the chance to continue learning their heritage language at school, especially if it's not French or Spanish but a less commonly taught language like, let's say, Swedish or Tagalog. So some communities start special language programs after school or on Saturdays to help keep the language alive. Being bilingual as a child doesn't automatically mean being bilingual for life.

Bilingualism is not the same thing as bilingual *education*, an approach to educating children who speak a language other than English. The thrust of bilingual education is to help such students learn school subjects through their native tongue at the same time as they're learning English. For a variety of reasons such programs have been very controversial.

In recent years, *dual* language education has become popular, and seems to show promise. Dual language programs offer monolingual kids the chance to speak and do schoolwork in two languages (one of which is always the majority language), and thus to develop *additive* bilingualism. Both language-minority and language-majority kids can become bilingual in classrooms where they learn together and help each other.

There are, of course, important reasons for new citizens of English-speaking countries, both adults and children, to learn English. But there are also important reasons for them to keep, nurture, and strengthen a language they learned at their mother's knee. In the U.S. and perhaps in other countries as well, new citizens have sometimes been so strongly encouraged to assimilate that they've been *discouraged* from retaining their original language.

That's a national loss, whenever and wherever it happens. True bilinguals—and by this I mean people whose skills in both languages are very strong—have an enormous advantage in society. They can function in more than one culture. They can be bridges for communication in their communities and the globalized world. We need to find ways to produce more of them.

About the author

Dora Johnson is an associate at the private non-profit Center for Applied Linguistics in Washington, DC. Her work at CAL has centered around the teaching and learning of less commonly taught languages. At present she is working on a project to develop a network of Arabic K-12 language teachers in the U.S.

Suggestions for further reading

In this book: Opportunities and requirements for professional use of language abilities are discussed in chapters 36 (America's language crisis), 42 (language-related careers), 43 (dictionaries), 44 (interpreting and translating), 46 (forensic linguistics), 53 (Russian), and 55 (Arabic).

Elsewhere:

Cunningham-Andersson, Una, and Staffan Andersson. *Growing Up With Two Languages: A Practical Guide* (Routledge, 1999). The authors of this manual for parents and professionals draw on the experiences of some fifty families from around the world. They provide practical advice on what to expect and how to plan, beginning before the birth of a child!

Baker, Colin. *A Parents' and Teachers' Guide to Bilingualism* (Multilingual Matters, second edition 2000). Poses and answers the most frequently asked questions about raising bilingual children.

Caldas, Stephen J. *Raising Bilingual-Biliterate Children in Monolingual Cultures* (Multilingual Matters, 2006). The author follows the bilingual and biliterate development of his own three children through adolescence. He sees this effort as a series of relationships that include family, school, the community, and peer groups. Lessons learned are a key component of this publication.

Center for Applied Linguistics Digest. *Raising Bilingual Children: Common Parental Concerns and Current Research* (Center for Applied Linguistics, 2006). This two-page digest is designed to address the many incorrect impressions parents, educators, pediatricians, and therapists have about raising bilingual children.

Web site:

http://www.bilingualfamilynewsletter.com
The Bilingual Family Newsletter. This quarterly periodical has short informative articles written in clear language. In addition to summarizing the latest research and information on language learning, bilingualism, biculturalism, etc., it presents real-life accounts of how families have developed solutions to the problems they encounter in raising bilingual children.

21

What is
'speaking in tongues'?

Walt Wolfram

*What happens when religious people 'speak in tongues'?
Is their speech a real language? What is its relationship
to natural language?*

The utterances flowed effortlessly from his mouth: *La horiya la
hariya, la hayneekeechee aleekeechi arateeli haya.* It sounded like
poetry in a foreign language, but no one else spoke the language
or understood it. That didn't make any difference; the speaker who
uttered these words in his private prayers considered them a special language for talking to God. Although it seems esoteric and
mysterious to those who encounter it for the first time, 'speaking
in tongues', or more technically, 'glossolalia', is not an uncommon
linguistic phenomenon. Millions of English speakers around the
world have spoken in tongues and speakers of many other languages
have experienced a similar form of linguistic expression. It has a
long history in Christianity and in other religions as well, perhaps

as long as humans have had language. In Christianity, it has been well documented since the Day of Pentecost, with the last century witnessing a significant revival in its use, especially in so-called holiness churches but also in some more liturgical churches such as Catholic and Anglican congregations.

Glossolalia has also been documented in other religions and in some non-religious practices. For example, practitioners of the Peyote cult among Native American Indians, shamans exercising witchcraft in Haiti, and Tibetan monks uttering various chants may also use a type of glossolalia. What exactly is it? Is it language? If not, what is its relationship to natural language? And how does it function in religious expression and in society?

Linguists have been studying the structure of glossolalia for some time now using the methods applied to the analysis of natural language. Studies include identifying the sounds, the sequencing of sounds into syllables, and the arrangement of segments into larger units similar to words and syntax in natural language. Glossolalic fluency may range from minimally organized, barely formed grunt-like sounds to highly organized streams of consonants and vowels that sound like highly expressive natural language.

The majority of sounds used in glossolalia come from a person's native language, though some speakers are capable of using other sounds as well. When compared with a speaker's native language, however, the inventory of sounds is restricted in ways that make it somewhat comparable to the speech of young children. For example, if a language has forty significant vowel and consonant sounds, only ten to twenty of those sounds might be used in the glossolalia. And syllables also tend to be somewhat simpler than in natural language, so that alternating sequences of a single consonant and single vowel are repeated. For example, notice how *lahoriya* in the sample alternates between a simple consonant and vowel. Glossolalia may, however, also exhibit traits of expressive or poetic language: rhyming and alliteration are found in some speakers' utterances. Notice, for example, the rhyming in phrases like *la horiya la hariya* or *hayneekeechee aleekeechi*.

In some worship traditions within Christianity, after one person utters glossolalia in a public meeting, another person will follow with a prophetic 'interpretation' into a natural language such as English or Spanish. Usually these interpretations reinforce religious themes shared by the group. An analysis of utterances and the interpretations using the techniques of translation theory, however, reveals that such interpretations are not literal translations. There are also reports of knowledgeable audience members recognizing the utterances of glossolalists as particular foreign languages ('xenoglossia'), but recorded documentation of such cases has proven to be elusive.

Linguistically, glossolalia is a kind of 'pseudolanguage'—nonsense syllables of a familiar language that are reminiscent of an earlier, prelanguage babbling stage. While most people stop using nonsense syllables in childhood, once they have acquired a natural language, glossolalists return to a stage in which sounds are used for purposes other than the communication of specific thoughts. Of course, not all adult language users completely give up uttering nonsense syllables. The writer J. R. R. Tolkien had a proclivity for speaking nonsense syllables throughout his life, and some modern music genres (think of 'scat' singing in jazz) are also characterized by the use of nonsense syllables. Speaking in tongues may also be an acquired capability, in which regular practice results in more fluently constructed strings of syllables. Tolkien, for example, apparently practiced his production of nonsense syllables regularly in order to refine the expressive effect of his utterances.

Though some psychologists have connected speaking in tongues with hypnotic trance, hysteria, or even schizophrenia, such assessments seem far too severe and judgmental. In fact, normal, well-adjusted people may speak in tongues in socially specified situations such as personal prayer, religious ritual, or public worship. The religious significance of speaking in tongues lies mostly in its demonstration that in such situations a speaker is able to transcend ordinary speech.

About the author

Although Walt Wolfram is most noted for his research on American dialects, his sociolinguistic career started with the study of speaking in tongues. In the mid-1960s, he conducted one of the first linguistic analyses of glossolalia based on an extensive set of tape recordings of its public and private use. Decades later he still thinks that the collection of naturally occurring samples of glossolalia was the most sensitive fieldwork situation he ever encountered.

Suggestions for further reading

In this book: The topic of how social contexts influence the way languages function and interact is addressed in chapters 8 (pidgins and creoles), 18 (language conflict), 38 (Cajun), 39 (German in the U.S.), and 40 (Gullah).

Elsewhere:

Goodman, Felicitas D. *Speaking in Tongues: A Cross-Cultural Study of Glossolalia* (University of Chicago Press, 1972). A comparison of speaking in tongues in different cultures that explains it as a kind of hypnotic trance. Though this psychological explanation does not hold up, the comparison of glossolalia across cultures is useful.

Nickell, Joe. *Looking for a Miracle: Weeping Icons, Relics, Stigmata, Visions, and Healing Cures* (Prometheus, 1993). A historical, forensic discussion of speaking in tongues along with other kinds of paranormal religious behavior. The focus is on explaining the need for the establishment of supernatural events within Christian religious tradition.

Samarin, William J. *Tongues of Men and Angels: The Religious Language of Pentecostalism* (Macmillan, 1972). Though somewhat dated, this still remains the most comprehensive linguistic description of glossolalia. Describes it as a kind of pseudolanguage comparable to prelanguage babbling.

Samarin, William J. 'Variation and variables in religious glossolalia', in *Language in Society* (1972) 1:121–30. A concise, technical linguistic description of glossolalia written primarily for linguists and sociolinguists.

22

What happens if you are raised without language?

Susan Curtiss

Are there really such beings as 'wolf children,' raised without human contact? Can a person raised without language catch up? When is it too late? Is it worse to grow up without hearing or without language?

It is almost impossible for most of us to imagine growing up without language—which develops in our minds so effortlessly in early childhood and plays such a central role in defining us as human and allowing us to participate in our culture. Nevertheless, being deprived of language occasionally happens. In recent centuries children have been found living in the wild, said to have been raised by wolves or other animals and deprived of human contact. It is hard to know the real stories behind these cases, but they are all strikingly similar with respect to language. The pattern is that only those rescued early in childhood developed an ability to speak. Those found after they were about nine years old learned only a few words, or failed to learn language at all.

One of the most famous of these cases is that of Victor, 'The wild boy of Aveyron', immortalized in a film by Francois Truffaut called *The Wild Child* (*L'Enfant Sauvage*). Victor was captured in 1800, when he was about ten or eleven. He was studied by a young physician named Jacques Itard, who creatively and painstakingly tried to teach him to speak, read, and write. But despite Itard's best efforts (many of which became the foundation of the Montessori Method for teaching), Victor never learned to speak; he learned to read and print only a small set of words.

We also know cases in which children grew up in social or linguistic isolation because of tragic family circumstances. One of the best-known of these is the case of Genie, whose childhood was one of extreme neglect, deprivation and abuse. For over twelve years, her father shut her away in a small bedroom, tied with a harness to an infant potty seat. When her blind mother finally escaped with Genie in the early 1970s and applied for welfare, the police intervened, and Genie was put in the rehabilitation ward of a children's hospital. She was thirteen and a half years old and knew no language.

Genie was studied by linguists for almost a decade. She was of normal intelligence; she rapidly learned words within a few months after her discovery, and soon began to combine them. However, she did not use grammatical elements like tense or agreement markers, articles, pronouns, or question words—the pieces of English that turn a string of words into grammatical speech. Most of her linguistic development consisted of learning more words and stringing them together into longer, semantically coherent utterances. In context, she could make herself understood. Her speech did not stick to standard English Subject-Verb-Object word order, but she performed well on word order comprehension tests: She differentiated sentences like 'The girl is pushing the boy' from 'The boy is pushing the girl', showing that she understood more than she could produce. Even after many years, however, she developed little knowledge of grammar. Interestingly, Genie was a powerful *non-verbal* communicator, providing strong evidence that language is not the same as communication.

Children without hearing are not as handicapped as Genie was. A deaf child can still have language and relate normally to others through signing—as long as language development starts early. There are a number of studies that show that the sooner a deaf child is exposed to a natural sign language, such as American Sign Language, the more proficient a signer he or she will become. As in other cases of linguistic isolation, the ability of deaf people to learn new *words* is not affected by the age at which they are exposed to language. But their ability to learn grammar is dramatically affected. Studies of deaf children exposed to sign language after the preschool years show that there is a critical window for grammatical development, which ends, perhaps, in the early school-age years.

Exciting recent evidence that a child brings something unique and necessary to language development comes from the creation of a new sign language in Nicaragua. After the Sandinistas came to power there, for the first time deaf teenagers and adults had the opportunity to come together as a community. This first generation created a rudimentary system of gestures for communication. But when young children, under the age of ten, joined this community, they transformed this system into a real language, embodying the structural elements and characteristics that define all human grammars. Over a short time, that language has become increasingly rich and complex grammatically.

People without hearing are typically normal and grow up in caring social environments that allow them to lead full lives. This is especially true for those who become part of culturally Deaf* communities and learn to communicate in sign. Hearing people

---

*In current usage, 'deaf' is lowercase when it refers to loss of hearing, capitalized when it refers to communities of deaf persons using sign language.

who are raised without language, on the other hand, typically grow up with no social community, in circumstances that have profoundly negative psychosocial effects. Therefore, while growing up without hearing poses many difficulties in life, growing up without *language* is significantly worse. Language is so central to being human that lacking it can mean a lifetime of social deprivation and isolation.

About the author

Susan Curtiss is Professor of Linguistics at UCLA. She is the author of *Genie: A Psycholinguistic Study of a Modern-Day 'Wild Child'*, as well as close to one hundred journal articles and book chapters. She has also authored numerous language tests, including the Curtiss-Yamada Comprehensive Language Evaluation (the CYCLE), used by researchers across the U.S. and overseas. Her research spans the study of language and mind, the 'critical period' for first language acquisition, Specific Language Impairment, mental retardation, adult aphasia, progressive demntia, and the genetics of language. Her current work has focused on language development following hemispherectomy (removal of one hemisphere of the brain) in childhood.

Suggestions for further reading

In this book: Other chapters discussing language acquisition by children include 8 (pidgins and creoles), 13 (babies and language), 15 (language and the brain), 23 (sign languages), and 33 (children and second languages). The importance of grammar as a part of full language capability is discussed in chapters 11 (grammar in gcneral), 12 (universal grammar), and 14 (animals and language).

Elsewhere:

Curtiss, S. *Genie: A Psycholinguistic Study of a Modern-Day 'Wild Child'* (Academic Press, 1977). A fascinating account of Curtiss's experiences and research with Genie and the implications of this work.

Lane, H. *The Wild Boy of Aveyron* (Harvard University Press, 1976). A rich, very readable description of the case of 'Victor' and the issues his case raises.

Newport, E. L. 'Maturational constraints on language learning', in *Cognitive Science* (1990) Vol. 14. Describes research on the effects of age on the acquisition of the grammar of American Sign Language (ASL) by Deaf individuals who were exposed to ASL at different ages, some not until adulthood.

Senghas, R. J., A. Senghas, and J. E. Pyers. 'The emergence of Nicaraguan sign language: questions of development, acquisition, and evolution', in J. Langer, S. T. Parker, and C. Milbrath, eds., *Biology and Knowledge Revisited: From Neurogenesis to Psychogenesis* (Lawrence Erlbaum Associates, 2006). Describes the emergence of a brand-new sign language in Nicaragua and the special properties young children bring to language learning.

23

Do deaf people everywhere use the same sign language?

Leila Monaghan

Is sign language really a language? Can you use it no matter what country you go to?

There are two widespread myths about sign languages. One is that they aren't languages at all. The second is that signing is a *universal* language—that any signer can understand all signers anywhere in the world. Both of these beliefs are false.

It's easy to understand why you might doubt sign languages are really languages—they're so different from what we often call 'tongues'. They have to be seen rather than heard. And some signs look like what they represent, making them easy to dismiss as mere gestures. But that view was refuted in 1960 when William Stokoe published the first scientific description of American Sign Language (ASL). Stokoe was an English professor at Gallaudet University (the world's only liberal arts university for Deaf* people) and found the

---

*See footnote on page 99.

language being used around him as systematic and as grammatical as any other language. He showed that (except for sound) sign languages have all the linguistic features that spoken languages have.

A word in spoken language, of course, is composed of sounds, made with your mouth and tongue. In ASL, the components of a word can include how you shape your hand, where you place it, and how you move it. For example, the signs for APPLE and CANDY are made at the same place, by the side of the mouth, but their handshapes are different: APPLE is made with a crooked index finger while CANDY is made with a straight index finger. Sign languages have complex grammars, so that words can be strung together into sentences, and sentences into stories. With signs you can discuss any topic, from concrete to abstract, from street slang to physics. And if you have any doubt, think about public events you've seen recently. After watching a signer interpret a political speech or a play, could anyone still believe it's not a language?

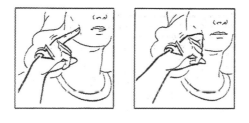

CANDY   APPLE

As for the second myth, people often don't realize that sign languages vary, just as spoken languages do. Whenever groups of people are separated by time and space, separate languages, or at least separate dialects, develop. This is as true for sign as it is for spoken languages: there are, for example, differing dialects of ASL. Like spoken English, it varies both geographically and across social groups. And the variations in sign language are even more

evident internationally. The signs used in Italy aren't readily understood by a signer using ASL, and vice versa. Even languages that
you might think are connected may or may not actually be. British
Sign Language and American Sign Language, for example, are
unrelated to each other, despite the fact that countries share English
as their spoken language: the histories of the British and American
Deaf communities are separate. American Sign Language is actually related to French Sign Language because a Deaf Frenchman
helped start many of the earliest schools for deaf children in the
United States. Although some signs in all sign languages are iconic
(they look like the object they are representing), even iconic signs
can differ. In ASL, the sign TREE is made by holding up a single
hand with fingers spread. The Danish version is done by tracing
the outline of a tree with both palms. Both signs are based on the
same image, a classic leafy tree, but they look quite different.

(a) American Sign Language   (b) Danish Sign Language

Whenever people can see each other but are somehow prevented
from communicating with speech or writing, they turn to signing
of some kind. Think about monks who have taken vows of silence
but need to cooperate on monastery business, or widows from
certain Australian Aboriginal groups, who are expected not to
speak during a long period of mourning. In cases like these, the
sign languages developed reflect the grammar of the languages the

monks or widows knew and could speak if they chose. But those are exceptions. Most sign languages are *not* based on the spoken language in the culture around them.

There are millions of sign language users around the world. For example, there are at least a half-million users of ASL in the U.S., and possibly as many as two million. It's routinely taught in schools across the country, and all fifty states recognize it in some way. At the last count, there were 147 colleges and universities whose language requirement could be satisfied by the study of ASL. In Britain, there are estimated to be around 370,000 sign language users and on March 18, 2003, the U.K. government officially recognized BSL as an official British Language.

Sign language is remarkable for its ability to express everything spoken language does, using completely different human capabilities. According to Hearing people who have learned it, communicating in sign opens a window to a different culture and can give you a totally different perspective—especially an understanding of how Deaf people perceive the world. So the next time you think about learning a new language, think about learning how to sign.

About the author

Leila Monaghan teaches in the Department of Communication and Culture at Indiana University, Bloomington. She received her Ph.D. in linguistic anthropology at the University of California, Los Angeles and her dissertation work was with the New Zealand Deaf community. Her other publications include a co-edited book *Many Ways to be Deaf* (Gallaudet University Press, 2003), a 2002 *Annual Review of Anthropology* article on Deaf communities with Richard Senghas, and a forthcoming *Deaf Worlds* issue co-edited with Constanze Schmaling, 'HIV/AIDS and Deafness'. She is also involved in literacy issues; in particular she works with local Bloomington residents, tutoring them in reading using a manual developed by William Labov and Bettina Baker.

Suggestions for further reading

In this book: Languages designed by their users are discussed in chapters 59 (Esperanto) and 60 (artificial languages in general). Other chapters discussing language acquisition by children include 8 (pidgins and creoles), 13 (babies and language), 15 (language and the brain), 22 (language deprivation), and 33 (children and second languages).

Elsewhere:

Klima, Edward, and Ursula Bellugi. *Signs of Language* (Harvard University Press, 1979). Classic and very readable introduction to sign language linguistics.

LeMaster, Barbara, and Leila Monaghan. 'Sign languages', in A. Duranti, ed., *A Companion to Linguistic Anthropology* (Blackwell, 2004). Introduction to the study of sign languages and Deaf communities in linguistic anthropology and sociolinguistics. Both disciplines look at the interaction between language and culture rather than just at languages themselves.

Monaghan, Leila, Constanze Schmaling, Karen Nakamura. and Graham H. Turner., eds. *Many Ways to be Deaf* (Gallaudet University Press, 2004). A collection of fifteen articles from fourteen countries on the history, culture and language of local Deaf communities. Includes a brief overview of five hundred years of Deaf history.

Padden, Carol, and Tom Humphries. *Inside Deaf Culture* (Harvard University Press, 2005). Latest book from two of the foremost experts on Deaf Culture in the U.S. Interesting and accessible.

Web sites:

http://library.gallaudet.edu/
http://www.signcommunity.org.uk/
http://www.sign-lang.uni-hamburg.de/bibweb/
http://www.signpostbsl.com/

24

Why do languages die?

Christopher Moseley

What do we mean when we speak of a language 'dying'? How does it happen? Can it be predicted? Can it be prevented?

This is not a happy subject. For those of us who love languages, it's terrible to see that they're dying at a very rapid rate. About half the world's languages have fewer than 10,000 speakers—about enough to fill a small-town football stadium. Even worse is that most of the languages spoken in the world today—nearly 90 percent, some think—may be lost by the end of this century. There are languages with only a handful of speakers left in the world—some have only one or two. When those last speakers die, the language dies too.

Why do languages disappear? The short answer is that they are no longer passed on to younger speakers, and eventually only the elderly speakers are left to die out. But what would make a community no longer want to pass on its spoken heritage to the younger generation? The circumstances vary from place to place.

Let's look at some examples. In the mountains of India we can find—if we hurry—the Sulung people, now down to only a few thousand, who've been driven to a remote area by constant warfare with neighbouring tribes. If they're wiped out by their enemies, their language will vanish. Wars destroy more than people.

You might ask, can there be any new languages left to discover? Surprisingly, yes. A few have recently come to light when previously uncontacted peoples were found in isolated places. In 1991, for instance, an ancient language known as Gongduk was discovered in the Himalayas. For linguists, this was like finding the fabled lost valley of Shangri-La. And in the deep Brazilian interior, there are still languages being discovered, some of them apparently unrelated to any other known tongue. But stories like that are rare. The overwhelming trend is in the direction of extinction.

For the most part, geographical barriers—high mountains, steep valleys, lack of infrastructure or roads—afford little protection, not even in the far corners of the earth. Think about the speakers of Rapanui, on Easter Island in the Pacific. After a millenium and a half of separation from the world, in the nineteenth century they were taken from their island as slaves to collect guano from the coast of South America. Very few came back; today there are just a few thousand people who have kept Rapanui alive in the face of Spanish, imported from Chile.

Thirty years ago, in Brazil, ranchers and illegal timber cutters drove the Jiahui people out of their traditional lands into the hands of hostile neighbors. The few that were left joined a less hostile group or drifted to the cities. Now the Jiahui have reclaimed some of their lands, but how many of them are left? Just fifty.

Or what about the Rikbatsá people in Brazil's Mato Grosso state? They were great warriors, but they couldn't fight epidemics of influenza and smallpox that were brought by Jesuit missionaries. Diseases imported from Europe decimated them and dozens of other native peoples of the Americas—and with them their native tongues.

And if human invasions aren't bad enough, nature itself can swallow up languages. In 1998 a terrible tsunami struck the north coast of Papua New Guinea, killing nearly all the speakers of the Warapu and Sissano languages. Just a few who weren't home at the time are the only ones left to keep the languages alive.

Finally, so-called 'killer languages'—like English or Spanish—are so dominant that people may *voluntarily* give up their mother tongue—for convenience or economic reasons. Indigenous peoples sometimes abandon their language to overcome discrimination, or fit into a majority culture. As children stop learning them, the languages slowly wither away.

Why should we care? Because with the loss of a language comes the loss of inherited knowledge, an entire thought-world. I've often heard it compared to losing a natural resource or an animal species. Yes, there are ways of reconstructing an extinct language from surviving evidence, and linguists are able to do that in some cases; but in the end what we have then is not much more than words on paper. We can't bring back from the dead a society that spoke the language, or the heritage and culture behind it. Once a language is gone, it's gone forever.

It's only in the past couple of decades that the urgency of the question of language extermination worldwide has been realised. Organisations have been set up to do what they can to preserve language diversity. There are the U.S.-based Terralingua and the U.K.-based Foundation for Endangered Languages, both dedicated to encouraging and supporting research into threatened languages and their maintenance; there is the UNESCO Endangered Languages Project; and recently a department for endangered languages was set up at the University of London.

About the author

Christopher Moseley (Chrismoseley50@yahoo.com) is a linguist at BBC Monitoring, part of the BBC World Service based near Reading, England, which translates news items from the world's media. He is also a writer and freelance translator, editor of the *Encyclopedia of the World's Endangered Languages* (Routledge, 2006), and co-editor of the *Atlas of the World's Languages* (Routledge, 1993). He has a special interest in artificial languages (and has created one himself).

Suggestions for further reading

In this book: The topic of how languages become extinct (or escape extinction) is discussed in chapters 2 (languages of the world), 25 (revitalizing threatened languages), 41 (Are U.S. dialects dying?), and 50 (Latin).

Elsewhere:

Nettle, Daniel, and Suzanne Romaine. *Vanishing Voices* (Oxford University Press, 2000). A serious and thoughtful study of the problems, causes and effects of language endangerment all over the world, relating the issue to biological diversity.

Crystal, David. *Language Death* (Cambridge University Press, 2000). An impassioned plea on behalf of the world's smaller languages, full of interesting anecdotal information about the treasures we are losing.

Abley, Mark. *Spoken Here: Travels Among Threatened Languages* (Heinemann, 2004). A personal travelogue of the author's visits to some of the world's smallest language communities to see how they are faring in the modern globalised community; quite appealing as a travel book as well.

Ostler, Nicholas. *Empires of the Word* (HarperCollins, 2005). Takes a sweeping overview of the's world recorded history from the point of view of the big victorious languages—the other end of the telescope— and shows how successive empires have claimed to spread their 'international languages' all over the known world. English is just the latest in a long line of conquerors.

25

Can a threatened language be saved?

Akira Y. Yamamoto et al.

Can threatened or dying languages be revived? What skills and resources does language revitalization require? Is it worth the effort?

Some languages die a natural death. Hittite, for example, once the language of a great empire, went the way of the saber-toothed tiger. However, many of the world's languages today are like the rare and beautiful whooping cranes—hanging on for dear life. Saving these languages takes a great deal of work, but it can be done.

Take Cherokee: In the past three or four decades, the number of children acquiring it as a first language has declined so sharply that it could disappear in just another generation. But here is a scene that provides hope: On a colorful carpet in a preschool classroom in Tahlequah, Oklahoma, three- and four-year-old children are sitting with their teachers, reading together from a picture book. It looks like a typical preschool anywhere—but the book is in Cherokee and Cherokee is the only language used in the classroom. The hope is that by the time they reach third grade, these children will be fluent enough in their ancestral tongue to become a new generation of Cherokee speakers.

Similar intensive programs—from infant day care through high school classes—are achieving success among the Mohawk people in New York State and Canada, the Blackfoot in Montana, the Arapaho in Wyoming, the Hawaiians, and in other Native American communities.

The challenge these programs must overcome is the 'Exposure Problem': simply put, you can't learn a language if you don't hear it and see it. In endangered language communities, learners are not getting enough exposure to their ancestral languages to become fluent in them. Successful revitalization programs have found both traditional and innovative solutions to this problem. Consider Gaelic, which was revitalized in Ireland; Maori, which has been made an official language in New Zealand; and Hebrew, which was used only for religious purposes for centuries before being revived to become the official language of Israel.

It has taken us a long time to realize the value of sustaining languages, but within the past twenty years, language revitalization has become an international movement. The U.S. (through the Native American Languages Acts of 1990 and 1992), the United Nations (through UNESCO), and various organizations and institutions (such as the Endangered Language Fund, the Foundation for Endangered Languages, and The Hans Rausing Endangered Languages Project of the School of Oriental and African Studies) have embraced the idea. In Africa, literature on AIDS is being used to teach literacy in local languages. In the Amazon rain forest, the Yanomami people are learning about hygiene through literature printed in their tribal language. Teachers in Siberia are being trained by linguists from Russia and the Netherlands to teach local languages to children.

Where there is any population of speakers and a willingness to keep the language alive, people are working to document, describe, and use endangered languages. In communities with only a few elderly speakers left, young language learners are spending time with them, doing everyday chores in the language so that they too can become speakers. And in places where the languages have not been spoken for years, language researchers are using archives and oral histories to revive languages, just as spoken Hebrew was revived from scriptures and rituals. Preservation efforts extend even to cross-cultural forms of speech like Gullah, a creole that combines English and African elements and is spoken on the coasts of Georgia and South Carolina. In the U.S., indigenous languages are being taught in colleges and universities in Arizona, Hawai'i, Kansas, New Mexico, and Oklahoma. It is a growing effort, and it may be our best hope to stem the loss of languages that are otherwise doomed.

Linguist Ken Hale has compared the loss of a language to 'dropping a bomb on a museum.' It destroys a culture, intellectual wealth, and works of art. It is a sobering thought that most of the languages alive today may not live to see the next century. This is why we need to care for the ones that are threatened … as if they were whooping cranes.

About the authors

Akira Y. Yamamoto (professor of anthropology and linguistics at Kansas University) has been active in bringing together language communities and professional communities for language and culture revitalization programs. Marcellino Berardo (Applied English Center, Kansas University) has been active in language revitalization programs in the U.S. Midwest; his specialties include language description, social aspects of language learning, and second language pedagogy. Tracy Hirata-Edds (Child Language Program, Kansas University) has been working with the Cherokee Nation's revitalization efforts, along with teaching revitalization workshops through the Oklahoma Native

Language Association. Mary S. Linn (Anthropology, University of Oklahoma; Sam Noble Oklahoma Museum of Natural History) works with native language teachers and programs in Oklahoma; as curator of native languages, she is building a language resource collection and revitalization programming in collaboration with Oklahoma tribes. Lizette Peter (Department of Teaching and Leadership, Kansas University) is an assistant professor of second language acquisition and serves as an advisor to the Cherokee Nation on several of their language initiatives. Gloria Sly (Culture Resource Center, Cherokee Nation, Oklahoma) has initiated and guided various language programs of the Cherokee Nation. Tracy Williams (University of Arizona) has been engaged in revitalizing her language, Oneida, and is currently pursuing a doctoral degree in indigenous language education. Kimiko Y. Yamamoto (Japanese Culture, Kansas University) works with Native educators in developing literature.

Suggestions for further reading

In this book: Language extinction is discussed from various angles in chapters 2 (languages of the world), 24 (language death), 41 (Are U.S. dialects dying?), and 50 (Latin).

Elsewhere:

Hale, Ken, and Leanne Hinton, eds. *The Green Book of Language Revitalization in Practice* (Academic Press, 2001). The editors have put together immediately usable examples of language revitalization programs for this magical book. The topics range from how to design a program to how to train language teachers, from one-on-one immersion to one-on-many classroom approaches. This is the starter book for anyone interested in language revitalization.

Hinton, Leanne. *How to Keep Your Language Alive: A Commonsense Approach to One-on-One Language Learning* (Heyday Press, 2002). A delightfully useful book on how one-on-one teaching can be used to ensure that new speakers of a severely endangered language will emerge. This is a must-have handbook for those working on revitalization.

McCarty, Teresa L., and Ofelia Zepeda, eds. *Indigenous Language Use and Change in the Americas* (International Journal of the Sociology of Language 132; Mouton de Gruyter, 1998). An excellent collection of articles concerning how indigenous language groups in the Americas are revitalizing their ancestral languages.

Nettle, Daniel, and Suzanne Romaine. *Vanishing Voices: The Extinction of the World's Languages* (Oxford University Press, 2002). Readable and comprehensive, this book covers the causes and effects of language extinction throughout the world.

Web sites:

http://portal.unesco.org/culture
UNESCO (see 'Intangible Cultural Heritage').

http://sapir.ling.yale.edu/~elf
The Endangered Language Fund.

http://www.ogmios.org
The Foundation for Endangered Languages.

http://www.hrelp.org
The Hans Rausing Endangered Languages Project of the School of Oriental and African Studies.

26

Why do American southerners talk that way?

Walt Wolfram

*Do all Southerners have the same dialect? What are the
ingredients of the way they talk? Where did the speech
of the Carolinas come from?*

No dialect in the U.S. is more noticed—and commented on—than
Southern English. This is where a person *totes* objects, but *carries*
friends to see a *show*. And where else do we *cut on* the lights and
mash the button on a machine? To quote the title of a recent book on
Southern terms, *Y'all is Spoken Here*. Nothing about the American
South is more Southern than its speech.

But is the South really united linguistically? Try telling people
from the Carolinas that they all talk alike. Along the coast, people
speak some of the most distinctive English dialects used anywhere.
Someone on the Outer Banks of North Carolina may say *It's hoi toid
on the saned soid*. That's *high tide on the Sound side* for those who

don't recognize the distinctive vowel sounds of the coast—or *hah tahd on the sound sahd* in the mainland South.

In South Carolina, traditional Charleston speech seems to have a vowel system all its own. The pronunciation of the vowel in *so* and *row* sounds like the /o/ of French or Spanish (which does not glide into an 'oo' ending as the 'o' sounds of most other English dialects do), and *out* and *about* sound like the Canadian *oat* and *aboat*. Travel to the Sea Islands and you find Gullah—a creole language, also known as Geechee, that goes back to the days of rice plantations populated largely by blacks from Africa and the West Indies. The sounds and rhythms of Gullah are popularized in the *Br'er Rabbit* stories and in George Gershwin's opera, *Porgy and Bess*. This variety of English is closer to the creoles of the Bahamas and Jamaica than to dialects of the Southern mainland.

Travel to Carolina's western mountains and the hollows of Southern Appalachia, and you'll find the imprint of the Scotch Irish. In the Smoky Mountains, you might be greeted with *Hit's nice to see you'uns*. The plural form *you'uns* is, of course the equivalent of the infamous Southern *y'all*. And *hit* for 'it' is a relic of an older English pronunciation. This is where a *boomer* is a red squirrel—not a thundershower as in other parts of Carolina. In the mountains, *si-gogglin'* (pronounced *SIGH-gahg-lin*) means something is crooked, while other Carolinians may use *catawampus* to talk about things that aren't quite plumb. And the term *dope* among older mountain people may still refer to a soft drink, thanks to some of its original ingredients.

Now add the sounds of African Americans in the Piedmont and Coastal Plain to the mix. And don't forget the unique dialect of the Lumbee Indians along the North and South Carolina border. With over fifty-five thousand members, they're the largest group of Native Americans east of the Mississippi. While the Lumbee no longer maintain a Native American Indian language, their dialect is ethnically distinct from both the white and the black dialects that are its neighbors. Put it all together and you have dialect differences greater than those in just about any other region of the United States.

Why such diversity? First, there's the so-called 'founder effect'. Groups of speakers came from different parts of the world and left their imprints on the speech of the region—the Scotch Irish influence in Appalachia, a Scots flavor in dialects of the Cape Fear valley; speech patterns from Southwestern England in the Outer Banks; and, of course, the African influence on the Sea Islands.

But there's also a cultural mix. In the antebellum South, aristocrats sent their children to England for a proper education. There they found a brand of English in which *r* sounds at the end of syllables (like *four*, *fear*, or *fair*) had gone silent around the seventeenth century; this British trend found a colonial home among the southern elite. At the same time, words like *tote* for 'carry', *goober* for 'peanut', and *cooter* for 'turtle' came from African languages through the Charleston port. The result was an ironic mixture in the South of African slave language and prestigious British pronunciation.

But the most intriguing aspect of speech in the south is that much of it is home-grown. Some of the most widely-known features of Southern speech are probably the pronunciation of the vowel in *tahm* for 'time', the pronunciation of *stick pin* and *ink pen* both as 'pin', and the thoroughly Southern plural *y'all*. Recent research shows that these traits were barely present in the antebellum South. They're relatively new. Over the past one hundred and fifty years, they germinated on their own, took root, and spread through the South like a linguistic kudzu.

About the author

Walt Wolfram, the William C. Friday Distinguished Professor of English Linguistics at North Carolina State University, describes himself as a dialect nomad. He has studied dialects ranging from African American varieties in large metropolitan areas to the speech of small, isolated island and mountain communities. He has authored more than twenty books and two hundred and fifity articles, in addition to producing a number of TV documentaries. More information on Dr. Wolfram's media productions is available at: http://www.talkingnc.com and http://www.ncsu.edu/linguistics

Suggestions for further reading

In this book: Dialects are discussed in chapters 3 (dialects versus languages), 18 (British, American, and other versions of English), and 41 (changing dialects in the U.S.). Various languages of America are discussed in chapters 25 (revitalizing threatened Native American languages), 35 (languages of the U.S.), 36 (America's language crisis), 37 (Spanish in the U.S.), 38 (Cajun), 39 (German in the U.S.), 40 (Gullah), and 49 (Native American languages).

Elsewhere:

Bernstein, Cynthia, Tom Nunnally, and Robin Sabino, eds. *Language Variety in the South Revisited* (University of Alabama Press, 1997). A collection of articles from a decennial conference dedicated to the study of language in the American South.

Nagle, Steven, and Sara Sanders, eds. *Language in the New South* (Cambridge University Press, 2003). An anthology on different dialects of the American South, including regional and ethnic varieties. Important overviews of major Southern dialects are included.

Wolfram, Walt, and Ben Ward, eds. *American Voices: How Dialects Differ from Coast to Coast* (Blackwell, 2006). A major section in this collection of brief, popular profiles of dialects in North America and the Caribbean is dedicated to the American South. The sections on sociocultural dialects and island dialects also include some Southern dialects.

Picone, Michael, and Catherine Davies, eds. *Language Variation in the South III* (University of Alabama Press, forthcoming). This collection includes papers from the most recent conference dedicated to language in the American South. Most major researchers in the field have articles in this collection.

27

What causes foreign accents?

Steven H. Weinberger

Where do foreign accents come from? What makes one foreign accent different from another? Can you learn to speak a foreign language without an accent?

Foreign accents have been around for a long time. The Old Testament tells us how the Gileadites destroyed the infiltrating army of their enemy, the Ephraimites: They set up roadblocks and made each man who approached them say the Gileadite word 'Shibboleth'. The Ephraimites couldn't pronounce the *sh* sound, so when they said the word it came out 'sibboleth'—and the Gileadites killed them on the spot.

The consequences aren't often that dramatic, but we're all experts at detecting things about people from the way they talk. Not only do we often make immediate biased judgments about a person simply based upon their accent, but even on the phone we know a person's sex, approximate age—even whether he or she is smiling. And like the Gileadites, we usually know right away whether the person is a native speaker of our language.

For example, if you heard a recording of someone saying a sentence including the words 'zeeze seengs', you might be able to recognize that the speaker meant 'these things', but you'd certainly know that she was a foreigner. You'd draw a similar conclusion if you heard a different voice say 'deeza tings'.

What is it about the speech of these two people that would let you immediately recognize them as non-native English speakers? And why would their accents be different from each other? While many factors influence foreign accents, much of the answer lies in something linguists call 'language transfer'. When you first learn a new language, you'd like to sound like a native, but you unavoidably carry over, or transfer, some of the characteristics of your own language to it.

The 'zeeze seengs' speaker, for example, wants to say 'these things', but her native language (which happens to be French) doesn't have the *th* sounds of English, so she uses the closest approximations to them that she can find in her inventory of French sounds: a *z* for the voiced *th* of 'these' and an *s* for the unvoiced *th* of 'things'. Another English sound missing from the French inventory is the short *i* vowel of 'things', so native French speakers will tend to replace it with the nearest handy sound, the long *ee*: 'zeeze seengs'.

The 'deeza tings' speaker has similar difficulties, but he's attempting the English phrase under the influence of his own native language (which happens to be Italian). He doesn't have a problem with the short *i* vowel, but he, too, lacks the voiced and unvoiced *th* sounds of English, and he substitutes a *d* and a *t* for them. He also seems to avoid ending a word with a consonant—English has lots of final *p t, k, b, d, g, f, s, v, z* sounds, but Italian does not—so he tends to tack a little neutral vowel after some English final consonants: 'deeza tings'.

It's the ability to recognize and reproduce these features of language transfer that enable professional actors to portray foreign speakers of English convincingly, and sometimes for comic effect. Think of Chico Marx portraying an Italian aviator, or Peter Sellers transforming himself into the incomparable Inspector Clouseau. Each of them filters his English through a foreign sound inventory, exaggerates a bit, and the results are humorous.

Does this mean that when foreigners speak English—and when we try to speak foreign languages—we're doomed to sound like comic caricatures forever? Of course not. We can't help starting out that way. But what Peter Sellers does to his English to give it a French flavor, we might be able to consciously do to our French, Russian, or Arabic to give it more of a native French, Russian, or Arabic flavor.

Can that make us sound like native speakers? Well, almost. Professional linguists say that people who start learning a new language after childhood can never completely get rid of traces of their original tongue: Some good listeners and certainly sensitive instruments in a linguistics lab can spot them. But we don't live in a lab. And many of us know someone who speaks a second language so well that they don't sound foreign at all. With hard work and good attention to sounds—maybe inspired by Inspector Clouseau—we may gradually develop an accent that sounds very close to that of a native. And that's a pretty good goal to shoot for.

About the author

Steven H. Weinberger (weinberg@gmu.edu) is Associate Professor and Director of the Linguistics program at George Mason University in Virginia. He teaches courses in phonetics, phonology, and second language acquisition. His principal research deals with language sound systems and foreign accents. He is co-editor of *Interlanguage Phonology: The Acquisition of a Second Language Sound System* (1987), and he is the founder and administrator of the *Speech Accent Archive* (http://accent. gmu.edu/), a Web database of hundreds of different accents in English.

Suggestions for further reading

In this book: Chapters relevant to language learning by adults include 15 (language and the brain), 29 (adult advantages in language learning), 30 (language-learning tips), 31 (history of language-teaching methods), 32 (study abroad), and 34 (language-teaching technology). Chapters discussing the sounds of language include 26 (English in the American South) and 28 (phonetics).

Elsewhere:

Blumenfeld, R. *Accents: A Manual for Actors* (Proscenium, 2000). A guide to producing more than eighty different speech accents for English speakers. It is designed for actors, but it contains insights into speech production and comparative linguistics.

Lippi-Green, R. *English with an Accent* (Routledge, 1997). A thorough analysis of American attitudes towards English accents. It focuses on language variation linked to geography and social identity, and looks at how institutions promote linguistic stereotyping.

Swan, M. and B. Smith. *Learner English* (Cambridge University Press, 2001). A practical reference text that presents and compares relevant linguistic features of English with about twenty-two other languages. It utilizes linguistic transfer to predict learners' errors, and is a valuable resource for ESL teachers.

Web site:

http://accent.gmu.edu
Weinberger, S. *Speech Accent Archive*. A Web-based phonetic analysis of native and non-native speakers of English who read the same paragraph that is carefully transcribed. The archive is used by people who wish to compare and analyze the accents of different English speakers.

28

How are the sounds of language made?

Peter Ladefoged

What kind of sounds make up languages? Do all languages have consonants and vowels? Do they all have the same ones?

Everyone knows that when you talk you use your tongue and lips. You probably also know that speech sounds often involve the action of the vocal cords—nowadays more usually called vocal folds, as they are two thin folds of muscle in the throat that vibrate when air is blown between them. To get the vocal folds to vibrate you have to push air out of your lungs. To talk, we then move parts of the vocal tract and, in various ways, alter its shape to produce consonants and vowels. Here are some examples of how it all works.

The lips are used to make the consonants at the beginning of the English words *pea, bee, me*. In the *p* sound, pressure is built up behind the closed lips. The vocal folds do not vibrate and there is usually a little puff of air (called aspiration) when the lips open and before any following vowel begins. This puff of air is missing when you say *b*, and there may even be some voicing (vocal fold vibration) while the lips are closed. There is always voicing during the lip closure for *m* in which the air comes out through the nose.

The English consonants *t*, *d*, *n* and *k*, *g*, *ng* are pronounced in ways similar to *p*, *b*, *m*, except that for *t*, *d*, *n* the air is stopped from flowing out of the mouth by raising the tip of the tongue to form a closure just behind the teeth; and for *k*, *g*, *ng* the closure is made by raising the back of the tongue to contact the soft palate, the fleshy part at the back of the roof of the mouth. Other consonant sounds, such as those in the words *fie*, *thigh*, *sigh*, *shy*, don't have a complete closure stopping air from flowing out of the mouth but are produced by forming a narrow gap through which the air hisses and hushes as it escapes. In these sounds the vocal folds are not vibrating. There is, however, another set of fricative sounds in which there *is* voicing, as in the sounds at the ends of the words *move*, *smooth*, *ooze*, *rouge*.

Most forms of English have twenty-two consonant sounds and anywhere from thirteen to twenty-one different vowel sounds. You can hear many of the different vowel sounds between the consonants *b* and *d* in the words *bead*, *bid*, *bayed*, *bed*, *bad*, *bawd*, *booed*, *bide*, *bowed*, *bode*, *Boyd*, *bud*, *bird*. It is very difficult to make accurate descriptions of vowels in terms of their tongue and lip positions, but they can easily be specified in terms of their acoustic overtones.

So how do languages differ with respect to the sounds they use? All spoken languages have consonants and vowels, but the sounds of the world's languages vary so extensively that altogether they may have as many as six hundred different consonant sounds and two hundred different vowels as modified by different pitches and voice qualities.

Sounds like *p*, *t*, *k* occur in 98 percent of all the languages in the world. Hawaiian is one of the languages that does not have all three; it lacks *t*. Interestingly, Hawaiian has only eight consonants, *p*, *k*, *m*, *n*, *w*, *l*, *h*, and a glottal stop (a closure of the vocal folds), written with an apostrophe, as in the word *Hawai'i*.

Other languages have consonants that don't occur in English. Spanish and Italian, for example, have trilled *r* sounds. Trills made with the lips occur in a number of small, endangered languages such as Melpa and Kele in Papua New Guinea. Lip trills preceded by a special kind of *t* occur in Oro Win, a language spoken by only half a dozen people living near the border between Brazil and Bolivia. American Indian languages have a wealth of sounds not found in English, sometimes including long strings of complex consonants. In Montana Salish the word for 'wood tick' in an English spelling would be something like *chchts'elshchen*.

The only speech sounds that can be made without using air from the lungs are the clicks that occur in languages spoken in central and southern Africa. These sounds are made by sucking air into your mouth, much as you might do when dropping a kiss on your grandmother's cheek. A language called !Xóõ, spoken in the Kalahari Desert has eighty-three different ways of beginning a word with a click sound. Zulu, a more well-known language, spoken in South Africa, has three basic clicks, each of which has five variants.

Where European languages stand out is in their number of vowels. French has vowels, not found in English, in which the lips are rounded while the tongue is in the position for the English words *tea* and *day*, forming the French words *tu* 'you' and *deux* 'two'. The largest number of vowels occur in Dutch and German dialects.

It falls to phoneticians to be concerned with describing the sounds of the world's languages: what sounds there are, how they fall into patterns, and how they change in different circumstances. Because there are so many languages and dialects, because the vocal apparatus can produce such a wide variety of sounds, and because each of us has a different way of speaking our own language, it is an infinitely challenging task—and one of most fascinating aspects of the study of language.

About the author

Peter Ladefoged, Professor of Phonetics Emeritus at UCLA, was the world's foremost linguistic phonetician and one of the most important figures in linguistics in the twentieth century. He published ten books and one hundred and thirty scholarly articles on various aspects of the theory and practice of phonetics and the phonetic properties of specific languages. The essay above was one of the last pieces he wrote before his death in early 2006.

Suggestions for further reading

In this book: Other chapters that talk about the sounds of language include 26 (English in the American South) and 27 (foreign accents).

Elsewhere:

Ladefoged, Peter. *A Course in Phonetics* (Harcourt Brace, 1975; Thomson/Wadsworth, fifth edition 2006). The standard textbook in the field, which has been used to train generations of linguists.

Maddieson, Ian. *Patterns of Sounds* (Cambridge University Press, 1984). A useful reference text that describes the distribution of sounds in more than three hundred languages of the world. Readers can look up a sound and find which languages contain it, or they can look up a language and find its particular phonetic inventory.

International Phonetic Association. *Handbook of the International Phonetic Association* (Cambridge University Press, 1999). A comprehensive guide to the phonetic alphabet used by linguists all over the world. The principles of phonetic analysis are described and examples of each phonetic symbol are given.

Web site:

http://www.phonetics.ucla.edu
Some of the sounds of the hundreds of languages Dr. Ladefoged has studied can be heard here.

29

Can monolingualism be cured?

Katherine Sprang

Is it possible to learn a new language as an adult? Isn't it a lot harder than it is for children? Are there any tricks to learning?

When was the last time you studied a foreign language? Some of us think about that experience with pleasure; others think of it as one we wouldn't *ever* want to repeat. If you're over sixteen and trying to learn a new language—or thinking about learning one (and I hope you are)—remember that adults and children learn languages in very different ways.

When we ask ourselves why it takes so long to learn a foreign language, it is easy for us, as adult language learners, to envy children. They learn language as part of learning about the world; their minds absorb the words, phrases, and sentences they hear while they are playing or exploring—and with no apparent effort. Language learning is the child's exciting full-time job for the first few years of life: no studying necessary, and no homework!

But don't forget that even with that sponge-like ability to absorb linguistic information, children have to hear and use their mother tongue for thousands of hours in order to master it; it typically takes them over ten years before they're fully capable of non-childish everyday language use. Adults usually don't have that much time to spare, but that doesn't mean that we can't learn languages and learn them very well. In some ways adults have an *advantage* over children. First, some elements of language can be categorized, analyzed, and explained, and these can be learned by adults more rapidly than by children learning their first language. Second, because we already have a language, adults can use what we know of our first language to organize our learning of the sounds, words, and grammar of the new one. We don't start from scratch when we learn another language.

For example, even if a language has some sounds that English doesn't (maybe a trilled *r* as in 'burro'—or an *ng* sound at the beginning of a word, like 'nga'), chances are that *most* of its sounds will be familiar. Adults can take advantage of this to prioritize their pronunciation effort where it is most needed.

Or the new language may use word orders like 'The boy brave with his rifle the tiger fierce shot.' That sounds unnatural to an English speaker, but foreign grammatical patterns are not so different from English that they can't be figured out and mastered, like a puzzle—again, a skill that improves with age.

Learning foreign vocabulary inescapably requires many exposures to the words in different contexts, but even here adults are well equipped to spot words related to words they already know and use them as stepping-stones into the new language. They can recognize prefixes and suffixes, and understand the roles that those parts of words play in the new language. Adult language students—especially when aided by good teachers, textbooks, and technical aids, have the knowledge, experience, and analytic ability to recognize what's already understandable in a new language and what's different from our first language. By focusing attention on the differences, we as adults can jump-start our learning.

By contrast, other elements of language need to be absorbed through continual and repeated exposure. When the mind is relaxed and not seeking explanations or patterns, it's capable of categorizing and sorting information about some elements of language without conscious effort. The aspects of language taken in best through this unconscious process—called implicit learning— tend not to be captured in textbooks, and they're seldom explained well by teachers. In fact, in some ways it can be more effective simply to watch TV or listen to the radio in the language you're trying to learn, rather than poring over rules and patterns and vocabulary lists.

The better we are at combining both approaches—explicit learning and implicit learning—the more effectively and quickly we can build our knowledge of a new language. And it's not enough just to acquire knowledge. To a great extent, speaking, writing, and understanding a foreign language are a matter of developing skills—like learning to play the piano—that you can't master without practice, practice, PRACTICE. Here again, children have it easier, if only because they're uninhibited. Practicing a foreign language means you have to get past the very adult fear of embarrassment, the discomfort of doing something you are not expert at. Are you willing to walk up to strangers from another country—say, a group of tourists—and try to talk with them in their language? To the extent that you are willing to try out your budding language skills, to practice them (even if your performance is not perfect), and learn from making mistakes, your ability in the foreign language will continue to grow.

Until around the middle of the last century, language learning in school was pretty dull. It was all about memorizing vocabulary, talking about grammar—in English—and translating as many paragraphs as you could stand. We've learned a lot about teaching languages since then. Since the 1970s, the new discipline of Second Language Acquisition, an interdisciplinary field combining cognitive science and applied linguistics, has also emerged. Through it we are gradually discovering which elements of a language are best taught through explicit instruction and which are best absorbed through sustained exposure to the language. As answers to these questions are uncovered through research, language instruction continues to improve, and adults are learning languages better than ever. So if you're a monolingual adult, there's no reason to continue in that sad condition. Monolingualism *can* be cured.

About the author

Katherine Sprang holds a Ph.D. from the German Department at George town University, with primary specialization in Second Language Acquisition (SLA). She is particularly interested in how excellence in teaching can help language students achieve superior foreign-language skills. She works currently at the Foreign Service Institute, U.S. Department of State, as director of the Instructional Support Division.

Suggestions for further reading

In this book: Language learning by adults is also discussed in chapters 15 (language and the brain), 27 (foreign accents), 30 (language-learning tips), 31 (history of language-teaching methods), 32 (study abroad), and 34 (language-teaching technology).

Elsewhere:

Byrnes, Heidi, and Hiram Maxim. *Advanced Foreign Language Learning: A Challenge to College Programs* (Heinle, 2003).

Larsen-Freeman, Diane. *Teaching Language: From Grammar to Grammaring* (Heinle, 2003).

30

What does it take to learn a language well?

Nina Garrett

*Do you have to be clever to learn a new language? How
long does it take to learn one well? Is 'total immersion'
the only real way to do it? Are there any shortcuts?*

People often say, 'I had four semesters of Language X, but I can't
speak a word.' That's a very common problem—in fact, it may be
the typical experience of adult classroom language learners. Why
is it so common? The implication seems to be that we're not very
smart, or we're bad at learning languages, or we had poor teachers.
But probably none of those are true.

We're talking here about speaking a language, speaking it well
enough to talk with other people in their native language about real-
world topics, with the confidence *both* that you're understanding the
cultural context of what they're saying *and* that you're representing
your own thoughts and feelings so that they'll understand you. That's
a very different matter from reading knowledge or even listening

comprehension, both of which can be learned to an advanced level without ever meeting a native speaker.

Speaking another language fluently isn't a matter of IQ or academic smarts: there are millions of people who have no formal education at all but who speak several languages fluently. Nor is it a matter of youth: it's too pessimistic to say that only children can learn languages. The Modern Language Association insists, 'Never too early, never too late.' Children can certainly pick up a new language easily when they're immersed in it, but they're not necessarily better than older learners when they take it as a school subject, because the latter have cognitive advantages.

Still, you don't want to massacre the language, sounding like Inspector Clouseau of the *Pink Panther* films. A language is not just a set of words and phrases that you can memorize to get simple here-and-now meanings across; it's a complex system for communicating—and even more fundamentally for structuring thought. So don't believe the ads in airline magazines for courses that guarantee 'mastery' of a language in just a few weeks—that's just nonsense. Language learning takes time, and the less similar the language is to English, the more time it takes. Think about this: in a typical four-semester course in college, you may well have fewer than two hundred hours of contact time with the language. In U.S. government schools, where languages are taught for real proficiency, courses meet for a minimum of six hundred hours of full-time study, and getting to proficiency in the languages most difficult for English speakers—Chinese, Japanese, Korean, and Arabic—takes twice as long as in the easier ones like French or Spanish.

In addition to a realistic amount of time, you need two things for success: a long period of regular interaction with people speaking the language, and some help with making sense of what's going on linguistically. It's *not* enough just to hang out for a month—or even a year—in a country where the language is spoken. Imagine a foreigner just starting to learn English, who hears an American acquaintance say 'Wutchagonnado?' There'll come a day when she can recognize that, and understand it, as a colloquially compressed version of the six-word sentence 'What are you going to do?' But as a beginner she's likely to hear just a single burst of sound. That's what any of us will experience with an unfamiliar language. How do you learn to make sense of those bursts of sound? Not through 'total immersion'; when you're in the country, the people around you—native speakers—are simply communicating with others who already know the language. They aren't speaking so as to teach you grammar—how to put words together to make meaning—and they probably don't know how to do that. (Most native speakers can't articulate why they say things the way they do.) But without someone explaining the system, your learning will be random and inefficient.

After puberty most of us need classroom work to create a framework for hearing sounds, figuring out how sentences work, and understanding the cultural context. Adults who pick up a language without that framework often end up with a kind of 'abominable fluency'—a lot of words, good speed, maybe even decent pronunciation, but typically mangled grammar and not much cultural sensitivity about how the words are used. They reach a plateau where they sound like Inspector Clouseau with a bigger vocabulary, and they often can't get beyond that plateau.

For adult learners it's ideal to have some solid academic background in the language before going abroad, but the classroom experience on its own isn't enough. If you took a language course and a few years later couldn't remember what you learned, it's probably because you left out the second step: prolonged interaction with people who speak the language. You can do that in the country, of course, but you can also do it by immersion in a summer language school or camp, or by dating a near-monolingual speaker of the language, or by finding intensive uses of the internet—listening to or watching news broadcasts, finding audio materials with transcripts, 'talking' with native speakers in chat rooms (which gives you 'spoken' language even in written form), reading, reading aloud to yourself, watching movies over and over, practicing the dialogues or songs that you hear. Emerging technologies are increasingly good at simulating—or even providing for real—the experience of communicating with native speakers. All of this takes serious motivation; but once you've gotten to the point of real comfort in another language, the excitement and the advantages of your fluency will give you all the motivation you need to keep it up.

About the author

Nina Garrett has taught French and German at junior high school, high school, and college levels, and has also taught graduate-level courses on Second Language Acquisition, especially as its theory underlies language pedagogy. Her first language was Dutch, and she has also studied Russian, Latin, and Spanish. She is internationally known in Computer Assisted Language Learning for her work in developing the use of computer technology both for teaching languages and for conducting research on how language is learned. She is currently Director of the Center for Language Study at Yale University (http://www.cls.yale/.edu), working with teachers of fifty languages.

Suggestions for further reading

In this book: Chapters relevant to language learning by adults include 15 (language and the brain), 27 (foreign accents), 29 (adult advantages in language learning), 31 (history of language-teaching methods), 32 (study abroad), and 34 (language-teaching technology).

Elsewhere:

Lightbown, Patsy, and Nina Spada. *How Languages are Learned* (Oxford University Press, 1993). A very readable account both of children's first-language learning and of second-language learning both in the classroom and in the immersion environment.

31

How has our thinking about language learning changed through the years?

June K. Phillips

What's the history of foreign-language teaching? Have there been a lot of different methods? How different are they? Are today's methods best?

The first language taught to anyone in America was, of all things, Algonquian. New arrivals from England learned native American languages so that they could survive in a foreign land. The goal: communication. But in the years that followed, language teaching became more formalized. The new settlers built schools. And when they, as good Europeans, started teaching languages in the schools, they wanted the best of European tradition. So before the 1800s, learning a language in America meant learning Ancient Greek or Latin—and often both.

When modern languages came on the scene—and that included only French, Spanish, Italian, and German at first—people studied them the same way they studied Latin and Greek, and for the same reasons. Here's what Thomas Jefferson said in 1824, a year before his new University of Virginia opened:

'The Latin and Greek languages constitute the basis of good education and are indispensable to fill up the character of a well educated man.' The next year he wrote, 'We generally learn languages for the benefit of reading the books written in them.' So much for interpersonal communication.

For the next century and more, Americans mostly studied languages, not to talk with native speakers but to learn to read. Language classes were all about reading, translating, and analyzing grammar—not just in Latin and Greek but in modern languages too. So if you studied a language before the middle of the twentieth century, you probably didn't learn to speak it, because no one intended that you should. Speaking wasn't the goal.

And then came World War II. Suddenly the U.S. urgently needed a way of mass-producing *speakers* of foreign languages—soldiers and civilians—who could not just conjugate French verbs or read *Don Quixote* but actually talk with people in all parts of the world. And what was needed included a dazzling *variety* of languages—everything from Dutch to Burmese.

The linguistic profession was pressed into war service ... and the teaching of languages dramatically changed. This time was also the heyday of behaviorism as an explanation for learning. Teachers were trained to use stimulus and response to imprint language patterns in student minds. Students were to learn by memorizing dialogues and producing rapid-fire responses in all kinds of oral drills, even though they rarely produced messages of their own.

It worked to an extent. More people became more fluent, in more languages, faster, through these 'audiolingual' courses than they ever could through the grammar-and-translation model with its emphasis on the written word. World War II needs carried over into the Cold War, and demand for language learning—Russian in particular—remained high. Ancient Greek fell off the charts. Latin experienced ups and downs in popularity and was widely taught for its potential to build vocabulary competency in English.

By the early 1960s, the audiolingual method was widely used across America. But its flaws began to show up. There were severe limitations on stimulus-response as a model for learning something as complex as a language. Researchers looked more closely at how language is acquired, and came to see acquisition as an evolving process rather than something one could master through thirty-minutes-a-day exercises. Language teaching changed again to reflect those insights.

In recent years teaching has changed further, because we now know more about how language is acquired for communicative purpose. We know more about how factors such as age, contexts (classrooms, immersion programs, or overseas study), and learning styles interact. And students are pushing the envelope. They talk across continents with instant messages. They read Web sites. They download news and entertainment. They want to learn more about the cultures that use the languages they study. So in classrooms today, students take on real-world tasks.

If Jefferson were brought back to see what's happened since 1824, he'd mourn the diminished status of Greek and Latin. But he'd no doubt be fascinated by today's students, the variety of languages they study, and the ways they develop language skills. If he could visit a typical classroom he'd see them working in pairs, moving around the room, chattering in short sentences, using imperfect but understandable grammar, and filling in meanings with gestures when necessary. Above all, communicating. I suspect it looked a lot like that when their ancestors were learning Algonquian.

About the author

June K. Phillips is Dean of Arts and Humanities at Weber State University in Utah. She has taught French (at the junior high school through college levels) and methods of foreign-language teaching. She served as President of the American Council on the Teaching of Foreign Languages (ACTFL) in 2001. She was ACTFL's project director for the National Standards for Foreign Language Education; she also co-chaired the development of Program Standards for the Preparation of Foreign Language Teachers, jointly promulgated by ACTFL and the National Council for Accreditation of Teacher Education. She has served as a consultant to the National Assessment of Educational Progress evaluation of Spanish teaching in the U.S. and to the WGBH/Annenberg Video Library for Foreign Languages, a non-profit educational resource. She has published and edited extensively on pedagogical topics.

Suggestions for further reading

In this book: Adult language-learning is also discussed in chapters 15 (language and the brain), 27 (foreign accents), 29 (adult advantages in language learning), 30 (language-learning tips), 31 (history of language-teaching methods), 32 (study abroad), and 34 (language-teaching technology).

Elsewhere:

National Standards in Foreign Language Education Project. *Standards for Foreign Language Learning in the 21st Century* (Allen Press, 1999). This book provides background information on the standards for foreign-language education that are now in part or in full adopted by most U.S. states. The standards, a wider set of goals than were aimed at in past language learning, are commonly called the 'Five Cs': Communication, Cultures, Connections, Comparisons, and Communities.

Omaggio Hadley, Alice. *Teaching Language in Context* (Heinle & Heinle, third edition 2001), Chapters 1–3. The introductory chapters of this text on language teaching trace the various instructional methods over time and set out the basic theories of language acquisition that dominate thinking today.

Shrum, Judith L. and Eileen W. Glisan. *Teacher's Handbook: Contextualized Language Instruction* (Thomson-Heinle, third edition 2005), chapters 1–2. The early chapters of this text explore theories of second-language acquisition and link them with the Standards for Foreign Language learning as the basis for instructional practice.

32

Why study languages abroad?

Sheri Spaine Long

Can you learn a language without going abroad? Isn't it easier to pick up a language by living in a country where it's spoken than by sitting in a classroom in your own country? Are there any pitfalls to 'total immersion' learning?

Are you one of those language learners who *love* to be plunked into an ongoing stream of talk, soaking it up, mimicking what they hear, unruffled if they do not understand what is being said? Or do you find yourself needing more structure, wanting to know what each word means before trying it out, and being frustrated when waves of incomprehensible speech wash over you?

As a language professor, I often hear people say: 'the only way to learn a language is to go abroad.' That assumption is not strictly true. And it is particularly not true if you are thinking that by being in another country you will automatically 'pick up' the language. I dislike that phrase—'pick up a language'—because it implies that language learning somehow happens without effort. Not so. It does take effort, and we probably all know people who spent two or three years in a foreign country but came home still monolingual.

Learning styles vary, so a good way to think about learning a language abroad is from the point of view of *readiness*. For most people, to parachute into a foreign culture with no previous study of the language, no preparation at all, is not only disorienting, it is inefficient. With no framework to help make sense of what you are hearing, progress is slow. Readiness differs from one person to the next, but for most of us, it is best to have *some* formal study of a language before you pull the ripcord. And once you are on the ground, it is best to enroll in a structured learning experience, a language class of some kind. You take the class to get knowledge about the language, and then use the street, pubs, and clubs of the community as your lab to practice speaking and hearing it.

The great advantage of studying and living abroad is that you can experience the language *in its cultural context*. Words and phrases that you hear in a sometimes 'sterile' classroom come alive, even change meaning, when you hear them coming from a native speaker over drinks in a café. Or when you join the crowds in a soccer game. Or deal with the local bureaucracy. However, be careful to avoid the 'dreaded anglophile', the local who wants to practice English with you and who takes advantage of your homesickness to do it. He or she gains—you lose. Your goal is to speak as little English as possible while abroad.

When a friend of mine was a junior in college—after a couple of semesters of Spanish—she signed up for a program in Spain, her first experience with language study abroad. After orientation on the first day, the instructor shifted to Spanish and told fifteen nervous Americans to take a 'no English' pledge. From then on my friend was immersed in a dialect of Spanish that she slowly adopted as her own. She spoke almost no English for five months. She did not socialize with English speakers. She watched Spanish TV and movies (with no subtitles), and spent as much time as she could with locals. At first she spoke broken Spanish; but by the end of the semester, she was using the language comfortably, expressing herself at an advanced level. That was *total immersion* in the language and culture. She spent all of her waking hours, seven days a week, speaking or thinking exclusively in the target language.

It is fatiguing at first to be confronted with a foreign language, because you are constantly listening, concentrating, trying to make sense of what you hear. And because it takes effort, it is easier than you think to spend a long time abroad and still come home monolingual. If your goal is to learn a language abroad, try for linguistic isolation. That means avoiding overseas phone calls, the Internet, satellite TV from home, and opportunities to speak your mother tongue. Even a little before you think you are ready, make a vow to yourself to communicate only in the target language, and do it as much as you can—around the clock.

There is an abundance of study-abroad programs, offered by a wide variety of providers who serve the business, health, and educational communities. Before selecting such a program, you will want to research the providers. Make sure that their goals are in line with yours and that the time abroad is focused on language learning. Ask questions, such as, Does the provider offer structured academic classes and immersion activities? Does the provider offer lodging and dining arrangements that enhance language and cultural immersion? If you are seeking documentation and measurement of the skills you acquire abroad, you should explore options for university or secondary-school credit, proficiency credentials or diplomas. Most people return from their time abroad enthusiastic about their linguistic gains and their new cross-cultural skills, and they express a fresh perspective on their home culture. Study abroad by itself is not the key to learning a language, but the combination of a structured class and total immersion cannot be beat.

About the author

Sheri Spaine Long teaches Spanish language, culture, and literature at the University of Alabama at Birmingham (UAB) and currently serves as chairperson of the Department of Foreign Languages and Literatures there. Dr. Long, who earned her Ph.D. at the University of California, Los Angeles (UCLA), writes about Madrid in the contemporary Spanish novel. She is the co-author of *Nexos: Introductory Spanish* (Houghton

Mifflin, 2005) and *Pueblos: Intermediate Spanish in Cultural Contexts* (forthcoming). She has published articles in *Associated Departments of Foreign Languages Bulletin, Dimension, Foreign Language Annals, Hispania, Modern Language Journal* and *Romance Languages Annual*. She serves on the boards of the American Council on the Teaching of Foreign Languages and the Southern Conference on the Teaching of Languages, and she is an Associate of the National Museum of Language. Dr. Long was recently named Editor of *Foreign Language Annals*, the scholarly journal of the American Council on the Teaching of Foreign Languages.

Suggestions for further reading

In this book: For other discussions of adult language-learning see chapters 15 (language and the brain), 27 (foreign accents), 29 (adult advantages in language learning), 30 (language-learning tips), 31 (history of language-teaching methods), and 34 (language-teaching technology).

Web sites:

http://www.studyabroad.com
Offers a comprehensive way to search for study abroad providers and compare options.

http://www.ciee.org/
This site, maintained by the Council on International Educational Exchange, specializes in options for academic international exchange.

http://www.nafsa.org/
This site is maintained by NAFSA: Association of International Educators (formerly known as the National Association of Foreign Student Advisors), and has a variety of useful publications about study abroad and general information about international education.

The following journals focus on study abroad and contain specialized case and research studies regarding individual study-abroad programs.

Frontiers: The Interdisciplinary Journal of Study Abroad
http://frontiersjournal.com.

Journal of Studies in International Education
http://jsi.sagepub.com.

33

Is elementary school too early to teach foreign languages?

Gladys Lipton

Is there any advantage to teaching languages in primary school? Is there a risk of overloading children's brains? Aren't other subjects more important at that age?

I recently got a note from a mother whose daughter's school had a program teaching Chinese and Spanish to elementary students. Will it result in linguistic confusion? she asked. It's a good question, but it's not a worry. Children under the age of ten are absolutely hard-wired to learn languages. In many countries they learn three or four, often at the same time—with no ill effects. In America, multilingual though it is, the tradition has been not to start language study until high school—and American children are poorer for it. Now, though, Americans are recognizing what a joyous thing language learning is for children, and early language programs are gaining momentum. The language profession calls them 'FLES' (Foreign Language in the Elementary School) or 'Early Language Learning' programs.

The theoretical underpinning for FLES comes from studies of the brain. Researchers say that it's most receptive to foreign language before the age of ten. (Readers fortunate enough to have started their study of a foreign language in childhood probably speak it without an accent.) After that age the brain begins to lose the plasticity it had in childhood. Does this mean that you can't learn a foreign language well if you wait until secondary school to start? Not at all, but you have to work harder at it.

In addition to this 'neurological' advantage, there's also a good deal of value in simply exposing children to the sounds and rhythms of other tongues. Part of learning languages is getting past the notion that English is the 'right' or only way to talk and other languages are 'funny'. Children who take FLES outgrow such attitudes rapidly, and don't have the inhibitions that teenagers often have when they start a language. Researchers have found that children under ten not only love to imitate new sounds, they're highly receptive to other people's customs, traditions, and different ways of doing things. FLES can open children's minds to other cultures, since culture goes along with language study. This is especially true in the early grades of elementary school, where songs, games, and the arts are part of the learning.

What results can you expect from a FLES program? Above all, greater proficiency: students who start a language early and stick with it achieve higher scores on Advanced Placement tests in the language than those who start in their teens. What explains this? A great deal of research has shown that success in language learning depends on three things: time on task, motivation, and frequency or intensity of learning sessions. All three flow from starting a foreign language early. Students who start early automatically get more exposure time; and because language learning in elementary school is *fun*, they're likely to look forward to continuing to study languages. They'll be more motivated.

But even if all that's true, some may ask, isn't the grade school day already full? How can we squeeze in another subject, even if it's worthwhile?

Part of the answer is that, according to emerging research, time spent on FLES is *not* subtracted from the rest of the curriculum. The interdisciplinary approach used by FLES teachers to teach languages reinforces what students learn in other classes: when a FLES teacher works on days of the week, weather, maps, shopping, and other real-life topics in the language class, she or he is reviewing what is taught by other teachers about numbers, dates, geography, temperature, colors, and money. In short, where FLES is integrated into the curriculum, students tend to do better on tests (in English) in Reading, Language Arts, Social Studies and Mathematics.

For all these reasons, many parents are interested in internationalizing the schools attended by their children, but they can be daunted by the perceived cost of establishing a FLES program. There is certainly no magical answer to this problem, but there are many options. Where regular classroom teachers are fluent in a foreign language and have been trained in language-teaching methods, they can form the nucleus of a program. Sometimes it makes most sense for several classes or several schools to share the services of one or more traveling language teachers. In some cases, videoconferencing technology can help stretch limited language-teaching staff to cover more schools. It is a good idea for parents, school administrators, and other community members to work together to identify appropriate program goals and realistic resource expectations.

To return to that mother's question, should we teach foreign languages in the elementary school? The answer is unequivocally: Yes!

About the author

Gladys Lipton is currently the Director of America's National FLES* (pronounced 'flestar') Institute. She has directed national teacher development at the University of Maryland, funded by many national grants. Her past positions include Program Coordinator in Foreign Languages and ESOL for Anne Arundel County Public Schools in Maryland and Director of Foreign Languages for the New York City Public Schools. She has taught foreign languages at all school (K-12) and university levels. Dr. Lipton has served as Editor of the newsletter of the Northeast Conference on the Teaching of Foreign Languages (NECTFL) and is currently a reviewer for *Foreign Language Annals*, a publication of the American Council on the Teaching of Foreign Languages (ACTFL). She has chaired the national FLES committees of both the American Association of Teachers of Spanish (AATS) and the American Association of Teachers of French (AATF); in addition, she has served as an Associate Editor of the AATS publication *Hispania* and as a board member, vice president, and national president of AATF. Dr. Lipton has presented many workshops, nationally and internationally, for teachers, parents, and administrators, and she currently serves as a foreign-language consultant for schools, school districts, and foreign-language organizations.

Suggestions for further reading

In this book: Other chapters discussing language acquisition by children include 8 (pidgins and creoles), 13 (babies and language), 15 (language and the brain), 22 (language deprivation), and 23 (sign languages).

Elsewhere:

Curtain, H. and C. A. Dahlberg. *Languages and Children: Making the Match* (Pearson/Prentice Hall, third edition 2004). This book offers information about FLES research, methods, and curriculum which may be of help to all those working with FLES programs.

Lipton, G. *Practical Handbook to Elementary Foreign Language Programs (FLES*)* (Blueprints for Learning, fourth edition 2004). This book offers assistance in planning and supporting FLES* programs, including rationale and research, differentiation of instruction for students, curriculum and assessment of programs and students, and suggestions for FLES* advocacy and promotion.

Lipton, G., L. Lucietto, and H. Saxon, eds. *Success Stories: Promoting FLES* Programs* (AATF, 2004). This publication contains successful practices in promoting and maintaining FLES* programs through creative and practical methods and by involving many members of school communities.

Web site:

http://www.gladys-c-lipton.org
This is a Web site of the National FLES* Institute and contains current information about FLES, including recommended references.

34

Can computers teach languages faster and better?

Frank Borchardt

*Can you converse with a machine? What technology
exists to help people learn languages?*

Douglas Adams's *Hitchhiker's Guide to the Galaxy* was filled with
wisdom. Big friendly letters on the cover advised, 'Don't panic!' The
book's best invention was the Babelfish, which, if you stuck it in your
ear, translated for you all the languages of the galaxy. When real-life
computers began to offer rudimentary versions of Babelfish-like
capabilities, language teachers would have done well to heed the
advice on the cover of Adams' *Guide*. Instead, for a very long time,
the language-teaching profession seemed to spin its wheels, unsure
about how to use the new technology.

It has been commonplace since the days of Marshall McLuhan
and Walter Ong to observe that new technologies emulate old ones,
at least for a while: printed books pretended to be manuscripts for a
good fifty years after Gutenberg's Bible; films at first looked like stage

plays; television news sounded like radio; and computer screens still haven't gotten beyond looking like paper. In the language-teaching world, electronic exercises and tests at first consisted largely of multiple-choice and true/false questions, fill-in-the-blanks sentences, and scrambled-sentence exercises, all of which came directly from the printed textbook.

Fortunately, things change. In recent years, the use of technology in language learning has dramatically increased, and its value is now abundantly clear.

An early example is the wholly glossed text, in which an audio or cinematic work is digitized and decked out with every imaginable resource for the learner. A complete transcript of a movie in the target language or a translation into English can be called up with a mouse click; a click on an individual word or phrase can bring up explanations of the grammar and syntax of almost every part of a paragraph, as well as its cultural background. The result is great savings in time, since there is no need for a learner to flip through the pages of a dictionary or grammar book. Examples of language-learning programs using this technology include *Interlex, Système D, Language Dynamics*, and *Transparent Language*.

More recently, the Internet and World Wide Web have brought remarkable new uses of technology. For the first time, without leaving the desk, a language learner can access reliable grammars, dictionaries, online formal courses, and authentic materials in great abundance.

There are also new ways to practice the language. Drill-and-practice programs, typical of 1960s language-teaching methods, were ridiculed by critics as 'drill-and-kill'; but eliminating such programs may not have been an altogether wise move. Drill-and-practice remains an unavoidable component of adult language learning, and it is something that computers do very well indeed. Now, as a low-end application of technology, instructors can use programs like *Hot Potatoes*, available at no cost, to quickly create exercises based on authentic media found on the Web.

The Web also permits contact—in the target language—with native speakers in countries wherever the language is spoken. One option, of course, is the electronic version of pen pals. Another is the emergence of audio and video 'podcasts'—created by people all over the globe with the express intent of being downloaded on computers—through which students can tune in subjects of their own interest. The existence of international 'blogs' (Web logs) offers a way for learners to read target-language prose, in informal language, which is easier to deal with than formal journalistic or literary prose. Text, audio, and video are available in countless combinations, as are e-mail services, chat rooms and instant messaging in many, many languages. If there is a drawback to such abundance, it is the difficulty of finding a pathway through these resources that will lead the learner rationally and gradually to the next level of proficiency.

To date, most computer-assisted language learning has focused on written language, with sound bytes added so learners can hear the pronunciation of native speakers. But a recent leap forward uses voice recognition technology to allow learners to 'converse' with a machine. It is not yet sustained conversation, but the computer can supply a video or audio prompt and gauge the comprehensibility of a student's response in narrowly-defined scenarios (such as greetings or ordering from a menu). Based on a database of acceptable responses and pronunciations, the machine will either accept the response and move ahead in the conversation, or ask for clarification.

This avalanche of computer-mediated linguistic resources benefits above all the highly motivated autonomous learner, who does well no matter what the circumstances, but it is also being used in structured language classes. Some teachers use 'discussion boards' (electronic bulletin boards) for students to work on the language collaboratively: students post comments in the target language, which their fellow students add to. Although it is still written, this kind of language practice is genuine communication which, after all, is what language learning is all about.

So, yes, the computer is in many ways helping to teach languages better, or at least more efficiently; and language study has become more interactive, more exciting. No one claims any longer that technology is going to solve all the problems of language learning. But neither is the new technology an oddity for the educational establishment. While the number of language teachers who use computers in their courses is still relatively small, it is growing daily.

We are a long way from creating artificial intelligence that will let us talk to a machine in the language of our choice. While many young people would not think of wandering about without iPods firmly planted in their ears, the Babelfish is even further off. But we are well launched, and the computer has set the course for a 'galaxy' of new approaches to language learning.

About the author

Frank L. Borchardt is Professor of German and Education at Duke University. From 1983 to 1997 he led the projects which produced the CALIS (Computer Assisted Language Instructional System) mark-up language for instructional exercises, and its successor WinCALIS. He was Executive Director of CALICO (Computer Assisted Language Instructional Consortium) and editor of the CALICO Journal from 1991 to 1997. He has served as Seminar Director at the Universidad de las Palmas de Gran Canaria (1993), as Visiting Professor at the Universidad Tecnológica Nacional of Argentina (1997), and as Advisory Professor to Shanghai's Jiao Tong University (1999). Currently he teaches language and literature in Duke's German Department and the occasional Educational Technologies seminar in the Program in Education at Duke. For further information, see http://www.duke.edu/~frankbo/frank1.html.

Suggestions for further reading

In this book: For other discussions of adult language-learning see chapters 15 (language and the brain), 27 (foreign accents), 29 (adult advantages in language learning), 30 (language-learning tips), 31 (history of language-teaching methods), and 32 (study abroad). Other linguistic/technological topics appear in chapters 35 (interactive map of U.S. language communities), 45 (machine translation), 46 (Forensic Linguistics), and 47 (the National Museum of Language).

Elsewhere:

http://en.wikipedia.org/wiki/Computer-assisted_language_learning
An excellent introduction and overview (like so much else in Wikipedia) of computer-assisted language learning.

http://www.ict4lt.org/en/index.htm
A general Web site on language-learning technologies. Good overview, good theory, good practice. Has a generally Eurocentric bias, understandable since the project was originally funded by the EU.

http://llt.msu.edu/vol8num1/net/default.html
Site of the online journal *Language Learning & Technology*.

http://www.tandf.co.uk/journals/titles/09588221.asp
The online journal for the professional organization devoted to Computer-Assisted Language Learning (CALL).

http://www.eurocall-languages.org/recall/
The online journal for the professional EuroCALL's ReCALL Journal.

http://calico.org/
Site of CALICO (Computer Assisted Language Instruction Consortium).

35

What's the language of the United States?

David Goldberg

Isn't the U.S. monolingual? What languages other than English are spoken there? How do you find out who speaks what languages where?

It always seems peculiar when you hear people say that the U.S. is an English-speaking country, and that Americans 'aren't good at languages.' Actually, tens of millions of people in the U.S. speak languages other than English—a lot of other languages. More than 47 million people speak languages other than English at home; about 93 percent of them also speak English. Did you know that people in Idaho speak over seventy languages, including almost a thousand who speak Shoshoni? That over 86 thousand people speak Polish in Chicago? Or that almost half of New York City's residents don't speak English at home? In fact, only the less populated or rural areas of the country are exclusively English-speaking: places like Appalachia, the deep South, and parts of the Midwest. In most of the country, and especially in the larger cities, multilingualism is the rule.

The language abilities of people in the U.S. are a valuable national resource in many ways, but the nation is not using this resource as well as it might to meet its language-related needs. People who know their family language only in part can be educated to strengthen their language skills, and those who are to any degree bilingual or multilingual have a leg up on learning other languages as well. Support for language education programs already in place would go far towards meeting language shortfalls in government and industry.

How do we know about how many Americans speak which languages and where? By referring to an online Language Map created by the Modern Language Association of America. Using data from the 2000 Census, the MLA has created interactive maps and tables that show the linguistic composition of the entire U.S., state by state, county by county, city by city—down to the neighborhoods defined by postal delivery codes—at the touch of a button.

You can see how languages are distributed across the country, and zoom in on places that have speakers of a language you're interested in. You can call up tables that rank the fifty states according to numbers of speakers for each language. If, for instance, you want to know where Vietnamese is most spoken you'll see that California, Texas, and Washington are the top three states. And tables in the MLA Language Map's Data Center will show you how well speakers of other languages speak English, too.

If you look at Minnesota, which you may think of as full of Scandinavians, you'll find that Spanish, German and the Southeast Asian language Hmong are the most spoken languages—there are three times as many speakers of Hmong as there are speakers of Swedish, Norwegian and Danish combined. You could look up Androscoggin County in Maine and find that it has 13,951 speakers of French and 271 speakers of German—not to mention well over thirty other languages. You can compare the number of

Yiddish speakers in New York with the number in Miami. The Map also gives a breakdown of speakers by age, separating those under the age of eighteen, those between eighteen and sixty-four, and those sixty-five and over. In Brooklyn, for instance, there are over 24,000 Yiddish speakers under the age of eighteen; in Miami, there are none. Data like these may provide clues to a language community's future—or perhaps to whether new immigrants have come by themselves to work and send money home, or have come with their families to stay.

There are dozens of ways planners, teachers and students, corporate researchers, librarians, or ordinary citizens can use the information presented in the electronic MLA Language Map. Marketers who want to reach speakers of Urdu or Korean can find the postal codes where a mass mailing might be most effective. Government agencies can use it for providing social services, or for disaster preparedness. The Map can tell Justice Department officials which languages they need to use to inform new citizens of their rights and responsibilities; it can tell officials in the Office of Trade and Information how it might help a company with interests in China find Americans who know the language. Perhaps most importantly, the Map can help language learners find a place in the U.S. where they can practice the languages they're studying without spending money to go abroad.

All this wealth of linguistic information existed in the U.S. Census Bureau's archives, but it was the MLA's work that made it public, easy to find and easy to use.

The U.S. has long been described as a cultural melting pot into which languages other than English disappear upon arrival. The Language Map reveals that this is far from being the case. You can investigate for yourself by going to www.mla.org, clicking on 'Language Map', and typing in the name of a town or a U.S. postal code (ZIP code). You may get a surprise.

About the author

David Goldberg is Associate Director of the Office of Foreign Language Programs and the Association of Departments of Foreign Languages at the Modern Language Association. He is responsible for the continuing development of the MLA Language Map. Goldberg holds a Ph.D. in Yiddish literature and has taught Yiddish language and literature in heritage language schools and at Columbia University and the University of Pennsylvania. He is the author of an intermediate Yiddish textbook published by Yale University Press.

Suggestions for further reading

In this book: The language landscape of the U.S. is discussed in chapters 25 (revitalizing threatened Native American languages), 26 (English in the American South), 36 (America's language crisis), 37 (Spanish in the U.S.), 38 (Cajun), 39 (German in the U.S.), 40 (Gullah), and 49 (Native American languages). Other linguistic uses of technology are the subjects of chapters 34 (language-teaching technology), 45 (machine translation), 46 (Forensic Linguistics), and 47 (the National Museum of Language).

Elsewhere:

McKay, Sandra Lee and Sau-ling Cynthia Wong, eds. *New Immigrants in the United States: Background for Second Language Educators* (Cambridge University Press, 2000). Discusses language issues from the perspective of the year 2000 in communities of Americans from Mexico, Puerto Rico, Cuba, Vietnam, Southeast Asia, China, Korea, the Philippines, Russia, and India. Includes studies on language and law, language and education.

McKay, Sandra Lee and Sau-ling Cynthia Wong, eds. *Language Diversity: Problem or Resource?* (Newbury House, 1988). Discusses language issues from the perspective of the year 1988 in communities of Americans from Mexico, Puerto Rico, Cuba, Vietnam, China, Korea, and the Philippines. Includes studies on language and law, language and education, and data from the 1980 Census.

Ferguson, Charles A. and Shirley Brice Heath. *Language in the USA* (Cambridge University Press, 1981). Discusses language issues from the perspective of the year 1981 in communities of Native Americans, African Americans, Filipino Americans, and American speakers of European languages, including Spanish, Italian, French, German, Yiddish, Russian, and Polish. Includes studies on language and law, language and education, and data from the 1970 Census.

36

Is there a language crisis
in the United States?

Catherine Ingold

*What kind of foreign-language capabilities does
America need? What gaps are there? What can be
done?*

Well, if it's not a crisis, it's certainly a serious problem. The U.S.
needs professional-level competence in well over a hundred different languages. While some skills are available, there are huge gaps,
including some in jobs of tremendous national importance.

Shortages in defense and intelligence have received the most
attention, but they aren't the only needs: the globalization of business
has radically increased demand for people who can move information from one language to another. You wouldn't be happy with
German-only instructions for your car radio, or a computer whose
help wizard understood only Japanese: the *localization* industry
(preparing products for use in another language and culture) is a
multi-billion dollar business. In addition, many U.S. residents need

language assistance for essential public services until they learn English; U.S. civil rights law requires in many cases that such assistance be made available—in as many as two hundred languages.

You might ask how there can be a problem when there are thousands of kids studying languages in high school and college every year. Well, first of all, America's schools and colleges rarely teach some of the world's most important tongues. How many schools do you know that teach more than a token amount of Mandarin Chinese, the most-spoken language on the planet? Or the languages of Afghanistan and Pakistan?—to say nothing of Arabic, the U.S. government's current highest priority.

Second, in terms of professionally usable skills, the output of America's education system is modest at best. It's not the fault of teachers or students; rather, it results from scant time allotted to language learning. In many countries, children start a foreign language in the fourth or fifth year of primary school and continue it through high school, adding a second foreign language along the way. Few U.S. schools have such programs. That's a real pity, since learning a language to a professional level takes a lot of time; it should include mastering not only general vocabulary but also the technical terms of one or more specific substantive fields—something that rarely happens in American schools. Think about the special language needs of the court interpreter, the social worker, or the hospital nurse.

Professional-level skill *can* come from living where a foreign language is spoken, but Americans who study abroad are far fewer than their counterparts from other countries, and they often choose English-speaking countries. (Learning to say, 'G'day, Mate' doesn't do much toward filling the gaps in U.S. language capabilities.) Of course there are exceptions: people who love languages and other cultures gravitate to the Peace Corps or diplomatic service. But they are relatively few. In general, professionally useful skill in a language requires a long sequence of education, at least some time spent in a country where it is spoken, and extensive, meaningful use of the language in real-world communication tasks.

Well, how about the immigrants who bring language skills to the U.S.? Aren't they filling the gap? In the 2000 census, forty-seven million people reported speaking a language other than English at home at least part of the time. That count includes two million speakers of Chinese, over 600,000 speakers each of Arabic and Korean, and 300,000 speakers of Hindi. People with skills in those less-taught languages are critically needed. But here's the catch: most language-related U.S. jobs demand professional-level skills in two languages, one of them English, and many newly arrived immigrants don't speak English well enough to fill them. The children of immigrants may speak the family language at home, but once they're in school they quickly switch to English, and by the third generation the family language is gone.

So despite being a nation of immigrants, the U.S. can't produce the capable, well-educated, bilingual professionals it needs without serious investment in training. The excellent Urdu, Chinese, or Persian of the first generation often needs to be complemented by advanced English—well beyond typical school and college offerings in English as a Second Language (ESL). For children of immigrants, high-quality ESL programs, parallelled by development of literacy in their family language, can achieve the goal. In such 'additive bilingual education' programs, strengths in one's best language can be used to leverage development in one's other language.

If its next generation is to fill critical roles in government, business, and community service, America needs to provide wider and deeper education in far more languages—both to introduce new languages to monolingual Americans and to bolster the skills of people who speak another language at home.

In 1958, the Soviet Union surprised the West by putting the Sputnik satellite into space. The U.S. Congress responded by creating a generation of scientists, engineers, and linguists who helped win the Cold War. September 11, 2001 was another Sputnik moment for America, and at least some members of Congress believe a similar response is needed. They've proposed a national commitment of resources to the teaching of critically needed languages of the Middle East and Asia, comparable to the commitment that was made half a century ago to the teaching of Russian.

About the author

Catherine Ingold is Director of the National Foreign Language Center (NFLC), an action-oriented language policy institute at the University of Maryland), where she is currently Principal Investigator of a large-scale project to develop online language-learning materials at advanced levels in more than thirty critical languages. Other grants include an online heritage language development resource for Spanish (NEH). Dr. Ingold holds an M.A. in Romance Linguistics and a Ph.D. in French from the University of Virginia. At Gallaudet University, she chaired the foreign-language department and served as Dean of Arts and Sciences and then Provost, learning American Sign Language. As President of the American University of Paris, she presided over a faculty with thirty-five native languages and a student body from seventy-six countries. She has been at NFLC since 1996.

Suggestions for further reading

In this book: Opportunities and requirements for professional use of language abilities are discussed in chapters 20 (bilingualism), 42 (language-related careers), 43 (dictionaries), 44 (interpreting and translating), 46 (forensic linguistics), 53 (Russian), and 55 (Arabic). Another view of U.S. language capabilities is presented in chapter 35 (languages of the U.S.).

Elsewhere:

Garcia, Ofelia, and Joshua A. Fishman, eds. *The Multilingual Apple: Languages in New York City* (Mouton de Gruyter, second edition 2002). For those interested in our heritage language capabilities and trends in minority language use and loss; provides a wealth of information, accessible to the general reader, on immigrant language communities in New York City.

Brecht, Richard, and William Rivers. *Language and National Security in the Twenty-First Century: The Federal Role in Supporting National Language Capacity* (National Foreign Language Center, 2000). A strategic analysis of this issue from NFLC that has greatly influenced public policy in the wake of September 11, although it was written shortly before that event.

Wiley, Terrence G. *Literacy and Language Diversity in the United States* (Center for Applied Linguistics, second edition 2005). Addresses a range of education policy issues related to speakers of languages other than English in the U.S. With emphasis on K-12 language and literacy issues, it complements the other two texts.

37

Is Spanish taking over the United States?

Maria Carreira

Is Spanish in the U.S. to stay? Will it remain the same as Spanish in other countries?

The story of Spanish in the United States is an amazing one. The U.S. is now the fifth largest and the third wealthiest Spanish-speaking country in the world. New York has as many Puerto Ricans as San Juan, the capital of Puerto Rico. Miami is the second-largest Cuban city, Los Angeles the second largest Mexican city.

But what's the future of Spanish in the U.S.? During more than three centuries of immigration, dozens of languages have landed on American shores, only to fade away in a generation or two. Think of Italian, Dutch, or Japanese. Judging purely from history, Spanish could be expected to follow the same path, gradually losing speakers and eventually disappearing. But will Spanish go the way of other immigrant languages—or will it find a way to survive?

As a general rule, immigrants to the U.S. strongly prefer their native language over English. This certainly applies to the millions of foreign-born Latinos now in the U.S. However, with each successive generation of Latinos, Spanish use declines sharply. By the third generation, few Latinos remain proficient in the language of their parents and grandparents. They overwhelmingly prefer English.

Latino youth abandon Spanish to fit in, or to attain the social status that comes with English. And practically speaking, some worry that Spanish will interfere with their ability to speak English, and their ability to make a good living. So it's only a matter of time before Spanish fades away. Or is it?

So far, the generational loss of speakers has been offset by a steady flow of new immigrants from Latin America—up to a million a year. But even if immigration declines as some experts predict, the sheer number of speakers in the country gives Spanish the advantage of critical mass—far larger than any other immigration in history—which will give it staying power. As of 2006, there were over 45 million Hispanics in the U.S., living in every state of the union.

There are parts of the country—places such as Texas, Florida, California, and New Mexico—where Spanish has a history dating back many decades, if not hundreds of years. Recently, Spanish is also making its presence felt in places as far away from the nation's southern contours as Washington State, Oregon, and Minnesota, as new waves of immigrants travel further into the country in search of a livelihood.

From the newly arrived to the native born, Latinos in the U.S. are avid consumers of all things in Spanish. In Los Angeles and Miami, Spanish-language television and radio have a larger audience than their English-language counterparts. Everywhere Latinos live, Spanish can be heard and seen in churches, businesses, schools, and government offices.

And let's not forget non-Latinos who, for many reasons, choose to become fluent in the language. From kindergarten to postgraduate programs, Spanish is the most widely-studied language in the U.S. At the secondary level, it is the language of choice of an astounding 70 percent of learners. But Spanish is not just for those in school. Professionals from all walks of life—including America's most powerful politicians—are flocking to learn the language. For members of the U.S. Congress seeking to attract the Latino vote, there's even a ten-week program titled 'Spanish on the Hill'.

However, the future of U.S. Spanish doesn't depend just on external factors like social pressures, economic incentives, and demographics. What becomes of it may also be affected by how it develops linguistically. Impressive as the numbers of speakers are, what's perhaps even more impressive is the variety of accents, usage and dialects, as Spanish-speaking immigrants arrive from places ranging from Buenos Aires to Tijuana. Mexicans are by far the largest national group, but there are sizable immigrant populations from all of the other Spanish-speaking countries, particularly in the Caribbean and Central America. There's been nothing like this in the history of the Spanish-speaking world.

In this new world, sometimes dubbed the 'United Hispanic States of America', Spanish is being negotiated and reinvented day by day, in part because of the mixing of dialects, in part because of the incorporating of elements of English. A U.S. mixture of Spanish and English is evolving, often referred to as 'Spanglish'. Think of '*Yo quiero Taco Bell*,' or '*Hasta la vista, Baby*.' Spanglish is both popular and contagious, and is even spreading to other Spanish-speaking countries.

Spanish in the U.S. is mutating, adapting to its linguistic environment, and therefore more likely to thrive. It is not the traditional Spanish of Mexico or, for that matter, the Spanish of any other country you know. Three generations from now U.S. Spanish will likely be a new blend, still understandable by people in Spanish-speaking countries, but different from what we hear today, enriched by the mixture of Spanish dialects that flow into it and by the influence of English.

Whatever new shape Spanish takes, we should recognize that it is no longer a *foreign* language in the United States. The state of New Mexico has acknowledged that by proclaiming itself officially bilingual in Spanish and English. The rest of the country, while not taking that official step, is rapidly adapting to the fact that Spanish now functions as a U.S. language second only to English.

About the author

Maria Carreira is professor of Spanish linguistics at California State University, Long Beach. Her publications focus on Spanish in the United States and Spanish as a world language. She is the co-author, with Sherri Spaine Long, of a beginning Spanish textbook (*Nexos*, Houghton Mifflin, 2005) and, with Michelle C. Geoffrion-Vinci, of a forthcoming textbook for teaching Spanish to bilingual Latinos (*Sí se puede*, Houghton Mifflin). Dr. Carreira received her Ph.D. in linguistics from the University of Illinois at Urbana Champaign.

Suggestions for further reading

In this book: Various languages of America are discussed in chapters 25 (revitalizing threatened Native American languages), 35 (languages of the U.S.), 36 (America's language crisis), 38 (Cajun), 39 (German in the U.S.), 40 (Gullah), and 49 (Native American languages). Chapter 52 discusses the relationship between Spanish and Portuguese.

Elsewhere:

Dávila, Arlene. *Latinos Inc.: The Marketing and Making of a People* (University of California Press, 2001). Documents the growing influence of Latino culture in the U.S. and explores Latino identity and ethnicity through the prism of the Hispanic marketing industry.

Carreira, Maria. 'Mass media, marketing, critical mass and other mechanisms of linguistic maintenance', in *Southwest Journal of Linguistics* (2002) Vol. 21, No. 4. Discusses the role that the Spanish-language media, Latino demographics, and commercial factors are playing in maintaining and promoting Spanish in the U.S.

Krashen, Stephen. 'Bilingual education, the acquisition of English, and the retention and loss of Spanish', in Ana Roca, ed. *Research on Spanish in the United States: Linguistic Issues and Challenges* (Cascadilla Press, 2000). Written by one of America's foremost authorities on foreign-language education, this article examines the impact of bilingual education in reversing the generational loss of immigrant languages in the U.S. It argues that American society and business, in particular, stand to benefit from stemming this loss.

38

What is Cajun and where did it come from?

Robyn Holman

Where did Cajun come from? Is it really French? How important is it today?

Did you know that French was once the language of everyday life in Louisiana? Claimed by France as a colony in 1682, Louisiana remained French territory until President Thomas Jefferson bought it from Napoleon in 1803—along with a great swath of land that has since been divided among fourteen other states—and it is still the place in the U.S. where French is spoken the most. According to the 2000 U.S. census, over a million Louisiana residents claim French ancestry, with around 200,000 saying they speak some type of French at home.

So how did all those French speakers get there? Some have ancestors who came from France as early colonists or who fled from Europe during the French Revolution, speaking 'official' French. The ancestors of others came from Africa, often by way of the Caribbean, and the French they brought with them was a creole, similar to the French creole of Haiti. But the most widely-spoken variety of French in Louisiana, and the one we hear the most about—probably because of the food and music that made it famous—is Cajun. Oddly enough, it came from Canada.

Here is how it happened: Around 1600, emigrants from France settled along the coast of present day Nova Scotia, in a colony they called *Acadia*. After struggles between France and England over the territory, it finally came under British control. But the Acadians refused to swear allegiance to the king of England, and in 1755, during '*le grand dérangement*', they were deported. Forcibly loaded onto boats and driven out, many Acadians died at sea. Some, with the help of Indians, took refuge in the forests of New Brunswick, while others found their way to settlements farther south, traveling by sea as far as Louisiana. This tragic episode in the lives of the Acadians attracted little attention at the time and was not brought to the forefront until a century or so later when Longfellow recounted in the poem *Evangeline* the story of an Acadian girl who was separated from her fiancé during the deportation and spent the rest of her life trying to find him.

The refugees from Nova Scotia who went to Louisiana came to be known as 'Cajuns', a local approximation of what they called themselves, 'Acadiens'. The language that the Cajuns spoke—and what they still speak—is French. But is it 'real' French? It is. The Cajuns may not always speak according to Parisian rules, but Cajun French doesn't differ from 'standard' French any more than other varieties do—like the French of Morocco, Quebec, or the West Indies. Cajun adds its own spice to the rich stew we call the French language.

Acadian French was somewhat different from the French spoken by the people who came to Louisiana directly from France, because the strains developed separately for up to 150 years. Over time, however, the two have blended together and most linguists no longer distinguish between Colonial and Acadian French, but use the term 'Cajun' to refer to the variety of French spoken in Southern

Louisiana today. Although generally homogeneous, Cajun varies slightly throughout Acadiana, with certain areas having distinctive pronunciations and idioms.

The majority of words and structures in Cajun are certainly recognizable to French speakers from other countries. The differences are like those between British and American English. Cajun has kept some words that have become obsolete in European French, and has produced new words to describe new situations. This includes borrowing words from other languages. For instance, *chaoui* from Choctaw names an animal that didn't exist in Europe, the raccoon. African languages contributed *gombo* to refer to okra, as well as *congo* ('black') to describe a poisonous snake, the water mocassin. Cajuns call shrimp *chevrette*, a word that sounds odd in France, where the Norman dialect word *crevette* replaced it.

Like many non-English languages in the U.S., Cajun faces an uncertain future. Members of the younger generation do not hear and use French as much as their parents did, and many Cajuns speak little or no French. Groups like CODOFIL (*Conseil pour le développement du français en Louisiane*), *Action Cadienne*, and *Les Amis de l'Immersion* are working to preserve the Cajun language and culture, primarily by emphasizing bilingual education programs in the schools.

French has been a part of American culture for as long as there has been a United States—even longer. It is an important part of America's linguistic heritage. Of course, Louisiana is not the only place in the U.S. where French is used. After Spanish, it is still one of the most widely-spoken foreign languages in the country. Even American passports are bilingual, bearing both English and French inscriptions.

About the author

Robyn Holman is an Associate Professor of French at the College of Charleston, South Carolina, where she also directs the graduate program for language teachers. She received her Ph.D. in French linguistics from the University of Colorado, and most often publishes in the field of medieval French language and culture.

Suggestions for further reading

In this book: Other languages of America are discussed in chapters 25 (revitalizing threatened Native American languages), 35 (languages of the U.S.), 36 (America's language crisis), 37 (Spanish in the U.S.), 39 (German in the U.S.), 40 (Gullah), and 49 (Native American languages). Other sociolinguistic topics are talked about in chapters 8 (pidgins and creoles) and 19 (language conflict).

Elsewhere:

Ancelet, Barry Jean. *Cajun and Creole Folktales: the French Oral Tradition of South Louisiana* (Garland Publishing, 1994). Includes three categories of Cajun French folktales: animal and magic tales, jokes and tall tales, legends and historical tales. Each story is accompanied by an English translation. Biographical information on the storytellers is also provided.

Brasseaux, Carl A. *Acadian to Cajun: transformation of a people* (UP of Mississippi, 1992, second printing 1999). Examines Acadian community life in the nineteenth century, including cultural evolution, demographic growth, and political involvement. Also available in electronic book format (Netlibrary, 2000).

Kein, Sybil, ed. *The History and Legacy of Louisiana's Free People of Color* (Louisiana State University Press, 2000). A collection of articles dealing with cultural and linguistic topics such as the origin of Louisiana creole, the use of creole in Southern literature, race and gender issues, Afro-Caribbean connections, and creole music and food.

Valdman, Albert, project director. *Discovering Cajun French through the spoken word* (Indiana University Creole Institute, 2003). Authentic samples of Cajun speech recorded on CD-ROM.

Web site:

http://www.artsci.lsu.edu/fai/Cajun/definition.html
Cajun French. Defines Cajun, presents information on the evolution and variability of the Cajun dialect, and addresses its preservation and perpetuation.

39

Did German almost become the language of the U.S.?

Nancy P. Nenno

*What part did German immigrants play in
eighteenth-century America? Did they come close to
making the young United States a German-speaking
country? What's 'Liberty Cabbage', and how did it get
its name?*

The official language of the United States of America was almost—
German? It's not true, but the so-called Mühlenberg legend is one
that never seems to die. As the story goes, the U.S. would have
become a German-speaking country in 1795 had it not been for
a single vote in the House of Representatives—ironically, a vote
putatively cast by a bilingual Representative from Pennsylvania,
Frederick Augustus Conrad Mühlenberg. What's the real story?
Well, it's true that German was widely spoken in Philadelphia when
the Congress met there. And it's true that a group of farmers from

Virginia in the 1790s petitioned for a German translation of some American laws. But the cliffhanger vote that saved English? It never happened.

So where did the fear that German might supersede English as America's language come from? It's not quite as far-fetched as it might seem. Germans began immigrating to the U.S. as early as 1683, and from then until the First World War, German was the most prevalent language in Pennsylvania after English. Not everybody was happy about that. Consider what one senior statesman from the Revolutionary period had to say about the Germans: 'Why,' he asked, 'should Pennsylvania, founded by the English, become a Colony of Aliens, who will shortly be so numerous as to Germanize us instead of our Anglifying them, and [who] will never adopt our Language or Customs, any more than they can acquire our Complexion?'

It might surprise you that these disturbing words came from the pen of none other than Benjamin Franklin.

Anti-foreign feelings persisted through the nineteenth century, but German continued to flourish in the U.S. Waves of English-only attacks, aimed at wiping German from the landscape, were countered by public displays of German identity. German-Americans celebrated their heritage in social clubs and societies all over the country. All of that ended with the First World War, when most states actually eliminated German from their schools. In some states during the war, it was illegal to speak anything but English in public. It is estimated that 18,000 people in the Midwest were charged during these years with violating English-only statutes. Even German foods came under attack. Sauerkraut wasn't outlawed, but it was renamed 'Liberty Cabbage'.

During the Second World War, attitudes toward things German, and toward Americans of German ancestry, weren't nearly so harsh. Perhaps this milder reaction was due in part to the fact that, like the first German immigrants to America, many of the German speakers who came to the U.S. before and during the war were fleeing religious and political persecution. Among the most visible of these refugees and exiles from Hitler's Europe were filmworkers such as the actors Conrad Veidt and Peter Lorre, and directors Otto Preminger, Billy Wilder, and Fritz Lang. Ironically, they became part of a Hollywood that for decades has used German accents as a kind of shorthand to represent evil. Ever since the 1940s, in scores of films from *Casablanca* to *Raiders of the Lost Ark* to *Saving Private Ryan*, the bad guys are always the ones who pronounce their W's like V's. There are, of course, a lot of exceptions to that stereotype. Marlene Dietrich's songs derived much of their sexy appeal from her German accent. And Arnold Schwarzenegger's Austrian cadences have become part of the U.S. cultural landscape.

It's really astonishing how many people of German heritage there are in America. The best known, probably, are the so-called Pennsylvania Dutch. (Their ancestors, by the way, came to the U.S. not from the Netherlands but from Germany. They called themselves 'Deutsch'—the German word for 'German'—but their English-speaking neighbors modified that to a more familiar-sounding word.) Beyond Pennsylvania, there are so many people of German ancestry in the U.S. heartland that the states from Ohio to Missouri and from Michigan to Nebraska are sometimes known as 'the German belt'. There are even pockets of German speakers in the Shenandoah Valley, where they are referred to as the 'Valley Dutch'. And in 1990, the so-called 'Texas Deutsch' emerged as the third largest ethnic group in that state. In fact, according to the 1990 census, more Americans of European ancestry claim German descent than Irish, English, or Italian.

On top of everything else, German has enriched English with marvelous vocabulary—from Autobahns to Zeppelins, from Frankfurters to Fahrenheit, from Wienerschnitzel to Wanderlust. And even though German never seriously challenged English as the primary language of the U.S., the ties between the two languages are long and deep. Shouldn't we be paying more attention to German?

About the author

Nancy P. Nenno is Associate Professor and Director of the German Program at the College of Charleston, South Carolina. She received her degrees at Brown University, in Rhode Island, and the University of California, Berkeley, and has studied at the University of Tübingen and the Free University of Berlin. Her research and publications focus primarily on twentieth-century German literature and film. Her current project examines the role of African Americans in German culture between the world wars.

Suggestions for further reading

In this book: Other languages of America are discussed in chapters 25 (revitalizing threatened Native American languages), 35 (languages of the U.S.), 36 (America's language crisis), 37 (Spanish in the U.S.), 38 (Cajun), 40 (Gullah), and 49 (Native American languages). Other sociolinguistic topics are talked about in chapters 8 (pidgins and creoles) and 19 (language conflict).

Elsewhere:

Adams, Willi Paul. *The German-Americans: An Ethnic Experience* (German Information Center, 1993). Part of the *Peoples of North America* series, this booklet offers an historical and cultural overview of German immigration and assimilation in the U.S. Includes an excellent chronology of Germans in America.

Crystal, David. 'A planning myth', in *The Cambridge Encyclopedia of Language* (Cambridge University Press, second edition 1997), p. 367. A concise description of the famous vote-that-never-was.

Gilbert, Glenn G., ed. *The German Language in America. A Symposium* (University of Texas Press, 1971). A collection of papers from a scholarly conference.

Heath, Shirley Brice, and Frederick Mandabach. 'Language status decisions and the law in the United States', a paper presented at the conference *Progress in Language Planning: International Perspectives* (Wayne, NJ, 1979), pp. 87–105. A scholarly but approachable article about British language politics in the Colonies through the nineteenth century.

Bussman, H., et. al. 'Pennsylvania Dutch', in *Routledge Dictionary of Language and Linguistics* (Routledge, 1996), p. 353. A concise history of the characteristics and continued existence of this dialect in the Eastern United States.

Web site:

http://www.watzmann.net/scg/germany-by-one-vote.html
Barron, Dennis. 'Urban legend: German almost became the official language of the U.S.' Barron demolishes the Mühlenberg myth and reveals that German-speakers were even blamed for the severe winters in Pennsylvania.

40

What's Gullah?

Elizabeth Martínez-Gibson

Where did Gullah come from? Does anyone speak it today?

Unless you are a linguist studying creoles or American dialects and languages—or you're lucky enough to live on the southeast coast of the U.S.—you may never have heard of the language called *Gullah* or *Geechee*.[1] Even some people who have heard of it think it's a Native American language, but in fact it is a hybrid from abroad: a creole blend of African languages with seventeenth- and eighteenth-century English, developed in the slave communities of the coastal South Atlantic. Even before the U.S. existed as a country, Gullah was spoken along the North American coast from southern North Carolina to northern Florida. Remarkably, the language has survived for over 300 years.

There is no exact count of how many Gullah speakers there are; but a good estimate is that at least 200,000 people speak it as their primary language and at least 7,000 as their only language. Most of

---

1 The term *Geechee* is synonymous with *Gullah*, but is applied mostly to speakers of the language outside South Carolina, primarily Georgia. In the past it was used as a derogatory term for anyone from South Carolina or Georgia; it is now a term of pride and identity.

them are older people who live in quiet isolation on a cluster of small islands off the Carolina, Georgia and Florida coasts. Beyond that, there is a substantial number of African-Americans on the coastal mainland who use English as their primary tongue but switch to Gullah when they are among friends and family. If you hear them speaking, you may mistakenly assume that what you are hearing is Jamaican. You may understand some of what you hear—because it contains so many English words—but the longer you listen, the more it comes clear that Gullah is not a kind of English but in fact a separate language.

There have been many theories about the origins of Gullah. Some thought it was a corrupted form of Elizabethan English. Some considered it 'broken English' or a 'baby-talk' which whites used to communicate with their slaves. Others thought it was a language deliberately created by slaves so their owners would not understand them. It was not until 1949, when Dr. Lorenzo Turner published research on *Africanisms in the Gullah Dialect*, that its origin in African languages became clear.

Recent studies have shown great similarities between Gullah and the creole language Krio spoken in Sierra Leone. The two languages have vocabulary in common, such as *bigyai* (greedy), *pantap* (on top of), *alltwo* (both), and *swit* (delicious); and many of the personal names in Gullah come from languages spoken in Sierra Leone. As evidence of that connection, we know that in 1988, when the President of Sierra Leone visited the Gullah Community in South Carolina, he at one point spoke in Krio and the audience understood him without the need for translation.

Nevertheless, Gullah is not the same as Krio or any specific African language. Most of its vocabulary is English, and major elements of its grammar and pronunciation resemble those of West African languages, such as Hausa, Igbo, Twi and Yoruba. It is a kind of pan-African mix, created by slaves who came from different tribes and different countries with no common language. Their need to communicate with each other led to the formation of a pidgin language, and ultimately to a creole. The word *Gullah* may have come from the name of a tribe in Angola who, as slaves brought to South Carolina, were called *N'gola* or Gullahs. Africanisms are most obvious in the sounds of Gullah, especially the consonants. For example, 'd' is used instead of 'th' (*dey*, for 'they'). There is also no 'v' sound in Gullah; English 'v' is usually replaced by 'w' (*willage*, for 'village') or sometimes by 'b' (*Debil*, for 'Devil').

While it is mainly a spoken language, Gullah also exists in written form: for example, the 1925 novel *Porgy*, the basis for Gershwin's musical *Porgy and Bess*, features characters speaking in Gullah. It's also the language of Uncle Remus in Joel Chandler Harris's *Br'er Rabbit* tales. And in 2005, a Gullah translation of *De Nyew Testament* appeared in U.S. bookstores.

So how did the language survive so long, surrounded by an English-speaking majority? First, a large part of the Gullah community, living on the Sea Islands, was physically separated from the U.S. mainland. There was not even a bridge to the mainland until the 1920s. Second, because of tropical disease in the area—against which the Africans had some resistance—whites tended to live away from the low-lying coast, leaving the slaves in isolation for much of the year. The numerical strength of the black community—and the Gullah people's strong community life—helped them preserve their language, unique identity, and cultural traditions.

Those traditions are still alive; and the Gullah take pride in their melodic language, seeing it as an important link to their African past. But speakers of Gullah are increasingly hard to find as the speech of new generations moves toward the American mainstream. Linguists and historians are working with a determined community to assure that the culture will be preserved, and that Gullah will be a living language for years to come. Some of the richest resources on the language and culture can be found at two South Carolina sites: the Avery Research Center at the College of Charleston and the Penn Center on St. Helena Island.

About the author

Elizabeth Martínez-Gibson is an Associate Professor of Spanish and Linguistics at the College of Charleston, in the heart of the Gullah region. Her area of specialty is Hispanic and general linguistics. She has taught courses in Spanish Phonetics and Phonology, Spanish Morphology and Syntax, Introduction to Spanish and General Linguistics, and Language Variation of Spanish and American dialects. She created and directs the Interdisciplinary Linguistics Minor Program at the College of Charleston.

Suggestions for further reading

In this book: Other languages of America are discussed in chapters 25 (revitalizing threatened Native American languages), 35 (languages of the U.S.), 36 (America's language crisis), 37 (Spanish in the U.S.), 38 (Cajun), 39 (German in the U.S.), and 49 (Native American languages). Other sociolinguistic topics are talked about in chapters 8 (pidgins and creoles) and 19 (language conflict).

Elsewhere:

Turner, Lorenzo D. *Africanisms in the Gullah Dialect* (University of South Carolina Press, republished 2002). An historical and linguistic perspective of the Gullah language and people. Turner's 1949 book is the main source and starting point for all research on Gullah.

Opala, Joseph. *The Gullah: Rice, Slavery and the Sierra-Leone-American Connection* (U.S. Park Service, 2000). A concise description of the links between Sierra Leone and the Gullah culture.

Holloway, Joseph E. *Africanisms in American Culture* (Indiana University Press, 1990).

Holloway, Joseph E., and Winifred K. Vass. *The African Heritage of American English* (Indiana University Press, 1993). Research on African-American language and culture—including Gullah—and their roots in Africa.

Web sites:

http://www.co.beaufort.sc.us/bftlib/gullah.htm
Basic information about Gullah, with samples of the language, recipes, and a bibliography of sources for further research.

http://www.gcrc.musc.edu/sugar/Gullah.html
Information about the Gullah people in South Carolina and links to other Web sites about the Gullah islands, language and culture.

41

Are dialects dying?

Walt Wolfram

Is shared popular culture wiping out dialects, in America and elsewhere? Can new dialects appear in today's world? Do you speak a dialect?

How do you say the word 'bought'? In the United States alone there are at least four distinct regional pronunciations of the vowel, from 'awe' to 'ah' to a rural southern version that sounds almost like 'ow' to the 'wo' used by comedians to lampoon dyed-in-the-wool New Yorkers (as in 'cwoffee twok').

Is the carbonated beverage you drink *pop, soda, tonic, co-cola*—or maybe even the older Appalachian mountain term *dope*? When you take the highway circling a city, do you drive on a *beltline*, a *beltway*, a *loop*, or a *perimeter*? And do you get cash at a *bank machine*, an *automated teller*, a *cash machine*, or an *ATM*?

Everyone notices dialects—we can't help it. But most of the time, we notice them in *other* people. 'We don't speak a dialect where we live, we speak normal English.' Speakers from Boston to Birmingham (Alabama and England) and from Medicine Hat to Melbourne (Florida and Australia) all echo the same sentiment.

Of course, they do this while pronouncing the vowel in words like *bought* and *caught* in quite different ways. Or while using different names for the same sandwich—a *sub*, a *grinder*, a *hoagie*, or a *hero*.

Dialects are everywhere, not just in those regions—like Appalachia, Liverpool, or the Outback—that seem to get the most dialect press. The fact of the matter is that it's impossible to speak the English language without speaking a dialect, some dialect. Everyone has an accent. When you pronounce the vowel in *bought* or *caught* (or was that *baht* and *caht*?) you've made a dialect commitment—you can't help it. We are all players in the dialect game, whether we like it or not.

But isn't this a different world? a global community where people move fluidly, travel frequently, and speak to each other by cell phone? Aren't dialects dying out, thanks to mobility and the media? Think again! Dialectologists counter the popular myth that dialects are dying by showing that major U.S. dialect areas like the North, Midland, and South remain very much alive—as they have been for a couple of centuries. But the dialect news is even more startling: Research shows that Northern and Southern speech in the U.S. are actually diverging—not becoming more similar. Blame those shifty vowels, which in large Northern cities like Buffalo and Chicago are acquiring sounds different from those we hear in other regions. So *coffee* becomes *cahffee*, *lock* sounds almost like *lack*, and *bat* sounds more like *bet*. Have you noticed? Don't worry if you haven't. The change is pretty subtle, and a lot of it flies under the impressionistic radar. But it's very real—and it's gradually making the speech of Northern U.S. cities quite different from that of the South and West.

How can this be? In today's compressed world it seems illogical that dialects could continue developing and diverging the way they did when language communities were more isolated. But language is always changing, and sometimes behaves as though it has a mind of its own. Yes, we all watch the same TV programs;

but most of us don't model our accents on TV newscasters—that's way too impersonal. We follow the lead of those we interact with in our daily lives—*they're* the ones who judge how well we fit in with the community.

And there remain plenty of regions where encroaching global culture is held at bay by a strong sense of community that includes local dialect. So working class Pittsburghers are proud to root for the Pittsburgh *Stillers*—instead of the *Steelers*; go *dahntahn*—instead of *downtown*, and put a *gum band* around their papers—instead of what other Americans would call a *rubber band* and Britons would call an *elastic band*. Part of being a Pittsburgher is speaking Pittsburghese.

But aren't *some* dialects dying?—like the ones once spoken in isolated mountain and island communities now flooded by tourists? Some may be, but there are also rural communities that (like Pittsburgh on a smaller scale) keep their dialects alive as a way of fighting back, and ensuring that they won't be confused with what they call 'furriners'.

Perhaps the most surprising news of all is that some areas of increasing prosperity and cultural influence—like Seattle and Northern California—are starting to express their new regional identity by developing dialect traits that didn't exist before.

So some traditional dialects may be disappearing, but they're being replaced by new dialects, in a process that can seem like the carnival game 'whack-a-mole'. The famous words of Mark Twain apply well to English dialects in America and elsewhere: rumors of their death are greatly exaggerated. Dialects remain alive and well—and an important part of the regional and sociocultural landscape.

About the author

Walt Wolfram, William C. Friday Distinguished Professor of English Linguistics at North Carolina State University, describes himself as a dialect nomad. He has studied dialects ranging from African American varieties in large metropolitan areas to the speech of small, isolated island and mountain communities. He has authored more than twenty books and two hundred and fifty articles, in addition to producing a number of TV documentaries. More information on Dr. Wolfram's media productions is available at: http://www.talkingnc.com and http://www.ncsu.edu/linguistics

Suggestions for further reading

In this book: dialects are discussed in chapters 3 (dialects versus languages), 18 (English in Britain, America, and elsewhere), and 26 (U.S. Southern English). Language extinction is discussed in chapters 2 (languages of the world), 24 (language death), 25 (revitalizing threatened languages), and 50 (Latin). Chapters talking more generally about how languages evolve include 7 (language change), 8 (pidgins and creoles), 11 (grammar), 41 (dialect change), 48 (origins of English), and 51 (Italian).

Elsewhere:

Labov, William, Sharon Ash and Charles Boberg, *The Atlas of North American English: Phonetics, Phonology and Sound Change* (Mouton de Gruyter, 2006). A major new work on the dialects of North American, based on the pronunciation of various vowel sounds. It is mostly intended for the dedicated scholar.

Wolfram, Walt, and Ben Ward, eds. *American Voices: How Dialects Differ from Coast to Coast* (Blackwell, 2006). This collection contains brief, popular profiles of major and minor dialects in North America. Both dying dialects and new dialect traditions of American English are included in the presentations by major researchers, as well as descriptions of sociocultural varieties of English.

Web site:

http://www.ling.upenn.edu/phonoatlas
A more accessible overview of some of the results from the project *The Atlas of North American English: Phonetics, Phonology and Sound Change*, listed above, can be found at the TELSUR (telephone survey) Web site.

42

Can you make a living loving languages?

Frederick H. Jackson

What kinds of careers are there for people who like
foreign languages? What should you do to prepare for
them?

Perhaps something like this has happened to you. Let's say you really
enjoy languages. At some time in your life—in school, on military
assignment, in the Peace Corps, or while traveling abroad—you
found that learning how a language works—and using it—was really
fun. But just as you were thinking that you might want to study
the language in depth, or maybe even learn another one, someone
looked at you with concern (or pity) and said: 'Foreign languages?
Hah!! How are you going to make a living with that?' This cynic
may even have asked whether you were planning to take a vow of
poverty.

Well, the answer is that there are *lots* of ways that people who know languages can use that ability to make a living—and a fairly good one, too.

There are two helpful ways of looking at the roles of language in making a living. On the one hand are professions centered around and dependent on language skill. Let's call them 'Careers in Language'. On the other hand are many more types of jobs where language ability is an important tool that enables you to do something else entirely; these we will call 'Language in Careers'.

Careers in Language are directly based upon outstanding ability in one or more languages. One of the first such careers that comes to mind is teaching a language, and there are certainly a lot of positions for language teachers in schools and colleges and other training institutions. Some states in the U.S. are importing teachers from other countries because they are in short supply locally. If you like languages and cultures, you should certainly think about teaching them. It is often a very rewarding career.

And then, of course, there are translating and interpreting. Both careers require extremely strong language skills and deep understanding of the cultures involved, plus special training. Both offer a wide variety of different jobs. For example, translators may be asked to translate all kinds of documents—from scientific articles or legal contracts to literature to a suspicious e-mail to an advertisement for peanut butter. (Translating advertising copy into another language is at least as demanding as translating more 'official' material because of the need to address a large audience in a way that doesn't run afoul of subtle cultural differences.)

Interpreters can help a monolingual patient describe symptoms to a doctor who doesn't speak his or her language; or travel with executives or diplomats on business abroad; or maybe serve on the 'language line', a telephone system that connects interpreters with people who need them. Really good translators and interpreters are not easy to find, so there are a great number of positions in national and regional government agencies as well as in international firms and other non-governmental organizations.

None of those 'Careers in Language' jobs can be done without truly advanced language skill. But most people, even those who speak and read other languages well, don't have those kinds of jobs. Many of them work at what we have called *Language in Careers*. Here the list is long: business people, social workers, police, actors, medical personnel, marketers, journalists, historians—a wide variety of professions in which language is not at the core, but in which knowing a language makes you a better performer. In these professions language is a tool that gives you leverage. The business person with a second language has an advantage in the global economy, so it's common for new hires with language skills to come in at higher pay (so much for the 'vow of poverty'); scientists can read the work of foreign researchers who may not write in English; librarians can work with books from other countries; environmentalists can fight more effectively to preserve the rain forests; doctors and nurses can understand the needs of their patients.

And think about government. Diplomats in all countries typically must have strong proficiency in at least one language to advance in their careers—more commonly two or three languages—and the U.S. military very recently established the same requirement for its officers. Intelligence and law enforcement agencies, courts, and even purely administrative organizations like census bureaus, are likely to have hundreds of positions that require language skill. In the U.S. more than eighty federal agencies need people with professional skills in more than a hundred languages. Jobs like these may not be *centered* on language, as teaching and translating positions are, but the agencies that offer them recognize that employees with language skills are more effective at whatever they do, and thus more valuable to the organizations that employ them.

One other field that attracts people interested in language is Linguistics. Linguists carry out research into language systems— either language in general or individual languages—and study how language functions in cultural and social contexts. The sub-discipline called Applied Linguistics uses the results of such research in practical tasks like developing language-teaching methods, designing voice recognition software, and helping people improve their communication skills. Professional linguists use their knowledge in many important kinds of work, from writing grammars and dictionaries to doing research on electronic communication, machine translation, or artificial intelligence, to training new linguists in colleges. Linguists investigate and give expert advice on effective political discourse, public relations, doctor-patient communication, and cultural differences in use of language in a courtroom. One linguist you may know is Professor Deborah Tannen, who has written several insightful books on how people may miscommunicate on the job, at home, or within the family.

So if you start learning a language, and you find that you love it, follow your heart. Give it the time needed to learn it well. One way or another your ability will pay off.

About the author

Frederick H. Jackson is Coordinator of the U.S. government's Interagency Language Roundtable (http://www.govtilr.org/). He is a language training supervisor at the Foreign Service Institute (FSI), the training arm of the State Department. He has an M.A. in English as a Second Language and a Ph.D. in Linguistics, both from the University of Hawaii. He has done research in the languages of Micronesia and Mainland Southeast Asia, and has taught at the University of Hawaii, Chiangmai University in Thailand, and the Pennsylvania State University.

Suggestions for further reading

In this book: Other chapters discussing professional opportunities for people with language skills include 20 (bilingualism), 36 (America's language crisis), 43 (dictionaries), 44 (interpreting and translating), 46 (Forensic Linguistics), 53 (Russian), and 55 (Arabic).

Elsewhere:

Crump, T. C. *Translating and Interpreting in the Federal Government* (American Translators Association, 1999). Prepared by a professional translator at the National Institutes of Health, this book describes jobs and careers in eighty federal agencies that involve translation and/or interpretation in more than one hundred languages.

Rifkin, B. 'Studying a foreign language at the postsecondary level', in *The Language Educator* (2006) Vol. 1, No. 2. Provides advice to college students about why to study foreign languages, how to do it successfully, and what you do with a language after graduation.

Tannen, D. *You Just Don't Understand: Women and Men in Conversation* (Ballantine, 1990). One of the first of Professor Tannen's important books on how communication often goes astray. Written for the lay reader.

Camenson, B. *Careers in Foreign Languages* (McGraw-Hill, 2001). This short book, together with the next two listed below, provide detailed information on jobs and careers that involve significant skill in foreign languages. There are more such jobs than you can imagine!

Seelye, H. N. and J. L. Day. *Careers for Foreign Language Aficionados & Other Multilingual Types* (McGraw-Hill, 2001).

Rivers, W. *Opportunities in Foreign Language Careers* (VGM Career Horizons, 1998).

Web sites:

http://flc.osu.edu/FLC_pages/careers_website/
'Careers in Foreign Languages.' Web site at the Ohio State University Language Resource Center. Provides numerous links for interested language students to explore.

http://www.atanet.org
American Translators Association.

43

How are dictionaries made?

Erin McKean

What's a lexicographer? How many of them does it take to make a dictionary? How do they decide what to put in and what to leave out? Why don't dictionaries tell us what's right and what's wrong?

Think of the language as an immense glacier, a giant shining mass of words, instead of ice. Like a glacier, language usually changes very, very slowly, with occasional huge surges forward. The English-language is moving—changing—very slowly, most of the time. Sure, there are sometimes surprising surges of new words, but most of the changes happen so slowly and gradually that they're almost imperceptible. A slightly different meaning here, a new ending on a word there–who notices? Well, lexicographers notice. Lexicographers keep track of language change and record it in the dictionaries they make—but they're always a step behind.

As recently as a few centuries ago it was possible for one very learned person to create a dictionary single-handedly. But these days virtually all dictionaries are built by *teams* of talented people. For each new dictionary, and each new edition of an existing dictionary, they collect huge amounts of written and spoken language—from newspapers, magazines, books, plays, movies, speeches, TV and radio shows, interviews and the Internet—and sift them for evidence of how language is being used: What words haven't been seen before? What words are changing their meanings? What words are used only in particular ways? What are their histories, pronunciations, grammatical quirks and foibles?

If you think this makes lexicographers sound like scientists, you're exactly right. Most of them see their primary job as data collecting. They try to capture as accurate a picture as possible of how people actually use a language at a given point in time.

But a lot of people in the dictionary-buying public are uncomfortable with scientific neutrality when it comes to language. They don't want their dictionaries to describe how people actually write and speak. They believe that some language is right and some is wrong, period. And they think the lexicographers' job is to tell us which is which. They want *prescriptive* dictionaries that omit vulgar language and condemn other words they disapprove of, like 'irregardless' or 'muchly'.

If you're one of those people, you'll be disappointed to learn that most modern dictionaries are basically *descriptive*. They don't prescribe what we ought to say or write; they tell us what people actually do. Like umpires, lexicographers don't make rules—they just call 'em the way they see 'em.

That doesn't mean that prescriptive views are completely left out. People's attitudes toward words are also a legitimate part of the dictionary. For example, the New Oxford American Dictionary doesn't forbid its readers to use the unlovely word 'irregardless', but it clearly notes that the word is 'avoided by careful users of English.' Because people no longer use words like 'fletcherize' (meaning to chew each bite at least fifty times before you swallow), and because you don't talk the way people did in eighteenth-century Williamsburg, you know that language is always in flux. So if research finds a lot of good and careful writers using 'irregardless', or creating sentences like

'Anybody could look it up if they wanted to'—using 'they' where you might expect 'he or she'—the dictionary can say with authority that it's becoming standard English—even if prescriptivists disapprove.

So don't think of dictionaries as rulebooks. They're much more like maps. They show where things are in relation to each other and point out where the terrain is rough. And, like maps, dictionaries are constantly updated to show the changing topography of the language—not just with shiny new words (like 'podcasting' or 'lo-carb') but new uses for old words (like 'burn' meaning 'record data on a compact disk') and even new parts of words (the suffix -*age* as in 'signage' or 'mopeage'—which is really just a funnier way of saying 'moping'). Dictionary-makers put as good a map as possible into your hands, but devising a route is up to you.

Knowing these facts about dictionaries and the people who make them will make you a better user of dictionaries; it will put the words and their meanings in the right context. You'll know that any particular definition is just what lexicographers have managed to find out—a picture, but not necessarily the whole picture, or the final picture. Words keep changing, lexicographers keep looking, and dictionaries keep updating to try to provide the best map of the language possible.

Remember: just because a word is in the dictionary doesn't mean you have to use it. And just because it isn't in the dictionary doesn't mean you can't. If it did mean that, there'd never be any new words. And lexicographers might be out of a job.

About the author

Erin McKean is the Editor in Chief of U.S. Dictionaries for Oxford University Press and the Editor of *VERBATIM: The Language Quarterly*. She is also the author of *Weird and Wonderful Words* and *More Weird and Wonderful Words*, both from Oxford University Press. She is on the editorial boards of *American Speech*, the journal of the American Dialect Society, and *Dictionaries*, the journal of the Dictionary Society of North America. She has a B.A. and M.A. in Linguistics from the University of

Chicago, where she wrote her M.A. thesis on the treatment of phrasal verbs (verbs like 'act up,' 'act out,' and, of course, 'look up') in children's dictionaries. She lives in Chicago. Please send her evidence of new words you've found, by e-mail, to dictionaries@oup.com.

Suggestions for further reading

In this book: How languages evolve over time is discussed in chapters 7 (language change), 8 (pidgins and creoles), 11 (grammar), 41 (dialect change), 48 (origins of English), 50 (Latin), and 51 (Italian). The concept of language rules is covered further in chapters 17 (prescriptivism) and 18 (British and American English). Other professional opportunities for people interested in language are discussed in chapters 20 (bilingualism), 36 (America's language crisis), 42 (language-related careers), 44 (interpreting and translating), and 46 (Forensic Linguistics).

Elsewhere:

Winchester, Simon. *The Professor and the Madman: A Tale of Murder, Insanity, and the Making of the Oxford English Dictionary* (Harper Perennial, 1999. Published in the U.K. as *The Surgeon of Crowthorne.*)

Winchester, Simon. *The Meaning of Everything: The Story of the Oxford English Dictionary* (Oxford University Press, 2003.)

The two Simon Winchester books are both wonderful introductions to the greatest dictionary of the English language, the Oxford English Dictionary. *Professor* recounts, with novelistic flair, the true story of some of the personalities involved in making the OED; *Meaning of Everything* has more detail and covers the entire scope of the project, which is ongoing.

Murray, K. M. Elisabeth. *Caught in the Web of Words: James Murray and the Oxford English Dictionary* (Yale University Press, reprinted 2001). People who are still intrigued can read this biography of James Murray, the original editor of the OED, written by his granddaughter, K. M. Elisabeth Murray.

Landau, Sidney I. *Dictionaries: The Art and Science of Lexicography* (Cambridge University Press, second edition 2001). This book is the best starting point for people interested in the nuts and bolts of how dictionaries are made.

44

Why do we need translators if we have dictionaries?

Kevin Hendzel

What does it take to be an interpreter? With a good dictionary, isn't translating something anybody can do?

I'm always impressed when I see someone standing behind a president or prime minister, interpreting a foreign visitor's comments into his ear. What *talent* it takes to translate one language into another—listening and speaking at the same time! You can't pick up a dictionary. And you can't just spit out words like a robot. The interpreter's job is to convey *meaning*. And since a lot of meaning is expressed by tone of voice or the nuance of words and phrases, his or her job is far more than translating word for word.

And what responsibility! Imagine the defendant in a court case who doesn't speak the language of the judge and the jury. If an interpreter gets it wrong, how can justice be done? Not everyone can move easily between two languages, but there needs to be somebody who knows how. That 'somebody' is a professional interpreter.

There's the same need for professional translators, who deal with the *written* word as interpreters deal with *spoken* language. Think about how important the choice of words or phrases is in, let's say, a business contract. Or on the famous 'hotline' between the White House and the Kremlin, which does not—contrary to what many people think—connect a bright red telephone on the U.S. President's desk to a similar one on the desk of the Russian leader. Instead, it's an encrypted high-speed data link that transmits written, rather than spoken, messages—and it requires a translator, rather than an interpreter.

So what does it take to be a professional translator or interpreter? And let me emphasize the word 'professional'. Because simply knowing two languages isn't enough—it's just a starting point.

Beyond skill in speaking a second language, an interpreter needs to know the two *cultures* involved, the use of slang or dialects of the languages, and the subject matter to be interpreted. To be really good at it, he or she has to have an exceptional memory—and a lot of training in the art of interpreting.

A *translator* needs somewhat different skills. But again, strong knowledge of two languages is just the beginning, because translating can get very complicated. This is why many professional translators and interpreters have advanced degrees in specific technical fields— many are trained engineers, architects, physicians and attorneys. To highlight why this is important, think of the technical terminology translators are called on to handle. Lawyers file *writs of mandamus*. Physicians treat *hypertrophic cardiomyopathy*. Terms like these can be pretty daunting, and for translation it's not enough just to look up their dictionary equivalents in another language—you need to understand what they mean. When a translator works from one language into another, that process involves first understanding the concept in one language, and then 'interpreting' or 'describing' that concept in another language. In a nutshell, translation isn't about words. It's about what the words are about.

So how do you get into one of these professions? Well, it's best if you've already had training in a substantive field—like engineering, medicine or finance—that you'll specialize in. It also probably helps to be born somewhere like Belgium, where virtually everyone grows up with two or more languages. But even if you're not bilingual from childhood, with hard work you can get close to it; after that, becoming professionally qualified is mostly a matter of training and practice. You'll need a minimum of a master's degree, which in the U.S. requires two years of study; in Europe, three years or more. And you'll have on-the-job internships before you're turned loose on society. The final step is certification by an organization like the American Translators Association.

Yes, it takes some time. But translation and interpreting are exciting and often lucrative careers. The language services industry is valued at $11 billion in the U.S. alone. And with the birth of the European Union, with easy movement of people, products and ideas across borders, there's huge demand for certified interpreters in Europe. Training programs for translators and interpreters are on the rise all over the world—and that's a good thing, because there are severe shortages of qualified interpreters and translators in every field.

If you would like to learn more about translation and interpreting as professions, to investigate training programs or to seek out professional translators or interpreters for your business or institution, one source is the Web site of the American Translators Association at www.atanet.org. This site provides comprehensive information on the profession and a searchable online database of translators and interpreters, as well as contact information for experts on many topics relating to translation and interpreting.

There have been interpreters for as long as people have spoken different tongues; and translators for as long as there has been writing. Contrary to the myth that everyone speaks English, as the world grows smaller we need translators and interpreters more than ever before.

About the author

Kevin Hendzel is a graduate of Georgetown University's School of Foreign Service and was formerly head linguist on the technical translation staff of the Presidential Hotline between the White House and the Kremlin. He is currently the national media spokesman for the American Translators Association. As such he is a well-known spokesman on translation and interpreting issues on national and international media, including National Public Radio. His translations from Russian into English include 34 books and 2,200 articles published in the areas of physics, technology and law. He continues to work as a translator, and his current field of expertise in translation is focused on national security areas ranging from nuclear weapons dismantlement and disposition programs in the former Soviet Union to U.S.-sponsored counter-proliferation programs to prevent the dissemination of nuclear, biological and chemical weapons worldwide.

Suggestions for further reading

In this book: Other discussions of opportunities and requirements for professional use of language abilities are discussed in chapters 20 (bilingualism), 36 (America's language crisis), 43 (dictionaries), 44 (interpreting and translating), 46 (Forensic Linguistics), 53 (Russian), and 55 (Arabic).

Elsewhere:

Robinson, Douglas. *Becoming a Translator: An Introduction to the Theory and Practice of Translation* (Routledge, second edition 2003). Designed as an introduction to translation, this work provides the best coverage of the practical and theoretical for the novice and also provides a view of the commercial aspects of becoming a translator.

Samuelsson-Brown, Geoffrey. *A Practical Guide for Translators* (Multilingual Matters, third edition 1998). A collection of nine essays on the craft of translation, with a strong emphasis on literary translation. A brilliantly rendered work that reminds us that translation is above all a creative art form.

Fuller, Frederick. *The Translator's Handbook* (University of Pennsylvania Press, 1984). An older work, but highly influential in its practical approach to translation and interpreting.

45

How good is machine translation?

David Savignac

How far in the future are computers like HAL in the movie 2001? Why aren't computers already replacing humans in tasks like translating foreign languages?

When the computer was invented, around the middle of the twentieth century, one of the first things people thought about was how it might be used to translate foreign languages. But early efforts at machine translation (MT) can most charitably be said to have fizzled. In the late 1960s and early 1970s the effort was almost completely abandoned. You've probably heard the funny mistranslation stories: The computer that rendered 'The spirit is willing but the flesh is weak' as 'The whisky is strong but the meat is rotten'; or the computer that transformed a pumping device known as a 'hydraulic ram' into a 'water goat'. Machines can indeed translate texts from one language to another, but the Holy Grail for humans who use them—'fully automated high-quality machine translation'—is still elusive. What's causing the problem here?

Well, the culprit is the complexity of language in general. This complexity begins at the word level. Take the word 'bark': a computer doesn't know that a dog isn't covered with wood, or that a tree doesn't make loud noises when someone approaches, so it's handicapped in deciding which possible translation of 'bark' it should choose in a given sentence. Or how about the Spanish verb *comer*? Depending on the sentence it appears in, it can mean 'eat', 'capture', 'overlook', 'corrode', 'fade', 'itch', 'skip', 'slur', 'swallow', or 'take'; picking the correct translation from such an array of possibilities puts significant demands on a computer's calculating abilities.

At the sentence level the complexity gets even worse. Take this sentence: 'John saw the woman in the park with a telescope.' It could mean any of half a dozen things. For starters, who do you think has the telescope, John or the woman in the park? Or is it John who's in the park? Or are there two parks, one with a telescope and one without? A human encountering such a sentence knows enough to look in nearby sentences for clues to the intended meaning, but a computer's mind may well boggle.

Underlying the challenges to machine translation is the fact that each language carves up pieces of knowledge in different ways, and there is no one-to-one mapping between them. The less two languages resemble each other, the harder the problems of translation between them are. Where English has three third-person singular pronouns, 'he', 'she', and 'it', Turkish has just one: *on*. Lacking any gender-related cues, how do you translate *on* into English? There are some languages which simply do not distinguish between green and blue, but Russian has two words for 'blue' where English has only one—so if you want to translate 'She's wearing a blue dress' into Russian, you have a fifty percent chance of choosing the right word, unless perhaps you can see the dress. There are many cases in which you just can't make an exact translation between languages.

And now for the good news. Despite its limitations, there are situations in which the machine does a very good job, particularly if the topic of translation is narrow. The Canadian Meteorological Centre, for example, uses machine translation for bilingual weather reporting. In the commercial world, technical writers have learned to write manuals and parts catalogs so that computer-based translations—let's say from Japanese to English—need only a little correction. Even on the Internet, the click of a mouse can translate entire Web pages with fairly good quality, at least for some languages.

And let's remember that machine translation doesn't always have to be perfect. It can be very useful even if it has some garbles. For instance, where human translators are scarce and the volume of material to be translated is great—as is frequently the case in the post-9/11 world—machines are widely used to 'triage' material before it reaches the desk of an overworked human. The National Security Agency's 'CyberTrans' software, created for the Department of Defense and the Intelligence Community, does precisely that: it identifies a language, corrects misspelled words, and translates some sixty-five languages into English, with quality that's usually good enough for scanning.

And the future looks good. Sparked by the events of 9/11 and energized by subsequent government funding, machine translation experts in academia, the commercial sector, and government are implementing new approaches to machine translation; and the results to date have been very encouraging. The quality of Arabic-to-English translation, for example, has improved dramatically in the past five years. Machines are making multilingual chat rooms possible on the web and helping multinational military forces talk to one another. Yes, a human translator is better. But even though the goal of 'fully automated high-quality machine translation' is still not in sight, we've come a long way. Steady progress is being made in quality, and the use of machine translation is increasing by leaps and bounds. The machine is here to stay.

About the author

David Savignac is Director of the Center for Applied Machine Translation at the National Security Agency at Fort George G. Meade, Maryland. A multilinguist by training and a bit of a medievalist in his spare time, he holds a Ph.D. in Slavic linguistics from the Slavic Department at Stanford University and has worked for the Department of Defense for over three decades.

Suggestions for further reading

In this book: For other discussions of linguistic/technological topics see chapters 34 (language-teaching technologies), 35 (interactive map of U.S. language communities), 46 (Forensic Linguistics), and 47 (the National Museum of Language). More on the subject of translation appears in chapter 44 (interpreting and translating).

Elsewhere:

Nirenburg, Sergei, Harold L. Somers, and Yorick A. Wilks, eds. *Readings in Machine Translation* (MIT Press, 2003). An outstanding collection of some landmark papers from the last fifty years by people who have thought a lot about machine translation, its potential and its limitations.

Somers, Harold, ed. *Computers and Translation: A Translator's Guide* (Johns Benjamins, 2003). Most books dwell on the technology, theory, taxonomy, evaluation, and other analytic issues involved in machine translation. This book is much more nuts-and-bolts about how to make productive use of it.

Styx, Gary. 'The elusive goal of machine translation', in *Scientific American* (2006) March. Written for a broad audience, this article focuses on the 'statistical approach', thought by many to hold great promise for significant improvements in machine translation.

Web sites:

http://www.essex.ac.uk/linguistics/clmt/MTbook/
Arnold, Doug, et al. *Machine Translation: An Introductory Guide* (Blackwells-NCC, 1994). Also available, in pdf or html, at the Web site above. The book is slightly dated, with limited coverage of current data-driven methods. But it's easy to browse, and freely accessible!

http://ourworld. compuserve.com/ homepages/ WJHutchins/
Hutchins, John. *Machine Translation (Computer-based Translation): Publications by John Hutchins*. John Hutchins has been the lead historian and documenter of the field of MT for twenty years. His Web site now has an encyclopedic collection of resources—papers and books by him and many others—all available as freely downloadable pdfs. The site is nicely organized, so it's easy to get general information or drill down to the level of one's interest.

(Note: The publications cited here are suggested by the author and do not represent the official opinions/endorsement of the National Security Agency/Central Security Service.)

46

Can you use language to solve crimes?

Robert Rodman

What's a voiceprint? Can language usage be analyzed to identify the author of an anonymous letter or a Shakespeare play? Or to catch plagiarists?

People who work with languages do a lot of things you probably never thought of. Think about this scenario: It's a dark and stormy night. You're leaving a party. After you slip behind the wheel and turn on the ignition, your car says, 'Count to five.' It won't start unless you do, so you count aloud: one, two, three, four, five. 'Sorry,' says your car, 'you've had too much to drink.' And it shuts off.

By analyzing your voice, the car's computer knows you're intoxicated. Your voice can tell a lot about you: where you grew up, your emotional state, whether you're lying—even who you are. Voice analysis is one of the things that linguists do; it's part of a field known as Forensic Linguistics. It's the application of linguistic science to matters concerning the law, crime, and the courts.

In computer voice analysis, speech is broken down electronically and then examined for clues about the speaker. You've probably heard this kind of computer product called a 'voiceprint'. Because your voice may change over time, or with illness, voiceprints aren't as accurate as fingerprints—which are unchanging from birth to death—but they're a very useful tool in solving crimes.

A notorious tape of the supposed voice of Osama Bin Laden was subjected to speaker authentication by voiceprint analysis late in 2002 in an attempt to determine conclusively whether the voice was that of the al-Qaeda leader. Fourteen known voiceprints of Bin Laden were parameterized and graphed along with sixteen voiceprints of Arabic male speakers known not to be Bin Laden. A decision boundary separated them into two distinct groups. The voiceprint of the 2002 purported Bin Laden voice was then similarly classified and guess what? The unknown found itself in the non-Bin Laden group. Whether correct or not, the entire world was informed that such linguistic evidence was possible and would play an important role in authenticating anonymous voices.

And then there's analysis of writing. Consider The Case of the Dog Club Letters. No, this isn't a Sherlock Holmes story. It's an actual case where the committee members of a dog club received threatening anonymous letters. Personal details in each letter hinted that the writer was actually a committee member, but which one? A forensic linguist compared the letters with writing samples from each member. Analysis of their writing styles, including punctuation, capitalization, and spelling, revealed that the letter writer was the committee treasurer. He was drummed out of the club.

Ranging from doggy letters to the text of stage plays that may or may not have been written by Shakespeare, *authorship* can be determined by comparing patterns such as word groupings, sentence length, grammatical usages, and much more. This, by the way, is how forensic linguists used computer programs to establish the authorship of some of the Federalist Papers, which had been in dispute for two hundred years.

Do you remember those letters containing anthrax germs that were mailed to U.S. government offices and news organizations after the September 2001 attacks? An obvious question was whether the letters were written by foreigners—if they were, it would suggest that they were connected to the 9/11 plot. Analysis of the letter sent to the Majority Leader of the U.S. Senate showed that the writer had far greater familiarity with the Roman alphabet than do most people whose languages are written in Arabic script. Forensic Linguistics revealed that the broken English and misspelled words were faked, and that the letters were in fact written by a native English speaker.

Plagiarism is a bane of Academia—often committed by students who take other people's writings from the Internet. Forensic Linguistics to the rescue! The same techniques used on the Federalist Papers can be used to detect whether material is plagiarized. Computer software reads a student's or scholar's paper, then scans millions of written works for duplication of specific words, phrases, sentences—even ideas.

Finally, a major concern of Forensic Linguistics is to clarify legal talk, so that people can understand the meaning of a law that may be couched in gobbledygook. For example, on the subject of expert witnesses, one law reads: 'Expert evidence presented to the court should be, and should be seen to be, the independent product of the expert uninfluenced as to form or content by the exigencies of litigation.' The forensic linguist simplifies this to say, 'Expert witnesses should be free from prejudice.' Today, linguists are designing computer programs that automatically translate legalese into ordinary English.

So there's a lot going on in this field. If you want to learn more, use an Internet search engine on the words 'Forensic' and 'Linguistics'. And the next time you think of crime-fighting superheroes, forget the cape and bulging muscles—and picture a laptop-toting linguist.

About the author

Robert Rodman is a UCLA-trained linguist who is currently a Professor in the Department of Computer Science at North Carolina State University. He is co-author, with Victoria Fromkin and Nina Hyams, of a popular linguistics textbook, *An Introduction to Language* (Thomson/Wadsworth, eighth edition 2007; available July, 2006).

Suggestions for further reading

In this book: Opportunities and requirements for professional use of language abilities are discussed in chapters 20 (bilingualism), 36 (America's language crisis), 42 (language-related careers), 43 (dictionaries), 44 (interpreting and translating), 53 (Russian), and 55 (Arabic). Other linguistic/technological topics appear in chapters 34 (language-teaching technology), 35 (interactive map of U.S. language communities), 45 (machine translation), and 47 (the National Museum of Language).

Elsewhere:

Olsson, John. *Forensic Linguistics* (Continuum, 2004). This is a core text for a rigorous introduction to the field of Forensic Linguistics. It is a carefully organized, clearly written book by one of Britain's most prominent forensic linguists.

Solan, Lawrence, and Peter Tiersma. *Speaking of Crime* (University of Chicago Press, 2005). This is a fascinating little book that examines the complex role of language within our criminal justice system. The authors have compiled numerous cases, ranging from the Lindbergh kidnapping to the impeachment trial of Bill Clinton to the JonBenét Ramsey case, that provide real-life examples of how language functions in arrests, investigations, interrogations, confessions, and trials.

Shuy, Roger. *Creating Language Crimes: How Law Enforcement Uses (and Misuses) Language* (Oxford University Press, 2005). Roger Shuy has given us a fascinating account with numerous illustrations of the centrality of language in all aspects of law enforcement, from arrest to arraignment to trial to sentencing. The author is a prominent American forensic linguist.

47

How can you keep languages in a museum?

Amelia C. Murdoch

What would there be to see and learn in a museum of language? Is there such a place?

As a matter of fact, in 1997 a National Museum of Language was established in the suburbs of Washington, D.C., scheduled to open to the public in stages through 2006 and later years. What a unique institution! Everyone is familiar with museums where you see (and sometimes touch) physical objects like airplanes, paintings, bleached bones and antique coins. But language, you might think, is mainly sounds and words and books. Don't libraries already exist to store and display them? What'll you do in a language museum? And why?

Language is a subject most of us want to know more about: how it developed, how languages differ, how the body works as a language machine. The Museum's purpose is to answer such questions. It will make clear why language is important; it'll demonstrate what we know about language and how we know it, and it'll give you a chance to explore linguistic knowledge—enjoyably.

There will of course be a library, America's most comprehensive collection of information on language. Some of that information will be in the form of printed books and journals, but much of it will be online—accessible wherever you are on the planet. Especially noteworthy will be the library's collection of speech samples—recordings of hundreds of languages and many dialects. This collection—with the eventual goal of having a sample of every language in the world—will be an extraordinary resource for language research.

But the Museum will also feature interactive multimedia displays of language-related objects and information. You'll see and hear how the science of speech analysis evolved from rudimentary techniques using gas flames to today's digital voiceprint technology. You'll be able to take home an image of your own speech from a sound spectrogram. Or learn how speech synthesizers work—from those annoying telephone voices to important devices that allow physically challenged people like Steven Hawking to speak. You'll be able to talk with a computer and see how well it does in understanding and creating speech.

There'll be an interactive wall-sized map showing where each of the world's languages is spoken. You'll see how languages develop and change. How they differ. How they spread over space and time. And how they die.

Complementing the world map, there'll be an interactive display using sound bites and video clips to demonstrate the linguistic heritage and diversity of America—including not only the dialects of American English but also the aboriginal tongues and the languages of centuries of immigrants. English-speaking visitors will even get a chance to see where their own dialect fits into the big picture.

There'll be an animated model of the human speech apparatus, showing how the lungs, vocal cords, lips, teeth, and tongue work together to create the infinite variety of sounds in thousands of languages and dialects.

And you'll see what we know about how language is *acquired*—the way babies learn their first language and the considerably different ways children and adults learn additional languages later in life.

Fascinating displays will trace the development of the Roman alphabet and other writing systems, with texts in each system and the tools used to produce them.

Other exhibits will explore the role of language in society, reaching back to the beginning of civilization. One topic will be the many ways in which language study and the law are intertwined, such as forensics and questions of access to justice in multilingual societies. Others will be be the importance of language in commerce, government, and technology—all demonstrated with historic documents, radio and television programs, and exhibits explaining things like how linguistic analysis can solve codes and ciphers. Language and religion have interacted with each other for many centuries, as will be shown in exhibits illustrating the role played by missionaries in the study of languages and linguistics.

You'll hear and see the story of dictionaries, from the earliest glossaries to the monumental Oxford English Dictionary. Paired with descriptions of the books themselves will be accounts of the lives of their makers—from learned scholars like Dr. Samuel Johnson (that 'harmless drudge') to the numberless, often anonymous, men and women whose work makes modern dictionaries possible. The Museum will trace the history of translation and interpretation and will demonstrate how the translators and interpreters of today practice their profession in the worlds of business, diplomacy and intelligence.

Yet another important subject is the preservation of *endangered* languages. Universities and other institutions in the U.S. and other countries—as well as the U.N.—devote considerable effort to collecting information on such languages. But there needs to be a coordinating point where all this information is brought together. The Museum's organizers see it as a candidate for fulfilling this role—as a central repository for preserving ethnic cultures through preservation of their languages.

There will be much, much more. This is only a peek at what the Museum eventually will become. As it grows, the National Museum of Language welcomes the ideas and participation of everybody to whom language is important—and that includes *you*. Why don't you help it grow by becoming a member?

About the author

Amelia C. Murdoch, Ph.D., founder and President of America's National Museum of Language, is a retired U.S. government linguist. She began her professional career as a specialist in Medieval French; after joining the federal government, she ventured into the Semitic languages. Over her long career she became convinced that the field of language had to be expanded from the academic and educational worlds into the cultural mainstream. Her experiences in guiding the creation of a seminal exhibit on language provided many insights that persuaded her that a museum of language was an ideal means to lead that expansion. Her appreciation of the value of language has grown through the years, as has her belief that everyone has an interest in some aspect of language, as well as a willingness and a desire to learn more about the subject.

Suggestions for further reading

In this book: The Museum of Language covers a range of subjects similar to that of this book. A sampling of chapters that may be of special interest to eventual Museum goers includes 2 (world language survey) and 35 (languages of the U.S.); 24 (language death) and 25 (language rescue); 34 (language-teaching technologies), 44 (interpreting and translating), and 46 (Forensic Linguistics); as well as chapters on individual languages, like 50 (Latin), 51 (Italian), 52 (Spanish, Portuguese, and others), 53 (Russian), 54 (Icelandic), 55 (Arabic), 57 (Chinese), and 58 (Japanese).

Elsewhere:

Comrie, Bernard, ed. *The World's Major Languages* (Oxford University Press, 1990). An authoritative presentation of the most interesting facts of the major languages of the world.

Crystal, David. *The Cambridge Encyclopedia of Language* (Cambridge University Press, second edition 1997). An invaluable comprehensive, indeed essential, reference treating all aspects of language.

McWhorter, John. *The Story of Human Language* (The Teaching Company, 2005). An outstanding series of 36 lectures (30 minutes each, available as DVD, videotape, or audio CD) on the history and development of language.

Wade, Nicholas, ed. *The Science Times Book of Language and Linguistics* (The Lyons Press, 2000). A collection of very readable essays. The topics, organization and style correspond to the approach of the National Museum of Language.

48

Where did English come from?

John Algeo

Was English originally a German dialect? If so, how did it get to be English? How did the Vikings and the French get involved? What can dictionaries tell us about the history of English?

English did come from the same ancestor as German, but there's a lot more to the story. In the fifth century, Celts lived in the British Isles. But warfare among them got so fierce that one local king asked for help from Germanic tribes living in southern Denmark and northern Germany. He got more than he bargained for: the tribes came as allies, but they liked the island so much they decided to take it over.

Two of the main tribes in this group came from regions called Angeln and Saxony, which is why we call the language they brought to Britain 'Anglo-Saxon'. The speech of the tribes who stayed on the European Continent eventually became modern German, Dutch, and Scandinavian languages; and Anglo-Saxon, also known as 'Old English', grew into the English we speak today.

On their new turf, these Germanic Anglo-Saxons started to talk in new ways. The tribes they drove to the fringes of Britain left them some Celtic place names. But more important, the newcomers were converted to Christianity, so a good deal of Latin crept into their language. Another influence showed up in the ninth and tenth centuries as Britain—which by then was called Angle-land, or England—was invaded again, this time by Scandinavian cousins of the Anglo-Saxons: Viking raiders, who ruled all of England for a couple of decades. Their contact with the Anglo-Saxons was so close that they've given us some of our most everyday words—like *sister*, *sky*, *law*, *take*, *window*, and the pronouns *they*, *them*, and *their*.

The greatest additions to English resulted from another invasion we all know about: '1066 and all that'. In that year England was conquered by descendants of a different group of Vikings—the 'Normans', men of the North, who had settled in the tenth century along the coast of France and become French speakers. The region of France they ruled still bears their name—Normandy. When they took over England, they made French the government language. So England became a trilingual country: officials used Norman French, the church used Latin, and the common people spoke a version of English we call 'Middle English'.

The common people were by far the majority, and by the late fourteenth century, their English reasserted itself over French as the language of Britain. But it was a different English from the Anglo-Saxon spoken before the Norman Conquest. Over the years it had absorbed an enormous number of French words for legal, governmental, military, and cultural matters—words like *judge*, *royal*, *soldier*, and a host of food terms like *fruit* and *beef*. And its grammar had changed in some dramatic ways.

At the end of the fifteenth century, printing was introduced in England, which helped standardize the language. And in the sixteenth century Englishmen began to explore the globe. They encountered new things that needed to be talked about with new words. They settled in North America, the Caribbean, Africa, South Asia, Australia, and the South Seas.

As it became a global language, English influenced other languages—and was influenced by them. Most of our core vocabulary comes directly from Old English: words like *mother*, *earth*, *love*, *hate*, *cow*, *man*, and *glad*. But we have borrowed words from many other languages: Greek (*pathos*), Welsh (*penguin*), Irish Gaelic (*galore*), Scots Gaelic (*slogan*), Icelandic (*geyser*), Swedish (*ombudsman*), Norwegian (*ski*), Danish (*skoal*), Spanish (*ranch*), Portuguese (*molasses*), Italian (*balcony*), Dutch (*boss*), German (*semester*), Yiddish (*bagel*), Arabic (*harem*), Hebrew (*shibboleth*), Persian (*bazaar*), Sanskrit (*yoga*), Hindi (*shampoo*), Romany or Gypsy (*pal*), Tamil (*curry*), Chinese (*gung-ho*), Japanese (*karaoke*), Malay (*gingham*), Tahitian (*tattoo*), Tongan (*taboo*), Hawaiian (*ukulele*), Australian Dharuk (*boomerang*), Australian Guugu Yimidhirr (*kangaroo*), Bantu (*goober*), Wolof (*jigger* or *chigger*), Russian (*mammoth*), Hungarian (*paprika*), Turkish (*jackal*), Algonquian (*possum*), Dakota (*tepee*), and Navajo (*hogan*). Most of the words in a large dictionary—perhaps as many as 85 or 90 percent—either are loanwords from other languages or have been invented in English using elements borrowed from other languages.

By now the language has expanded far beyond its tribal beginnings. It's a first language in countries settled by the English. It's a second language in countries like India and the Philippines, which were part of the British Empire or under American influence. And it's a foreign language used around the globe for business, science, technology, and commerce. A Scandinavian pilot landing his plane in Greece talks with the air controller in English. It's also the main language of the worldwide Internet.

So did English come from German? No—it's closely related to German, but what began as the tongue of a small Germanic tribe in northwestern Europe morphed over time into something very different—a blend of dozens of languages that came to be spoken in virtually every country in the world.

About the author

John Algeo is Professor Emeritus at the University of Georgia. He is the author of *British or American English? A Handbook of Word and Grammar Patterns* (Cambridge, 2006), co-author of *The Origins and Development of the English Language* (Heinle, fifth edition 2004), and editor of *The Cambridge History of the English Language: Volume 6, English in North America* (Cambridge, 2002) and of *Fifty Years Among the New Words* (Cambridge, 1991). He is past president of the Dictionary Society of North America, the American Dialect Society, and the American Name Society. He and his wife, Adele, wrote 'Among the New Words' in the journal *American Speech* for ten years and now are gathering material for a Dictionary of Briticisms.

Suggestions for further reading

In this book: Other chapters on the origins and history of languages include 4 (earliest languages), 5 (language relationships), 8 (pidgins and creoles), and 54 (Icelandic); chapters that discuss various aspects of how languages evolve include 7 (language change), 11 (grammar), 41 (dialect change), 50 (Latin), and 51 (Italian).

Elsewhere:

Algeo, John. *British or American English? A Handbook of Word and Grammar Patterns* (Cambridge University Press, 2006). A guide to the many, often unnoticed, grammatical differences between the two principal national varieties of the language.

Algeo, John, and Thomas Pyles. *The Origins and Development of the English Language* (Heinle, 1993). A detailed history of the English Language from prehistoric Indo-European to present-day developments in vocabulary and usage.

Hogg, Richard M., ed. *The Cambridge History of the English Language* (Cambridge University Press, 1992–2001). A six-volume history of English written by some of the leading scholars in the subject, dealing with all aspects of the subject and including extensive bibliographies.

Leech, Geoffrey, and Jan Svartvik. *English—One Tongue, Many Voices* (Palgrave Macmillan, 2006). A masterful and up-to-date survey of the English language: its global spread, international and local varieties, history from obscurity to primacy, usage and uses, standards and creoles, style and change in progress, politics and controversy.

49

How many Native American languages are there?

Marianne Mithun

*Do the Native American languages have any connection
with languages in Europe or Asia or Africa? Are they all
related to each other? Are they dying out? Is there any
point in trying to save them?*

A surprising number of people think there's just one language native
to the U.S.: 'Indian'. Nothing could be further from the truth.

In fact, we know of nearly three hundred languages that were
spoken north of Mexico before the arrival of Europeans. Many have
disappeared, but there are still about one hundred and eighty of
them. They are not demonstrably related to Indo-European or to any
other large language family. They constitute between fifty and sixty
different families of their own—and the languages are as different
from each other as English is from Arabic or Japanese.

Some of the language families are quite large. The Athabaskan-
Eyak-Tlingit family, for example, contains thirty-nine different lan-

guages, spoken from Alaska through western Canada into Oregon, California, and the Southwestern U.S. This family includes Navajo, the most widely used indigenous language on the continent, with about 100,000 speakers.

A family called Algic is best known for its largest branch, Algonquian, which is spoken along the Atlantic seaboard from Labrador to Virginia. It was Algonquian speakers who met the Pilgrims and Sir Walter Raleigh, and gave American English such words as *caribou*, *skunk*, *moccasin*, *hominy*, and *raccoon*. Algonquian languages are also spoken across most of Canada and down into the Plains in the U.S. Midwest: languages like Shawnee, Fox, Potawatomi, Cree, Cheyenne, and Blackfoot.

The Iroquoian family consists of eight modern languages, among them Mohawk—which is still spoken in Quebec, Ontario, and New York State—and Cherokee, which in the seventeenth century was spoken in the southern Appalachians. Like several other indigenous peoples, the Cherokee were forced to march westward in 1838–39 along the so-called 'Trail of Tears', so the largest Cherokee community is now in Oklahoma. Iroquoian languages gave us place names like *Schenectady*, *Ontario*, *Ohio*, and *Kentucky*, as well as *Canada*.

The languages indigenous to North America are so diverse that it is hard to make generalizations about them. But they are far from simple, or 'primitive'. In fact, their grammars are very complex. If you saw the 2002 film *Windtalkers*, for example, you know that the U.S. Marine Corps in World War II had speakers of Navajo use their language as a secret code to baffle the Japanese.

Many Native American languages use sounds unfamiliar to English speakers, such as ejectives, consonants with an extra popping sound. Some use distinctive tone, so that the same syllable spoken with different pitches can mean entirely different things. Navajo has both of these features.

And words in some of the languages can be very long, sometimes carrying as much meaning as a complete sentence in English. The Mohawk word *wa'tkenikahrá:ra'ne'*, for example, means 'they saw it.' This word consists of several parts. The first is the factual prefix *wa'-*, which indicates that the speaker feels that this is a fact, that the event actually happened. It is usually translated as the past tense in English. The second part is the prefix *t-*, which indicates duality. The third is the pronomial prefix *keni-* ('they'), but it is more specific than the English translation. It tell us that just two females were involved. The fourth part is an incorporated noun *-kahr-* ('eye'). The core of the word is actually the verb root *-r-* 'be on'. Next is the suffix *-a'n-*, which means 'come to' or 'become'. Finally we have the suffix *-e*,' which tells us that the event happened all at once. The word thus means literally 'the girls came to be visually on it,' that is, 'their eyes fell upon it,' or 'they saw it.'

Each of the languages shows us a unique way of looking at the world, of packaging experience into words, of making subtle distinctions. If you speak an Eskimoan language, for example, and you want to say 'that caribou,' there is no single word equivalent to English 'that'. You first have to notice whether the caribou is standing or moving. If it is stationary, you have to specify whether it is visible or out of sight. If you can see it, you must specify whether it is near you, near the person you're talking to, or far away, or whether it's above or below you. Or that it's approaching, or that it's the same caribou you were talking about earlier. Each of these ideas is packaged in just one word—translated simply 'that' in English.

Unfortunately, the world is losing the melodies and unique perspectives of these aboriginal tongues. The languages are dying. Some have already disappeared because their speakers perished in warfare or epidemics; others, because their speakers chose to use other languages instead. Human heritage has been enriched by these languages, but it is likely that no more than a dozen of them will survive this century. And like an environmental disaster, this will be a great loss.

About the author

Marianne Mithun is Professor of Linguistics at the University of California, Santa Barbara. Her work covers such areas as morphology (word structure), relations between grammar and discourse, language typology, and language change, particularly the mechanisms by which grammatical structures evolve. She has worked with speakers of a number of North American languages, including Mohawk, Tuscarora, Seneca, Lakhota, Central Alaskan Yup'ik, and Navajo, as well as several Austronesian languages. She has also worked with a number of communities on projects aimed at documenting their traditional languages and training speakers to teach them to younger generations.

Suggestions for further reading

In this book: Chapters on how groups of language are related include 5 (language families), 48 (origins of English), and 56 (languages of Africa). Languages of the U.S. are discussed in chapters 25 (revitalizing threatened Native American languages), 26 (English in the American South), 36 (America's language crisis), 37 (Spanish in the U.S.), 38 (Cajun), 39 (German in the U.S.), and 40 (Gullah).

Elsewhere:

Grenoble, Lenore A., and Lindsay J. Whaley, eds. *Endangered Languages: Language Loss and Community Response* (Cambridge University Press, 1998). A collection of articles on various aspects of language loss around the world, including discussions of what is lost when languages disappear, the processes by which languages disappear, and community responses to the loss of heritage languages.

Mithun, Marianne, *The Languages of Native North America* (Cambridge University Press, 1999/2001). An encyclopedic compendium describing the languages and language families indigenous to North America, along with the special structures and areas of complexity and elaboration found in these languages.

Silver, Shirley, and Wick R. Miller. *American Indian Languages: Cultural and Social Contexts* (University of Arizona, 1997). An introductory textbook on the languages of the Americas with special emphasis on the cultural and social contexts in which they have developed and are used.

50

Is Latin really dead?

Frank Morris

Didn't people stop speaking Latin after the barbarians sacked Rome and ended the Roman Empire? Why should anybody but a specialized scholar be interested in a language that's dead?

Dead? Well, lovers of Latin will tell you that the language is still living and quite well—and our list of evidence is long.

First, of course, it is alive at the Vatican. We have quite recently witnessed, for example, the Latin funeral mass for John Paul II, the announcement of the new Pope's election with the words *Habemus Papam* ('we have a Pope'), and a speech delivered in Latin to the Cardinals by the newly elevated Pope Benedict XVI. Lexicographers at the Vatican also regularly coin Latin words to keep Latin in touch with the modern world. As it has for many hundreds of years, Latin continues to serve ceremonial purposes. Some colleges and universities grant Latin diplomas. We may hear a student deliver a Latin oration at Harvard graduations or the President of the College of Charleston confer in Latin the *Artium Baccalaureatus* degree.

But beyond these traditional uses, Latin increasingly is finding a place in popular culture. The Harry Potter books are replete with Latin phrases. In the film *Life of Brian*, characters scrawl Latin graffiti on public walls; Mel Gibson's *Passion of Christ* has characters speaking in Latin. We can hear weekly radio broadcasts of the news in Latin from Finland. And growing numbers of enthusiasts around the world are carrying on Latin conversations, a good number of them through the Internet. In all these examples Latin is doing what all living languages do: communicating information from one human to another in the modern world.

Lovers of the language would also argue that Latin lives through its influence on other languages. For example, about 80 percent of words in Romance languages come from Latin. Roughly 60 percent of all English words—and 90 percent of our multisyllabic words—are borrowed or derived from it. Almost all medical and scientific terms come from Latin or its cousin, ancient Greek. Of course legal terms and some of our most common abbreviations are Latin, e.g., *in loco parentis*, *habeas corpus*, etc. (yes, even the phrase *et cetera*).

Headlines in various media report on the vitality of Latin in schools: 'Latin Makes a Comeback' (*Education World*), 'Schools Reviving a Dead Language' (CNN.com/education) and 'Latin: A Language Alive and Well' (*The Washington Post*). Indeed, in U.S. schools at all levels enrollments in both Latin and Ancient Greek have increased sharply. According to a recent survey by the Modern Language Association, undergraduate college enrollments in Latin increased 13 percent from 1995 to 2002. In secondary schools, enrollments in Latin grew 8 percent from 1990 to 2000, and have doubled since 1985 in U.S. middle schools. While comprehensive figures for the lower grades are not available, we know that elementary school programs prospered in Philadelphia and Los Angeles from the 1970s into the 1990s (at one time there were 14,000 students in Philadelphia alone). The steady production of elementary school materials such as *First Latin, Salvete, Minimus, Charleston*

Latin and *The Keepers of Alexandria* are a good indication 'from the marketplace' that enrollments in Latin are continuing to grow.

What, you ask, explains this remarkable resurgence of interest in Latin and Greek among so many people? One driving force is the so-called 'Back to Basics' movement. Administrators, teachers and parents see benefits in the study of Latin: it disciplines the mind, provides insight into western civilization and its values, expands English vocabulary, gives an understanding of grammar that results in better use of English, and provides a fruitful basis for the study of other languages. The study of Latin is linked with the achievement of higher scores on standardized tests. In the 1970s Latin students in the fifth grade in America's inner-city schools scored one year higher in vocabulary on the Iowa Test of Basic Skills than their peers who did not take Latin. On the 2005 Scholastic Aptitude Test (a standardized examination for college applicants), secondary school students with two or more years of Latin had a median score that was 173 points above that of all other students. An analysis of Graduate Record Exam scores from 1996–1999 shows that undergraduates in classics ranked first in verbal scores among the 270 fields in which students take the test.

But there is more to the resurgence of Latin than just returning to the basics. New audiences and wider curricular applications have been developed. As is clear from the reference above to the study of Latin in inner-city schools, innovative materials and teaching methodologies are making Latin and Classics accessible to all students, not just a traditional elite. For children of Hispanic origin, Latin can serve as a bridge between Spanish and English and enhance the learning of English. Furthermore, teachers can capitalize on the vast cultural legacy of Greece and Rome to make interdisciplinary connections between Latin and subjects such as language arts, social studies, art, literature, mythology, mathematics, and science. Teachers can use the history of Rome and its multicultural empire to provide an ethnically-neutral means to develop cross-cultural understanding and respect for diversity. But the ultimate reason for Latin's comeback is that, with new, more interactive ways to teach it, students are finding the study of Latin and the Romans to be fun. There are even reports of grade-school children who beg teachers to skip recess … so they don't have to stop their Latin lesson.

So is Latin really dead? Surely not. We can find it at the Vatican, on the radio, on the Internet, in contemporary books and films, at happy occasions like graduations, in elementary school class-rooms, and among a growing number of enthusiasts around the world. Speakers of English and many other tongues draw on it for their everyday words and for terminology needed in their technical and professional lives. Although there were decades, not so long ago, when Latin was less frequently taught in schools and was thought of as dull or out of fashion, those days are obviously over. As it has many times before, Latin is making a comeback—and it's coming on strong.

About the author

Frank Morris holds a Ph.D. in Classics from the University of Cincinnati and teaches Latin and Greek at the College of Charleston in Charleston, SC. He is Director of *Charleston Latin*, and has been training teachers to teach Latin in elementary schools since the mid 1980s. Prior to joining the faculty at the College of Charleston he taught Latin and Greek at Orange Park High School in Florida.

Suggestions for further reading

In this book: Latin is a vivid case study in the endangered-language issues that are the subjects of chapters 2 (languages of the world), 24 (language death), and 25 (language rescue), 35 (languages of the U.S.), and 41 (Are dialects dying?). Its long history (which continues on into chapter 51, on Italian) exemplifies the ways of language evolution discussed in chapters 7 (language change), 8 (pidgins and creoles), 11 (grammar), 41 (dialect change), and 48 (origins of English).

Elsewhere:

LaFleur, Richard A., ed. *Latin for the Twenty-First Century: From Concept to Classroom* (Foresman, 1998). A survey of trends in the teaching of Latin.

Pearcy, Lee T. *The Grammar of Our Civility* (Baylor Universtiy Press, 2005). A history of the teaching of Classics in the U.S.

Web sites:

http://www.yleradio1.fi/nuntii
A source for radio broadcasts in Latin.

http://www.promotelatin.org
http://www.promotelatin.org/greek.htm
Both sites provide many informative links on Classics and Classics teaching.

51

Who speaks Italian?

Dennis Looney

*When did Latin turn into modern Italian? Do all
Italians speak the same language? How many dialects
are there in Italy?*

Fragmentation defines the linguistic history of the Italian peninsula more than you can imagine. Shortly after the modern state of
Italy was founded in 1861, a politician famously reflected, 'With
Italy made, we must now make the Italians.' Making Italians meant
first and foremost giving citizens of the new country—who spoke
hundreds of dialects—one voice, an official national language. This
project took another century to complete.

The earliest example of written Italian appears in a legal document from 960 A.D. The document, about a debate over property
boundaries, is mostly in church Latin, but embedded in the judicial
commentary is the statement of a plaintiff in his own vernacular:
'I know that those lands … [have been held by the Benedictine
monks].' A monastic scribe dutifully recorded the speech phonetically, beginning '*Sao ke kelle terre ...*'—four words strikingly similar
to the standard language of today: *so che quelle terre*. Somewhere

around the end of the first millennium, Latin was changing into what we now think of as Italian.

But, of course, the two languages co-existed for many, many years. This posed a problem for writers, especially educated ones. Should they write in Latin, the revered and long-established language of scholars and the church? Or in the vernacular? This later became known as 'the question of the language', and it was not completely resolved until modern times.

In the early fourteenth century, Dante Alighieri considered writing *The Divine Comedy* in Latin but ultimately chose to use the language of the people, specifically the dialect of his town, Florence, and the region around it, Tuscany. Dante's *Comedy* became the touchstone and starting place for most of the subsequent debates about the language. For scholarly Renaissance humanists, as for Dante, the first choice was between Latin and the vernacular. If one chose the vernacular (as most writers did), there was a second decision: which regional version of it? The dialect of Florence or that of Venice or Rome or Milan or some other city or region?

The prestige and political clout of Florentine culture heavily influenced such linguistic decisions. The powerful precedent set by Dante and other Tuscan authors, including Petrarch and Boccaccio, influenced writers from many other parts of Italy. In 1525, Pietro Bembo, a Venetian, proposed a standard Italian vocabulary, grammar, and syntax modelled after Tuscan. Tuscan's dominance over other dialects was reflected in a common saying: 'the Florentine tongue [should be] in a Roman mouth.'

The debate over linguistic models raged into the nineteenth century, when the influential writer Alessandro Manzoni chose the dialect of contemporary Florence for his great historical novel *The Betrothed*. This required Manzoni, whose native dialect was that of Milan, to 'rinse his clothes'—as he colorfully put it—'in [Tuscany's] Arno River.' In the 1860s Manzoni lobbied successfully for educational policies that established the dialect of Tuscany as the standard to be used in schools. By the middle of the twentieth century most Italians spoke a form of the language updated from Dante's medieval Florentine.

In the 1920s and 1930s, Italy's Fascist government undertook, with no great success, a campaign to rid Italian of all foreign influences. The word *sandwich*, for example, was to be ousted by a new made-up word, *tramezzino*, meaning 'the small thing in between'. Legislation in 1938 banished the respectful pronoun *lei* ('you'), requiring instead the 'more Italian' pronoun *voi*. But *lei* and *sandwich* survived and Italian continued to absorb words from other languages, especially English—or more precisely Anglo-American—throughout the second half of the twentieth century and into the twenty-first. For example, the new English word 'to google'—with an Italian verb ending attached—has recently joined the vocabulary of Italy's computer literate: *googleare*. Italians are not as squeamish about foreign influences on their language as their neighbors in France, and many languages other than Italian are used in Italy; fifteen of them (including German, French, Provençal, Slovenian, Albanian, and Greek) were granted official status as linguistic minorities in 1999.

So, with regional dialects and the infusion of words from other languages, is there now a 'real' Italian, universally understood throughout Italy? Yes, there is: approximately 57 million of the country's 60 million inhabitants communicate in the standard language, as do millions of Italian speakers in other countries. People in Argentina speak a version of standard Italian, making Buenos Aires the second largest Italian city in the world. Standard Italian is also an official language of the European Union, Switzerland, and Vatican City. The rise of mass media has spread the standard language into the country's furthest corners, threatening to extinguish the approximately one hundred dialects that still give the peninsula linguistic richness. Between 1955 and 1995 the percentage of speakers who used only dialect dropped from 66 percent to 6.9 percent. The fragmentation of the language is all but over.

Like all languages, Italian has changed a great deal as its national standard emerged, enriched by its many dialects and by foreign borrowings—and it will continue to change. But at bottom its origins are in Tuscany, and Dante would probably have little trouble understanding it even today.

About the author

Dennis Looney (Ph.D., 1987, Comparative Literature, University of North Carolina at Chapel Hill) is an associate professor of Italian at the University of Pittsburgh, with a secondary appointment in Classics; he currently serves as Assistant Dean in the Humanities. He has published articles on Dante, Petrarch, Boiardo, Ariosto, Tasso, Herodotus, Ovid, and Pinocchio. *Compromising the Classics: Romance Epic Narrative in the Italian Renaissance* (Wayne State, 1996) won Honorable Mention for the MLA's Prize for Italian Literary Studies, 1996–1997. He is co-editor of *Phaethon's Children: The Este Court and Its Culture in Early Modern Ferrara* (MRTS, 2005) and editor and co-translator of Sergio Zatti, *The Quest for Epic: From Ariosto to Tasso* (Toronto, 2006).

Suggestions for further reading

In this book: The history of Italian, which grew out of Latin as described in chapter 50, demonstrates many of the same kinds of issues covered in chapters 7 (language change), 11 (grammar), 41 (dialect change), and 48 (origins of English). Other chapters on modern languages include 52 (Spanish, Portuguese, and others), 53 (Russian), 54 (Icelandic), 55 (Arabic), 56 (languages of Africa), 57 (Chinese), and 58 (Japanese).

Elsewhere:

Lepschy, Anna Laura, and Giulio Lepschy. *The Italian Language Today* (Routledge, 1994, second edition). Provides a brief outline of the history of the language with a focus on the evolution of the modern standard language. Includes reference grammar of contemporary Italian.

Maiden, Martin. *A Linguistic History of Italian* (Longman, 1995). A study of the historical development of the elements of Italian. Assumes some knowledge of the language.

Migliorini, Bruno; abridged, recast and revised by T. Gwynfor Griffith. *The Italian Language* (Faber, 1984). Comprehensive work on the history of the language from its origins to the twentieth century.

Web sites:

http://www.accademiadellacrusca.it/
Web site of the active linguistic academy founded in the late sixteenth century to create a dictionary of standard Italian based on the rules of Pietro Bembo. English portal.

http://www.dialettiitaliani.com/
http://www.dialettando.com/
Both Web sites provide examples of dialects from around Italy (poems, stories, recipes, anecdotes, and proverbs) in addition to dictionaries for translating dialect into standard Italian. In Italian.

http://www.italica.rai.it/principali/lingua/bruni/mappe/flash/regionalok.htm
Web site in Italian that provides an interactive linguistic atlas of the principal dialects of the Italian peninsula.

52

How different are Spanish and Portuguese?

Ana Maria Carvalho

*Are Spanish and Portuguese really dialects of the same
language? What differences are there between them?
How did they come about?*

Well, if Portuguese and Spanish aren't varieties of the same language,
they're surely sister languages, and very close sisters at that. If we
define dialects as speech varieties that are mutually understood,
we can say they are, in fact, dialects of the same language. It's not
uncommon to find a speaker of say, Brazilian Portuguese, talking
to an Argentinean at an airport—each speaking his own language,
both understanding each other, with just occasional need to stop
now and then to clarify the meaning of a word. They communicate
very well most of the time, as long as they avoid using slang or
talking too fast.

Communication works because Spanish and Portuguese share
around 80 percent of their vocabulary, and most of the same gram-

matical structures, things like the endings on nouns and verbs. Where communication breaks down, it's often because of differences in pronunciation. Look at these two sentences, the first in Spanish and the second in Portuguese:

Mis hermanos alemanes cantan bien.

Meus irmãos alemães cantam bem.

It's pretty obvious that these are differently spelled and pronounced versions of the same five words (meaning 'My German brothers sing well'). Usually the difference that jumps out right away when one hears someone speaking Portuguese—whether from Portugal or from Brazil—is the nasal vowels that Portuguese often uses in words (like *irmãos*) whose Spanish versions use 'n' sounds (as in *hermanos*).

There are also some differences in grammar and word order, as well as some words that sound the same in both languages but have different meanings. The verb 'pegar' in Portuguese, for example, means 'pick up'; in Spanish it means 'hit'. Put that in the context of a babysitter getting instructions for taking care of an infant ... and you can imagine some confusion.

In reading—where, of course, pronunciation isn't a factor—the great amount of overlap in words and grammar means that a speaker of Spanish can read Portuguese with little difficulty. A recent study found that educated native speakers of Spanish with no previous exposure to Portuguese could understand as much as 95 percent of an academic text written solely in Portuguese.

But there are other criteria for distinguishing dialects from languages. As the saying goes, a language has an army behind it, but a dialect doesn't—and Portuguese has had its own army since the founding of Portugal in the twelfth century. It's had an official grammar book, giving it the status of a separate language in the eyes of the Portuguese, since 1536. Like Spanish, Portuguese came from the colloquial Latin spoken by the Romans occupying the Iberian Peninsula, but it emerged on the western side of the peninsula, largely separated by mountains from Spain. With separation came differences in the two languages.

We shouldn't forget that those are not the only languages of the Iberian Peninsula. Catalan, another Latin descendant, spoken by some eight million people along the eastern coast of Spain, has a long-established literary heritage and is widely agreed to be a language separate from both Spanish and Portuguese. Just above Portugal in the northwest corner of Spain is Galicia, a mountain region of around three million people. They speak what some call a dialect of Portuguese; I'd describe Galician as a Portuguese heavily influenced by Spanish, but there are those who consider it a language in its own right. And of course there are the Basques, who occupied the peninsula before the Romans came and have outlasted the Empire. They speak Euskera, a language not genetically related to any other European language.

You may be surprised to hear that Portuguese is used on four continents and is at least a candidate for the position of fifth most widely-spoken language in the world. Outside the Portuguese homeland in Europe, it's the language of Brazil, an emerging economic powerhouse and one of the few countries in South America where Spanish is not spoken. In Africa, you'll find Portuguese in Mozambique, Angola, Guinea-Bissau, and Cape Verde. Finally, you can hear it in Asia: the islands of East Timor, Macao in southern China, and Goa on the west coast of India.

So there are a lot of reasons why you might want to learn Portuguese. Above all, if you already speak Spanish, it won't be hard to add Portuguese to your repertoire, and then you'll be able to talk to lots more people in the world!

About the author

Ana Maria Carvalho is an Assistant Professor of Portuguese and Spanish linguistics at the University of Arizona, where she also directs the Portuguese Language Program. She studies the sociolinguistics of languages in contact, especially the contact between Spanish and Portuguese in the bilingual communities of Northern Uruguay. In addition to her work on sociolinguistics, she has published on the acquisition of Portuguese by Spanish speakers. Dr. Carvalho received her Ph.D. from the University of California, Berkeley.

Suggestions for further reading

In this book: Other chapters covering various languages of the world include 2 (world language survey), 50 (Latin), 51 (Italian), 53 (Russian), 54 (Icelandic), 55 (Arabic), 56 (languages of Africa), 57 (Chinese), and 58 (Japanese). Also of particular interest may be chapter 37, on Spanish in the U.S.

Elsewhere:

Thogmartin, Clyde, and Joanna Courteau. *A Checklist of Phonological, Grammatical and Lexical Contrasts between Spanish and Portuguese* (U.S. Department of Education, Education Resources Information Center, 1985). This work provides a short, accessible, and practical checklist of the most important contrasts between Spanish and Portuguese. It should be highly useful for someone trying to understand the main differences between the languages.

Ulsh, Jack L. *From Spanish to Portuguese* (U.S. Foreign Service Institute, 1971). Ulsh's seminal work is beneficial for anyone who already has achieved some competence in Spanish and wishes to build on that in order to develop familiarity with Portuguese.

53

Should we be studying Russian?

Benjamin Rifkin

Is Russian less beautiful than other languages?
Now that the Cold War is over, is there any reason
for non-Russians to learn it?

A colleague of mine who's a professor of Russian tells me that whenever he's on an airplane he likes to read Russian mystery novels. Typically, the person sitting next to him sees that he's reading something with unusual letters, and says something like: You teach Russian? But that's so hard! Or maybe: But Russia is so bleak! Or: It's kind of an ugly language, isn't it? Or: What can your students can do with it? Or even: Russian? Don't they spend most of their time drinking vodka?

Let me say a few things about those myths.

First, Russian isn't as hard as you might think. It does have a different alphabet, but if you've been in a fraternity or sorority, or if you studied mathematics in college, you might be surprised at how many of the letters you already know. They're borrowed from Greek. There are thirty-three letters, and they take only about ten hours to learn. And remember that Russian is a cousin of English in the Indo-European language family, so there are many connections. For instance, the root of the verb 'to see' in Russian is *vid*, related to the English words *video, vision*, and *visual*. And of course Russian words have crept into English, like *sputnik, babushka*, and *intelligentsia*. Students of Russian are also helped by the language's very logical system of roots, prefixes and suffixes. Once you learn that the word 'to write' is *pisat'*, for example, a whole series of verbs becomes predictable, created by combining the root of this verb with various prefixes. Adding prefix *vy-* ('out') makes *vypisat'* ('to write out'); adding *pro-* ('through') makes *propisat'* ('to prescribe'); adding *pod-* ('under') makes *podpisat'* ('to sign'); adding *pri-* ('adhering to') makes *pripisat'* ('to attribute'); adding *s-* ('from') makes *spisat'* ('to copy'); and adding *do-* ('up to' or 'until') makes *dopisat'* ('to finish writing').

As to the second myth, Russia is in no sense a bleak country. Yes, it has long winters, but the winters are beautiful: most of Russia is not only snowy in the winter, but also sunny. Imagine Russia's many churches, with their golden cupolas, laced in snow, gleaming in the winter sun. Russian villages are beautiful, often nestled on rivers near deep forests. Moscow and St. Petersburg are world-class, cosmopolitan cities. And consider these names as representatives of Russian culture: Dostoevsky, Tolstoy, Chekhov, Pasternak, Chagall, Tchaikovsky, Stravinsky, and Prokofiev, to name just a few. If you're not sure of Russia's role in the arts, check out the Bolshoi Theater in Moscow and the Hermitage Museum in St. Petersburg. Even the Russian subway systems are dazzling.

As for the third myth, about the sound of Russian—well, beauty is in the ear of the listener, but I find it hard to imagine anyone hearing, for example, Alexander Pushkin's poem 'I loved you once' or Anna Akhmatova's poem 'Lot's Wife' as read at www.russian-poetry.net without agreeing with me that the Russian language is exceptionally beautiful.

Some of the beauty of Russian results from the fact that it's spoken by people who are passionate about friendship. People who take the time to learn Russian and travel to the country are always struck by how intense Russian friendships can be. It's a national characteristic: the weather may be cold, but the people are very warm and hospitable.

The fourth myth suggests that foreigners who study Russian can't use it professionally now that the Cold War is over. The truth is that demand for speakers of Russian is growing and will continue to grow. The Russian economy is booming, and foreign companies are investing like never before. Russia is a top producer of oil and natural gas, with reserves second only to Saudi Arabia's. The energy sector will be of increasing importance to the Russian economy as new pipelines are built to Nakhodka, on Russia's Pacific coast, and Murmansk, on the North Atlantic. The Russian middle class is growing exponentially, thanks in part to revenues from the energy sector and foreign investment from the U.S., Germany, Japan, and the U.K., among other countries.

Russia is huge: it spreads across eleven time zones from Kaliningrad to Kamchatka. Roughly 140 million people in Russia consider Russian their native language, making it one of the most-spoken languages in the world. Russian is spoken as a native or second language by millions of people outside Russia, too, including many in the former Soviet Republics of Central Asia, as well as Ukraine, Belarus, and the Caucasus. There are large communities of Russian speakers in every major European and North American city.

We come at last to the story about vodka. Well, there might be some truth to that one. Legend has it that Prince Vladimir of Kiev chose Christianity as the official religion of the Slavs partly because Islam prohibited alcohol and because, as the Prince put it, 'drink is the joy of the Russians.' On the other hand, not every Russian drinks vodka, but almost every Russian drinks tea. Tea is definitely the number one national beverage and tea-drinking the national pastime.

So if you're ready to start a new language, think about Russian. And the next time you hear someone speaking with a Russian accent, offer him a glass of tea. You might make a friend for life.

About the author

Benjamin Rifkin is Professor of Slavic Languages and Vice Dean for Undergraduate Affairs of the College of Liberal Arts at Temple University, in Pennsylvania. He is a recent past president of the American Association of Teachers of Slavic and East European Languages and is a long-standing member of the board of directors of the American Council of Teachers of Russian. He is also the author of numerous articles about the learning and teaching of Russian; a manual for learning the Russian alphabet, *START* (Focus Publishers, 2005); and an intermediate-level Russian textbook, *Grammatika v kontekste* (McGraw-Hill, 1996). E-mail: benjamin.rifkin@temple.edu

Suggestions for further reading

In this book: Other chapters covering various languages of the world include 2 (world language survey), 50 (Latin), 51 (Italian), 52 (Spanish and Portuguese), 54 (Icelandic), 55 (Arabic), 56 (languages of Africa), 57 (Chinese), and 58 (Japanese). Opportunities and requirements for professional use of language abilities are discussed in chapters 20 (bilingualism), 36 (America's language crisis), 42 (language-related careers), 43 (dictionaries), 44 (interpreting and translating), and 46 (Forensic Linguistics).

Elsewhere:

Billington, James. *Face of Russia* (TV Books, 1998). A review of Russian culture.

Massie, Suzanne. *Land of the Firebird* (Hearttree Press, thirteenth edition 1980). A review of Russian culture.

Rzhevsky, Nicholas, ed. *The Cambridge Companion to Modern Russian Culture* (Cambridge University Press, 1999). A review of contemporary Russian culture.

Web sites:

http://www.russnet.org/why/index.html
'Why study Russian?' Information about studying Russian.

http://russnet.org
Interactive (Web-based) materials for learning Russian.

http://slavica.com/teaching/rifkin.html
A review of materials available for the study of Russian.

54

What's exciting about Icelandic?

Pardee Lowe Jr.

Why do linguists love Icelandic? Is it related to English?

It's too bad the pop singer Björk does most of her songs in English, rather than her native tongue. Icelandic is a really interesting language, with sounds not heard in most of the major languages of the world. Icelandic and English *are* related—they're both Germanic languages, and speakers of Old English could understand Old Norse, the ancestor of modern Icelandic—but there have been so many changes over time that you'd have to be a linguist to spot the connection. As one of the Icelandic sagas puts it: 'Our languages were mutually intelligible until the coming of William the Bastard!' (The Icelanders evidently didn't much like William of Normandy—whom most of us know as William the Conqueror.)

Of the two languages, it was English that changed more down through the centuries. Icelandic isn't much different now than it was when the Vikings, whose language it was, came to Iceland in the ninth century. Think about that. We need a college course to get us through the thousand-year-old Old English poem *Beowulf*, and even Shakespeare's plays, only a few hundred years old, can be difficult going for us. But a modern Icelander can still read eleven-hundred-year-old stories from the Middle Ages with ease—and without a dictionary. The pronunciation of the language has changed through the years, but not much else has. Yes, and despite the changes in English, its sometimes still possible to see the relationship between the two languages. For example, the Modern Icelandic sentence *Það er klukka-n tólf* (literally, 'That is clock-the twelve') is the equivalent of Modern English 'It's twelve o'clock.'

How is it that the past is still so accessible to modern Icelanders? Well, one way languages change is that the endings of words can disappear. Think of how English lost the '-st' verb ending in phrases like 'thou hast'. That happened to Swedish and Norwegian, too. They're sisters of Icelandic, but their grammar is quite streamlined. Icelandic grammar, in contrast, remains rich and complex. It didn't lose many of its early forms, mostly because its speakers lived for centuries in relative isolation, not much influenced by other languages. This old-fashionedness makes Icelandic harder to learn if you're not an Icelander, but it's one of the reasons linguists love the language: Icelandic offers a window on the early Germanic past.

The Icelanders love it too, and want to keep their language just the way it is. There is, of course, pressure to change it because of global communication, but Icelanders resist. Unlike the Germans, who by the late twentieth century had pretty much adopted modern international terms like *Telephon* (replacing its 'pure German' equivalent, *Fernsprecher*), the Icelanders continue to create new vocabulary from native words or parts of words. For example, a 'telephone' is *talsími*, that is 'speech wire', and 'telegraph' is *ritsími* or 'write wire'. They're constantly producing dictionaries to provide Icelandic terms for new words from abroad.

The language is also traditional in the way it handles personal names. Most Icelanders don't use surnames, that is, names that are shared through generations by all members of a family. Instead, each person has a given name and a patronymic, based on his or her father's given name. For example, a brother and sister named Eiríkur and Þórdís, whose father's name was Haraldur, would be called Eiríkur Haraldsson and Þórdís Haraldsdóttir. Tryggvi, the son of Eiríkur and grandson of Haraldur, would be called Tryggvi Eiríksson. And when you look them up in the phone book, you'll find Haraldur, Eiríkur, Þórdís, and Tryggvi alphabetized under their *given* names.

Maybe because of their long winter nights, Icelanders read more books per capita than any other people in the world. Their ancient poetry, known as the Eddas, and their ancient prose, the Sagas, are where much of the early history of the country is preserved. They're also one source Richard Wagner drew on for the Germanic myths he wove into *The Ring of the Nibelung*. The Eddas include one of Iceland's most famous poems, *Völuspá* (The Song of the Sybil), which is worth listening to for its beauty, even if you need a translation to understand the words.

Old Norse prose is particularly rich, the main genre being the sagas. These exist in several series, but two are particularly noteworthy: the Sagas of the Kings of Norway and the Sagas of the Icelanders. The former tell the history of where most Icelanders originated before immigrating to Iceland and of the many reasons why these fiercely independent people didn't want to stay living in Norway under a king.

The latter series, the Sagas of the Icelanders, tell of the island's settlement and of the families and their subsequent history after their arrival in Iceland. Probably the most famous of these is *Njal's Saga* (see the bibliography below).

One of the reasons you might want to read the Sagas is that they record the first discoveries of America, which the Vikings called Vinland. Read *The Saga of Leif Erikson* or *The Saga of Erik the Red* for details. No, Columbus wasn't the first to discover America. To be honest, the ancient Icelanders may not have been either. But they were the first to write the discovery down! And now those accounts are out in paperback.

About the author

Pardee Lowe Jr., of Falls Church, Virginia, has a Ph.D in German with Linguistic Emphasis from the University of California, Berkeley. He is a specialist in foreign language proficiency testing and an independent scholar and writer. He has taught Ancient Icelandic (also known as Old Norse) and has long enjoyed the delights of Old Icelandic language and literature.

Suggestions for further reading

In this book: Icelandic's historical role is an example of processes also discussed in chapters 5 (language relationships), 7 (language change), 11 (grammar), 41 (dialect change), and 48 (origins of English). Other chapters on languages in current use include 50 (Latin), 51 (Italian), 52 (Spanish, Portuguese, and others), 53 (Russian), 54 (Icelandic), 55 (Arabic), 57 (Chinese), and 58 (Japanese).

Elsewhere:

Smiley, Jane, ed., with introduction by Robert Kellogg. *Sagas of the Icelanders: A Selection* (Penguin Books, 2001). This 782-page paperback offers an excellent selection of nine sagas (among them the Vinland Sagas about the discovery of North America) and seven Old Icelandic tales.

Brønsted, Johannes. *The Vikings* (Penguin, 1960).

Cook, Robert, translator. *Njal's Saga* (Penguin, 1997).

Forte, Angelo, Richard Oram, and Frederik Pedersen. *Viking Empires* (Cambridge University Press, 2005).

Hjálmarsson, Jón R. *History of Iceland: From the Settlement to the Present Day* (Icelandic Review, 1993).

Larrington, Carolyne, translator. *The Poetic Edda: A New Translation by Carolyne Larrington* (Oxford University Press, 1996).

Sturluson, Snorri, translated by Jean I. Young. *The Prose Edda: Tales from Norse Mythology* (University of California Press, 2001).

55

Do all Arabs speak the same language?

Jerry Lampe

What is Arabic like? Should we be studying it?
How hard is it to learn? What can you do with it?

Arabic is all around us these days. On news broadcasts we hear words like *mujahideen*, *intifada* and *al-Qaeda*. Middle Eastern foods like hummus and falafel are considered gourmet delights. And, if you look closely you'll see small ads in Arabic script—for some reason often on the sports page—seeking people who can read and speak the language.

It has an exotic sound to western ears. But we'd better get used to it. Because it's not just for linguists and gourmets anymore. It promises to be part of our lives for a long time to come.

Arabic is spoken by more than 250 million people in an area extending from the Persian Gulf to the Atlantic Ocean. It's the language of the Qu'ran, the holy book of Islam, so more than 700 million people have it as a spiritual component of their daily lives.

The governments of nineteen countries list Arabic as their principal language, and the UN made it one of its official languages in 1974. By any of several measures, Arabic is one of the most important languages in the world.

And yet it's been pretty much neglected in countries that should know better. A prime example is the United States. You've probably heard that the FBI and other government agencies—more than eighty of them—have huge needs for Americans proficient in Arabic. And that military and civilians serving in Iraq don't have the language or cultural skills to deal with the Iraqis. Arabic is now the foreign language most critical to U.S. national security, but nowhere near enough people with Arabic skills are available to fill the multitude of job vacancies: translators, interpreters, diplomats, business consultants, market analysts, intelligence analysts, and of course, teachers and researchers.

You've probably heard it said that Arabic is hard to learn. What's the hard part? Well, the writing system takes a little getting used to, because words and sentences are written from right to left, meaning that what you might think of as the back of a book is actually the front. The alphabet has just twenty-eight letters, with a few extra dots that float above and below them. I've heard the letters described as a collection of 'worms and snails,' and to the western eye they can look, well, vermicular. But they're really quite beautiful, and they, in fact, constitute the principal form of art in the Arab and Islamic worlds. And it doesn't take more than a couple of weeks to learn them if they are studied systematically.

Also, Arabic pronunciation can be tricky in spots, because there are a number of sounds that we don't have in English; some in the back of the throat remind me a little of German.

Probably the most challenging thing about Arabic is that you have to learn two variants of the language to get along well: One is Modern Standard Arabic, known as MSA, which is the language of literature and media throughout the Arab world. In addition to that you need a colloquial variant of Arabic, a dialect, which is the language used in everyday talk in a given country. Most people learn either the Egyptian dialect or the Levantine dialect because they are the two variants most often taught in the West, and most American and European students of Arabic attend study-abroad programs in Egypt and the Levant.

Why do you need both Modern Standard and a dialect? If you speak only MSA, you'll be understood by most Arabs, who hear it in formal situations and in films or TV. But many Arabs don't speak it on a daily basis, so you won't understand them unless you learn the dialect of the country you go to. In fact, local speech varies so much from country to country in the Arabic-speaking world that even Arabs may not always understand one another when they travel.

So yes, it takes some time and dedication to learn Arabic. But it's well worth doing. Arabic is a centuries-old language and is part and parcel of a very rich culture. Learning it is a truly enriching, mind-opening experience, and the diligent study of Arabic can lead to exciting careers in a variety of fields. Shouldn't the non-Arab world be teaching it more often in schools?

About the author

Jerry Lampe is Deputy Director of the U.S. National Foreign Language Center (NFLC: http://www.nflc.org) and President of the American Association of Teachers of Arabic. He is currently working on projects intended to increase language capacity in the U.S. These include the National Flagship Language Initiative (a program to get more people into the pipeline of students learning critical languages in the U.S. and to enable them to reach high levels of professional proficiency) and LangNet, an online language-learning support system.

Suggestions for further reading

In this book: Other chapters covering various languages of the world include 2 (world language survey), 50 (Latin), 51 (Italian), 52 (Spanish and Portuguese), 54 (Icelandic), 53 (Russian), 56 (languages of Africa), 57 (Chinese), and 58 (Japanese). Opportunities and requirements for professional use of language abilities are discussed in chapters 20 (bilingualism), 36 (America's language crisis), 42 (language-related careers), 43 (dictionaries), 44 (interpreting and translating), and 46 (Forensic Linguistics).

Elsewhere:

Brustad, Kristen, et al. *Alif Baa: Introduction to Arabic Letters and Sounds* (Georgetown University Press, 2001); and

Brustad, Kristen, et al. *Al-Kitaab fii Ta'allum al-'Arabiyya: A Textbook for Beginning Arabic, Part One* (Georgetown University Press, 1995). These are the textbooks most widely used in the U.S. for beginning Arabic.

Nydell, Margaret. *Understanding Arabs: A Guide for Modern Times* (Intercultural Press, fourth edition 2005). The most popular guide for people who want to know more about the Arabs, their language, and their culture.

Web sites:

http://www.wm.edu/aata
American Association of Teachers of Arabic (AATA). See the following sections: About Arabic, Manuscripts, Arabic Programs, Arabic Software, and General Links.

http://www.langnet.umd.edu
National Foreign Language Center (NFLC). A database composed of brief reviews of some of the best resources for learning/teaching the Arabic language and culture.

56

Is Swahili the language of Africa?

Donald Osborn

What languages do people speak in Africa? Are they all related, like the European languages? Are they less complex and advanced than European languages?

'Say something in African.' That's a question you might hear from a college freshman talking to an African exchange student. But of course there is no single 'language of Africa'. According to *Ethnologue*, the widely-cited reference on languages, there are 2,092 separate tongues on the continent. Some are spoken by very small groups of people, maybe in only one village; others are spoken by millions. The thing to remember is that Africa, especially south of the Sahara, is one of the most multilingual regions in the world.

But what about a shared 'language of Africa' like Swahili? Well, a large number of people do speak Swahili, but it's limited mostly to east Africa. Africa is a vast continent and even the most widely spoken languages cover only subregions.

Because of the sheer number of African languages there's a lot that we're still learning about them. Since most are only spoken tongues, with an oral tradition but no written record, they're not easy to document. And to what extent are they related? It wasn't until 1963 that the linguist Joseph Greenberg, building on earlier work such as that of Diedrich Hermann Westermann, suggested that they fall into just four separate families: a huge one of over 1,300 languages spread across most of sub-Saharan Africa; a north African family that includes Hebrew, Arabic, and Amharic; a group in the middle around Chad and Uganda; and a small group called Khoisan, near the Kalahari desert.

So what are these languages like? Because of their diversity, no language represents them all. You've probably heard an occasional word like *harambee*, from Swahili, meaning 'pulling together', which was a rallying cry in Kenya. Or maybe the songs of Miriam Makeba or Ali Farka Touré. Or dialogue in the film *Amistad*, in which actors portraying enslaved Africans speak Mende, a language of present-day Sierra Leone. Perhaps the most exotic to the ears of English speakers are the clicking sounds used as consonants in some southern African languages. You can hear them in a recent film version of Bizet's opera *Carmen*, spoken and sung entirely in Xhosa.

The sounds and grammar of African languages are often very different from what we English speakers are more familiar with. For instance, many of them, such as Yoruba in Nigeria, use *tones* to distinguish meaning of words, much as Chinese does. These tones, by the way, are what permits the famous 'talking drums' of the region to convey messages.

And the structures of some African languages are quite intricate. We might think of German as complex, with three genders to classify nouns; but the Fulani language of West Africa has over *two dozen* noun classes. In this case, however, the noun endings and the indicative particles harmonize so that learning them is actually simpler than remembering, say, the gender of an object or abstraction in a continental European tongue.

Other languages have unique sounds, such as that click in Xhosa, which linguists believe was borrowed from neighboring Khoisan tongues. It has been suggested that the clicks are surviving remnants of the earliest sounds our human ancestors made in communicating—which would make these languages some of the oldest ones we know in terms of their phonetics.

Old, yes, but in no sense primitive. Many non-Africans still believe that African languages are less capable of expressing complex thought than European tongues. It was in reaction to such attitudes a half-century ago that Senegalese scholar Cheick Anta Diop translated an explanation of Einstein's theory of relativity into Wolof, a language of Senegal and Gambia.

And what about writing? It is often said that African cultures are oral, but this is an oversimplification. A number of African languages have also been written for a long time: a few in indigenous scripts like the one used for Amharic and Tigrinya in Ethiopia and Eritrea, several in West Africa as well as Swahili in Arabic script (though this is less common today), and many in the Latin alphabet, sometimes with added letters to represent additional sounds used in these tongues. However, the number of people actually using the written form of their language tends to be limited.

Now, with all those different languages, how do people communicate? The answer is: they find a way. Close to home, Africans commonly use more than one language in daily life. Further away, they may rely mainly on a *lingua franca* like Swahili, English, or French—or maybe a pidgin language.

But this answer hides another set of questions—how distinct are all these languages, or how many are there really? Many of the over 2,000 languages *Ethnologue* counts in Africa are in fact very closely related—some groups of them might alternatively be categorized as dialects of one language. For instance, the

Mandinka of *Roots* author Alex Haley's ancestor Kunta Kinte is similar enough to languages called Malinke, Bambara, and Jula that fluent speakers of one can understand the others to varying degrees. On this basis some suggest that Africa is not really the Tower of Babel it seems to be.

Nevertheless, with population growth and social change, the multilingual situation, already complex, becomes even more so. African languages are in flux, especially in cities, where diverse peoples come together. Some that are no longer taught in schools—or never were—are losing speakers. Economic incentives favor English or French. But African tongues are firmly part of the daily life, cultural identities, and economic activity of the continent. So what's the future of 'saying something in African'? There are probably as many answers to that as there are languages in Africa.

About the author

Donald Osborn is an independent scholar living in China, who works on a project for localizing information technology in African languages. He is a specialist in environment, agriculture, and development who has studied and speaks two African languages and has published a lexicon of one of them, Fulfulde. He has lived and worked eleven years in West Africa. He also runs *Bisharat*, a small initiative to facilitate use of African languages on computers and the Internet.

Suggestions for further reading

In this book: Other chapters covering various languages of the world include 2 (world language survey), 50 (Latin), 51 (Italian), 52 (Spanish and Portuguese), 54 (Icelandic), 53 (Russian), 55 (Arabic), 57 (Chinese), and 58 (Japanese). Chapters on how groups of language are related include 5 (language families), 48 (origins of English), and 49 (Native American languages).

Elsewhere:

Batibo, Herman M. *Language Decline and Death in Africa: Causes, Consequences, and Challenges* (Multilingual Matters, 2005). An introduction that focuses on endangered languages in Africa.

Childs, G. Tucker. *An Introduction to African Languages* (John Benjamins, 2004). An introduction to African languages and linguistics.

Heine, Bernd, and Derek Nurse, eds. *African Languages: An Introduction* (Cambridge University Press, 2000). A compilation of eleven articles by noted linguists expert in the study of different aspects of African languages.

Webb, Vic, and Kembo-Sure. *African Voices: An Introduction to the Languages and Linguistics of Africa* (Oxford University Press, 2000). A compilation of articles on African languages and their importance to African societies.

57

Do you have to be a masochist to study Chinese?

Barry Hilton

Some western missionaries felt it was invented by Satan
'to keep the gospel out of China.' Is Chinese the most
difficult language in the world? Is it worth the trouble?

If you ask professional linguists questions like these, most will probably say that every language is complex in some ways and simple
in others, and that they average out to around the same level of
complexity. But that's probably not the kind of answer you're looking
for. If we rephrase the question, though, and ask which language is
hardest for native English speakers to learn, well, yes, a pretty good
case can be made for Chinese. (Background note: the name 'Chinese'
refers to at least half a dozen regional languages that are closely
related but as different from each other as French, Spanish, and
Italian. What I have to say applies to all of them, especially to the
one most widely spoken, called 'Mandarin' by foreigners. It is the

official language of both Mainland China and Taiwan.) Let's look at some of the reasons.

One difficulty is that Chinese is unrelated to English. When you study a cousin of English in the Indo-European language family, like Spanish, Russian or Hindi, you find plenty of cognates—related words, similar in sound and meaning—to use as stepping-stones. To learn Chinese you have to acquire a vocabulary totally new except for a few borrowings like 'typhoon', 'gung ho', 'coolie', and 'kowtow'.

As a second obstacle, Chinese has a phonetic feature that can be difficult for English-speaking learners to hear and reproduce. Like English words, Chinese words are made up of consonant and vowel sounds, but each Chinese syllable also has an *intonation* pattern that's *not optional*. Mandarin syllables come in five patterns: (1) high level (think of a cartoon opera singer warming up: 'mi-mi-mi'); (2) rising (like answering a knock at the door: 'Yes?'); (3) dipping-and-rising (like a drawn-out, pensive 'we-e-ll'); (4) sharply falling ('Stop!'); and (5) toneless or unaccented (like the second syllable of 'cattle'). The Chinese word *lyou*^{4} (falling tone) means 'six'; *lyou*^{2} (same consonant and vowels but rising tone) means 'remain'. *Ying*^{2}*mu*^{4} means 'tent'; *ying*^{1}*mu*^{3} means 'acre'; *jya*^{4}*jr*^{5} means 'value'; *jya*^{3}*jr*^{1} means 'artificial limb'. Learners of Chinese who get tones wrong can sound as odd—or incomprehensible—to native ears as learners of English sound to us when they mix up the vowel sounds in words like 'fit' and 'feet', or 'hall' and 'hull'.

Now, many other languages—like Hungarian and Arabic and Indonesian—have no cognates for English-speaking students to rely on. And some, like Vietnamese and Thai and various African languages, are also tonal. But there's another obstacle that puts the difficulty of Chinese on an entirely different level: its writing system.

If you've ever done volunteer work in a literacy program, you know what a frustrating handicap illiteracy is, and how empowered an adult learner feels as he or she masters the 'code' that links familiar sounds with the few dozen squiggles that represent them on paper. People learning Chinese have a very complicated 'code' to master, which impedes not just their ability to read but their ability to broaden their vocabulary and develop other linguistic skills.

The squiggles the Chinese writing system uses—usually called 'characters'—don't represent simple consonant and vowel sounds, the way English letters do. Each one stands for a whole one-syllable word or word element, combining sound *and* meaning. For example, if a Chinese-like system were used to write English, the word 'unbearable' might be written with three squiggles, one for 'un', one for 'bear', and one for 'able'. And *that* 'bear' squiggle would be different from the squiggles representing the same sound in 'polar bear', 'childbearing', and 'the right to bear arms'—to say nothing of 'barefoot', or 'Bering Strait'. That adds up to a *lot* of squiggles for learners to memorize—several thousand characters instead of a couple of dozen alphabet letters. Not surprisingly, illiteracy is a major problem in China.

And when you meet a new character (or one whose sound and meaning you've learned and forgotten), how do you look it up? There are hundreds of Chinese dictionaries, and almost as many different systems for arranging characters. Without alphabetical order, tracking down an unknown character is much more labor-intensive than flipping pages while silently mouthing the ABC song. Even when you find the character, you won't necessarily know—without still more dictionary research—whether it's a standalone word or part of a compound like 'unbearable'.

I hope these comments serve less to discourage than to challenge people interested in learning Chinese. Learners can take heart from the fact that the *sound* system of Chinese is pretty simple except for the tones, and Chinese grammar poses no real difficulties for English speakers. Even the writing system, devilish as it may seem, has fascinated foreigners for centuries, and offers a key to understanding the classical literature and modern economic vitality of one of the great civilizations of the world.

About the author

Barry Hilton is the Associate Editor of this book and was a member of the review board of the radio series from which it was adapted. He is a freelance writer/editor and independent scholar living in Maine and working as a marketing specialist for a small publishing company. He is an honors graduate of Harvard College who after graduate studies at Cornell, Yale, and George Washington Universities and the Foreign Service Institute has travelled extensively and lived in both Europe and Asia. In a variety of U.S. government assignments he has made professional use of Vietnamese, Chinese, Japanese, French and German. He describes himself as an 'armchair philologist and recovering polyglot.'

Suggestions for further reading

In this book: Other chapters covering various languages of the world include 2 (world language survey), 50 (Latin), 51 (Italian), 52 (Spanish and Portuguese), 54 (Icelandic), 53 (Russian), 55 (Arabic), and 58 (Japanese). Writing systems are also discussed in chapters 9 (scripts) and 10 (history of writing).

Elsewhere:

Kratochvil, Paul. *The Chinese Language Today* (Hutchinson University Library, 1968). Although some of the vocabulary examples are very dated by their political flavor, as a brief introduction to Chinese for the serious general reader this book has not been superseded.

DeFrancis, John. *The Chinese Language: Fact and Fantasy* (University of Hawaii Press, 1984). The grand old man of Chinese instruction in the U.S. authoritatively debunks a number of myths about Chinese—particularly about the writing system—in a highly entertaining style.

McCawley, James D. *The Eater's Guide to Chinese Characters* (University of Chicago Press, 1984). There are many lightweight 'teach yourself Chinese characters' books on the market, some superficial to the point of being misleading. McCawley's guide provides practical exercises in reading and looking up Chinese characters, while limiting itself to the useful aim of showing general readers how to find their way around a Chinese menu.

Web site:

http://www.pinyin.info/readings/texts/moser.html
Moser, David. 'Why Chinese is so damn hard'. An accurate and amusing detailed account of the difficulties of Chinese, which almost in spite of itself serves as an invitation to potential learners: 'The more you learn about Chinese characters the more intriguing and addicting they become.'

58

Is studying Japanese worth the effort?

Blaine Erickson

Is Japanese really the world's hardest language? Is it related to Chinese?

No one language is the 'world's hardest,' but any language takes longer to learn the less it has in common with your native tongue. By that measure, Japanese is one of the hardest languages for English speakers.

However, not everything about Japanese is difficult: its *sounds* pose little problem. Many of them are much like English, though as you probably know, Japanese has only a single sound corresponding to both 'l' and 'r' in English—so that comedians imitating Japanese-accented English get cheap laughs by simply reversing the two sounds. On the downside, Japanese is absolutely unrelated to English, so you don't get a free startup vocabulary of cognates, as you would if you were learning, say, German or French. While Japanese has borrowed plenty of words from other languages, you might not recognize them. For example, the name 'Smith' becomes *Sumisu*, and *kuruunekku seetaa* is a crew-neck sweater.

Japanese grammar isn't too complex, but it's definitely un-English. For example, English sentence order is usually subject, then verb, then object. Japanese sentences put verbs at the end, and subjects and objects, especially words for 'you' and 'I', are often left out. Japanese sentences also sometimes end with mini-words that can change a statement into a question, or make a sentence more emphatic, or seek agreement.

Interestingly, some of these mini-words are used only by men, others only by women. Male/female speech differences, while not as strong as they used to be, are noticeably greater than in English. In fact, male and female vocabularies are different enough that dialogue between a man and a woman in a Japanese novel can omit 'he said' and 'she said.'

Besides using 'female' words, women usually speak more politely than men, demonstrating another un-English aspect of Japanese: an elaborate system of polite, respectful, and humble speech. When you talk to superiors or strangers, you refer to them and their actions with 'respectful' words, like *irassharu* for 'go' and *ossharu* for 'say'; for your own going and saying you use the 'humble' *mairu* and *mooshiageru*. (This is part of why 'you' and 'I' can be omitted.) When you talk with friends and family you can use 'neutral' words like *iku* and *yuu*, no matter whose actions you're referring to. How do you know when to use respectful or humble language? Well, it's not easy, even for Japanese, who get exposed to it as they grow up. Japanese college graduates newly hired by big companies are often sent off for training in polite speech, so don't worry if you can't quite master it overnight.

Another thing sometimes bewildering for foreigners is that the Japanese so often seem to cut linguistic corners. They talk about 'that' without ever mentioning what 'that' refers to, and even leave verbs, subjects, objects, and even entire phrases out of sentences, once everyone knows what the topic of conversation is. To an outsider, a social conversation can be as cryptic as a Mafia telephone call.

Still, these are all things you can master with a reasonable amount of time and effort. It's the Japanese writing system that gives learners fits. By some accounts, it's the most complex writing system in current use.

Like many other Asian peoples, the Japanese were enormously influenced by China. When they began writing their own language—which is not at all related to Chinese—they adapted Chinese characters. They took a system already challenging for learners—thousands of characters to memorize—and added a new difficulty: they used one character for several different words. If English were written using Chinese characters in the Japanese way, the same character, let's say the one used to write 'horse,' might appear as part of the written versions of 'chivalry', 'cavalier', 'horseman', and even 'knight'. The reader would have to deduce from context which of those the writer meant. It's not as hard as it could be, though. The Japanese commonly use only about 2,000 characters (as opposed to 3,000, 4,000, or more for Chinese), and they spell out quite a few things phonetically. But just to keep you on your toes, they do it with two different home-grown systems, plus the Roman alphabet! Even for people born in Japan, it can become confusing.

The Japanese sometimes seem to take perverse pride in the obstacles their language poses, but the fact is that foreigners can and do learn it—some even become Japanese TV celebrities. Learning it well will take more study than a European language, but the effort is really worthwhile. Japanese has 127 million native speakers, which makes it the eighth most-commonly spoken language in the world, ahead of German, French, and Italian.

The time is long past when the Japanese were feared as an imperialist power or the label 'Made in Japan' was thought to mean cheap imitation goods. Today, the world beats a path to Japan's door to do business, buy its products, and enjoy its culture, including pop music and animation—everything from sushi to sumo. The gateway to understanding and appreciating that fascinating culture is the Japanese language.

About the author

Blaine Erickson is Assistant Professor of Japanese at the Defense Language Institute Foreign Language Center at the Presidio of Monterey, California. He was educated at the University of Oregon, Waseda University (Tokyo), the Chinese University of Hong Kong, the University of Tokyo, and the University of Hawaii at Manoa. He specializes in both modern and historical Japanese phonology and morphology, with additional interests in historical Chinese, modern Cantonese, and modern and historical English. He has lived in Yokohama, Sapporo, Kanazawa, and Kumamoto, and has travelled in many other regions throughout Japan. His favorite food is *unagi* (broiled freshwater eel), though *basashi* (raw horse meat), a Kumamoto specialty, is a runner-up.

Suggestions for further reading

In this book: Other chapters covering various languages of the world include 2 (world language survey), 50 (Latin), 51 (Italian), 52 (Spanish and Portuguese), 54 (Icelandic), 53 (Russian), 55 (Arabic), and 57 (Chinese). Writing systems are also discussed in chapters 9 (scripts) and 10 (history of writing).

Elsewhere:

Miller, Roy Andrew. *The Japanese Language* (University of Chicago Press, 1967). While this book is old, it is a classic. It covers a wide range of topics, some of which are of more interest to specialists than the general reader. It's still a good read.

Shibatani, Masayoshi. *The Languages of Japan* (Cambridge University Press, 1990). More recent than Miller's book, it covers not just Japanese but also Ainu, a nearly-extinct language spoken in northern Japan. Again, some topics may be too specialized for the general reader, but it is still accessible.

McClain, Yoko Matsuoka. *Handbook of Modern Japanese Grammar* (Hokuseido Press, 1981). An excellent reference for the student of Japanese, with topics logically divided by grammatical pattern and type.

Makino, Seiichi, and Michio Tsutsui. *A Dictionary of Basic Japanese Grammar* (*The Japan Times*, 1989). Another reference work, alphabetically arranged. Though it covers fewer topics than McClain's reference, each topic is treated in greater detail.

Haig, John H., ed. *The New Nelson: Japanese-English Character Dictionary, based on the classic edition by Andrew N. Nelson* (Tuttle, 1997). The definitive reference work for those who are serious about learning to read Japanese. It also has extensive appendixes, making it an important tool.

There are also a huge number of resources on the Internet, not all equally reliable.

59

Whatever happened
to Esperanto?

E. M. Rickerson

Whatever happened to the idea of a universal language?
Is Esperanto still alive? And if so, who speaks it?

Wouldn't it be wonderful if everyone in the world spoke the same
language? Or wouldn't it be almost as good if everyone could speak
their own language at home but agree to learn the same *second*
language for international communication; a language that didn't
belong to any one country; and so easy you could learn it in just a
few weeks?

If you like that idea, you're in good company. Starting as early as
the seventeenth century with philosophers such as Bacon, Descartes
and Leibniz, there have been hundreds of proposals for an international language—and people are still trying to create one. For a
variety of reasons, however, the only one that had lasting success
was Esperanto, invented in Poland in the late nineteenth century

by Ludwig Zamenhof, an idealist who understood the power of language to unite or divide.

What kind of a language is Esperanto? People who have heard of it but never heard it spoken are sometimes led to believe that it is based on Spanish, which is not true. The name 'Esperanto' has a Spanish flavor, but the vocabulary of the language is a mix of European tongues; it includes Slavic and Germanic words, as well as words from Latin and Romance languages. To me Esperanto has a kind of eerie, interplanetary sound, which is no doubt one of the reasons it was once used in a film with a science-fiction theme. *Incubus* is a 1965 cult classic—the only feature-length film ever made with a sound track entirely in Esperanto—featuring a young, pre-*Star Trek* William Shatner. If you can find it in a video-rental store, it will take only a few moments of listening to confirm that Esperanto is not a form of Spanish—or any other language that you know.

When he first thought about a universal language, Zamenhof felt that spoken Latin might be a good choice, because there were Latin-based words in so many European tongues, including English. But as marvelous as Latin is, its grammar is fairly complicated—not the kind of thing to be learned quickly as a second language for everyone in the world. Esperanto, on the other hand, can be learned in a few weeks or months by just about anyone who wants to do so. It uses a Latin alphabet like ours (slightly modified), with phonetic spelling, and a very simple grammar. Its beauty, above all, is that it is deliciously predictable. It has no irregularities, none of those pesky exceptions that make natural languages so slippery and so … natural.

So whatever happened to Esperanto? It was created in 1887, got a big boost in popularity from the war-weariness of the 1920s, even became a serious candidate to be the official language of the League of Nations—and then seemed to fade away. But it did not, in fact, disappear. Although it had ups and downs throughout the twentieth century, the language quietly survived. And as the twenty-first century gets under way, Esperanto has emerged again, robust and gaining in popularity—in part because of the Internet.

There are now Esperanto novels and magazines. There's a translation of the Bible, as well as *The Lord of the Rings*. There are Esperanto poems, an International Esperanto museum, and—best of all—online chat rooms, where you can talk to people all over the world. You can hear broadcasts in Esperanto on over twenty radio stations, among them Radio Beijing and Vatican Radio. There's an Internet station that plays nothing but music—with vocals in Esperanto—24 hours a day.

There are even a few hundred people for whom Esperanto is a native tongue. Since a native language is one you learn at your mother's knee, and Esperanto is a language *constructed* for people who already have a native tongue, you may wonder how anyone could speak it natively. Answer: Mother learned Esperanto as a second language, then taught it to the child or children at her knee. At international World Congresses of Esperanto, attended largely by people of child-bearing age, there are some who fall in love, marry, have children, and speak to their children mainly in Esperanto. It is an unusual choice, perhaps; but Esperantists are passionate about their language and find an extraordinary number of ways of to use it.

Esperanto speakers are dispersed, so it's hard to get an exact count of them. But most estimates put the number at more than a million speakers on the planet—and growing. In recent years the language has moved into places where it was never heard before, such as Mongolia, Indonesia, and the Congo. One of its strongholds is Hungary, where Esperanto has become the third most-popular foreign language in the country's high schools, ahead of French.

Given the rise of globalization, it should not be surprising that there is a strong and growing interest in universal languages. English covers a broad area, but Esperanto provides a means to reach beyond the English-speaking world. With Esperanto already thriving in many places and in so many ways, the time may be right to think again about its possible role in international communication. In a newly-interconnected world, why shouldn't more of us learn Esperanto as a second language? It's quick, it's easy, and—thanks to the Internet—it can be used worldwide.

About the author

E. M. ('Rick') Rickerson is the General Editor of this book. He is Professor Emeritus of German, Director Emeritus of the award-winning language program at the College of Charleston (South Carolina), a former Deputy Director of the U.S. government's Center for the Advancement of Language Learning, and an Associate of the National Museum of Language. In 2005 he created the radio series on languages (*Talkin' About Talk*) from which *The Five-Minute Linguist* has been adapted. He is currently a consultant on the development of language programs at the university level.

Suggestions for further reading

In this book: Other chapters on languages consciously created by humans include 23 (sign languages) and 60 (survey of artificial languages).

Elsewhere:

Richardson, David. *Esperanto—Learning and Using the International Language* (Esperanto League for North America, third edition 2004). Includes chapters on the history of Esperanto, a complete course in the language, an annotated reader, and a bibliography.

Jordan, David. *Being Colloquial in Esperanto* (Esperanto League for North America, second edition 2004). A complete overview of Esperanto grammar plus a listing of words which may mislead speakers of English.

Web sites:

http://www.Esperanto.net
General information about Esperanto, in sixty-two different languages; with links to other relevant Web sites. To questions you may have about the language, it provides answers from Donald Harlow, who is past President of the Esperanto League for North America and an important contributor to the essay above.

http://www.lernu.net/lernu.php?lingvo=en
A multilingual Web site that will help you learn the language, easily and free of charge.

60

Does anybody here speak Klingon?

Christopher Moseley

Why do people invent artificial languages? Can invented languages be more scientific than natural languages?

With well over six thousand languages already in the world, what possesses people to make up new ones? For some, the motive seems to be idealistic, to create a single language to unite mankind in mutual understanding. But there may be a flaw in that reasoning: some of the bloodiest conflicts in history have been fought among people who speak the same language. Think of Vietnam or, for that matter, the English civil war, the American civil war, and the two British-American wars in between!

Another motive seems to be to create an exclusive secret society. Children make up languages all the time to do that.

Then there are languages created as backdrops for fictional civilizations. Good examples are the Klingon language in the *Star*

Trek television series, and the languages Tolkien devised for the Elves, Dwarves, and other inhabitants of Middle Earth in *The Lord of the Rings*.

Still another reason is that thinkers have been frustrated at how imperfectly natural languages represent the world. Beginning at least as early as the seventeenth century there have been attempts to create a 'logical' language, using symbols—as in mathematics—that could be understood regardless of what language a person spoke. But while the invented languages were logical, they were also complicated, arbitrary, and hard for anyone but the inventor to learn.

The late nineteenth century saw a great flowering of attempts at a universal language, starting in 1880 with a language called Volapük. Then came Esperanto, and languages with names like Novial, Interlingua and dozens of others. Almost all of them were based on Western European tongues, usually German, French, English, or Spanish. And most of them are extinct. Once an invented language is launched onto the stormy seas of language *usage* it rarely survives the death of its inventor, no matter how clever or systematic it may be.

Of these idealistic nineteenth-century ventures, Esperanto became the best-known and the most widespread; it now has a body of literature of its own and still has many enthusiastic speakers around the world today. But there have been other artificial languages that have embodied more unusual concepts. Two of the most intriguing made-up languages are based on extraterrestrial or musical ideas. Even though it's fictional, Klingon is known even to non-linguists, and—like Esperanto—may be one of the rare languages that does outlive its creator. If you want to learn it, there are things to help, such as a grammar book and audio tapes, a multimedia Klingon tutor, and dictionaries—in Portuguese and German, as well as English. There are even some international societies that try to keep the language alive. All of this for a made-for-TV invented language of roughly two thousand words, designed to sound as alien and harsh as possible to capture the nasty nature of the Klingons.

The second language, which was one of those invented in the nineteenth century, reminds me of the film *Close Encounters of the Third Kind*. You may remember the scenes in which an alien spacecraft begins its efforts to open communications with Earthlings by teaching them to reproduce a haunting series of five tones. The invented language Solresol was based on a very similar principle: starting with the do-re-mi system used to teach singing, it created words by combining the seven notes of the scale in particular sequences. For example, *fa-fa-do-fa* was the word for 'doctor' and *fa-fa-do-la* meant 'dentist'. Solresol was relatively easy to learn, and what made the language unique was that it could be sung, played or whistled as well as spoken! It was popular for quite a long time.

There have also been languages created for a scientific purpose, such as Loglan, which was invented in 1960 to test whether grammar rules based on mathematical logic would make a language's speakers more precise thinkers. And a language invented in 1962 called 'BABM' (pronounced 'Bo-A-Bo-Mu'), with a writing system in which each letter represents a syllable. Or one from 1979 that uses a system of icons instead of letters to represent concepts and sounds. The list goes on.

Dr. Zamenhof's creation, Esperanto, and the languages like Ido and Novial that competed with it in the late nineteenth century were all created on the basis of natural European languages. European empires encircled the globe at the time, and it was only natural for Latin and its daughter languages to be taken as the basis for these languages. They are what linguists call 'a posteriori' languages—created out of a blend of languages already existing. Solresol, Klingon and a host of others, some using familiar alphabets, some with scripts of their own, are what we call 'a priori' languages—created from scratch.

You can find a lot of these languages—including the newest ones—at www.langmaker.com. Would you like to create your own language, better than the ones we already have? If so, join the club. Among people who like languages, it seems to be a universal urge.

About the author

Christopher Moseley (Chrismoseley50@yahoo.com) is a linguist at BBC Monitoring, a part of the BBC World Service based near Reading, England, which translates news items from the world's media. He is also a writer and freelance translator, Editor of the *Encyclopedia of the World's Endangered Languages* (Routledge, 2006), and co-editor of the *Atlas of the World's Languages* (Routledge, 1993). He has a special interest in artificial languages (and has created one himself).

Suggestions for further reading

In this book: Other chapters on languages consciously created by humans include 23 (sign languages) and 59 (Esperanto).

Elsewhere:

Alan Libert. *A Priori Artificial Languages* (LINCOM, 2002).

Andrew Large. *The Artificial Language Movement* (Blackwell, 1985). Large's book is the best overview of this complicated story in one volume; if you want to explore the individual languages further, you must seek out the textbooks and manuals of their authors and propagators. These can be very hard to find; hardly any are still in print.

Web site:

http://www.langmaker.com
For a look at the lively competition to create languages today, either for fun or to further an ideal, the above Web site is the place to look.

Scripts and audio files for
Talkin' About Talk

For those who would like more background about the book and the *Talkin' About Talk* project, we refer you to a Web site permanently maintained by the College of Charleston (www.cofc.edu/linguist). Not all the essays from *The Five-Minute Linguist* are on the site, because several were added as the fifty-two broadcasts grew into the book's current sixty chapters. The book chapters also differ somewhat from the radio essays. They were not only recast for a different medium but, in many cases, lengthened a little when the constraints of radio were no longer a factor. Scripts and audio files of the original *Talkin' About Talk* broadcasts are available to interested readers and can be downloaded at no cost. For the convenience of those who may not have time or equipment to download the broadcasts, the College will make them available at low cost on attractively packaged compact disks. There is an order form on the Web site.

Index

CPSIA information can be obtained at www.ICGtesting.com
Printed in the USA
BVOW072132170112

280710BV00001B/6/A